D1584319

Flight 93 Revealed

What really happened on the 9/11 "Let's Roll" flight?

Flight 93 Revealed

What really happened
on the 9/11 "Let's Roll" flight?

Rowland Morgan

ROBINSON
London

Where the rights owner is known, every effort has been made to locate the person/s having rights in the pictures and figures appearing in this book and to secure permission for usage from such persons. Any queries regarding the usage of such material should be addressed to the author c/o the publisher.

Constable & Robinson Ltd
3 The Lanchesters
162 Fulham Palace Road
London W6 9ER
www.constablerobinson.com

This edition published by Robinson,
an imprint of Constable & Robinson Ltd, 2006

Copyright © Rowland Morgan, 2006

The right of Rowland Morgan to be identified as the author of this work has been asserted by him in accordance with the Copyright, Designs and Patent Act 1988.

All rights reserved. This book is sold subject to the condition that it shall not, by way of trade or otherwise, be lent, re-sold, hired out or otherwise circulated in any form of binding or cover other than that in which it is published and without a similar condition including this condition being imposed on the subsequent purchaser.

A copy of the British Library Cataloguing in Publication Data is available from the British Library.

ISBN-13: 978-1-84529-464-9
ISBN-10: 1-84529-464-5

Printed and bound in the EU

1 3 5 7 9 10 8 6 4 2

Contents

Introduction

Five years after the event, the 9/11 attacks seem both very distant and only too close. Distant, as we recall that innocent world where the deaths of many hundreds of US citizens seemed like a terrorist outrage of unprecedented scale, a world that had never heard of Abu Ghraib, that had not seen the leaders of the US and the UK launch an illegal bloody war to occupy Iraq or heard them threatening a nuclear attack on Iran on much the same flimsy pretext used to attack Iraq.

But every time the US/UK issues a new threat, every time a government tightens up a little more on citizens' rights, every time a Washington politician reminds the public that "we" are at war, one is reminded that 9/11 is still close. Whatever you think about the sketchy facts of 9/11, about the truth of Washington's official story, one thing is certain: 9/11 was a godsend for US arms contractors, the Washington media, the Pentagon, Israeli settlers, the enemies of civil liberties and indeed for governments everywhere, and they all know it. This is why everyone else should take a very close look at the official 9/11 story.

Rowland Morgan has laid bare many of the unexplained contradictions in the official 9/11 narrative. The story of the 9/11 attacks has varied so much by now, with Bush's "Independent 9/11 Commission" only adding to the confusion, that it is reasonable to say there is no official narrative. Morgan has conducted a meticulous examination of the Flight 93 story that gave rise to the 9/11 war myth and found that, whatever the truth may be, most of the Flight 93 story is just that: an unproven story written around some scraps of evidence, much of it contradictory. The questions concerning this central, but highly dubious, legend are to be found in the following pages.

Why have the media failed to raise the alarm? Rowland Morgan, himself an experienced Fleet Street columnist, has plenty to say about that, too. His description of the tiny ownership base and flagrant partisanship of the key media outlets will come as a shock to many readers.

No doubt this book will be dismissed as misinformation (our co-authored overview of the 9/11 attacks, *9/11 Revealed*, led to a high-profile "misinformation" page on the US State Department's website). It may even, to use the lazy shorthand of establishment figures confronting unwelcome facts, be described as "conspiracy theory" – as if the official story was not in itself an unlikely conspiracy theory. But this book is nothing if not a work of journalism and so, like *9/11 Revealed*, it will be condemned by some sectors of the 9/11 Truth Movement too. Its exacting scrutiny, not only of the official story, but of the alternative theories, will puncture egos. Its pessimistic assessment – that Washington might be able to keep its dirty secrets under wraps for many years – poses a challenge to campaigners.

No honest reader can deny that Morgan has dared to go down a path that too many others have flunked. Everyone who cares about the truth should applaud that. Everyone who cares about a war that is planned to last "beyond our lifetimes" (Cheney) should not only applaud Morgan's courage but do what they can to confront the warmongers and their supporters in the media with the questions they need to answer.

A planet facing environmental pollution, climate change, the AIDS epidemic and mass starvation in the midst of plenty now has in addition to confront a highly indebted militarized state using naked military threats to demand, in effect, an unfair share of dwindling global resources. As Rumsfeld puts it in Washington speak: US military spending is not an expense but an investment.

9/11 sceptics say that if the Pentagon and the intelligence agencies can avoid any scrutiny of their role in 9/11, whatever it was, then they will only be emboldened in the future. Just as the Reichstag Fire was the lie that launched Hitler, 9/11 is the lie at the heart of Washington's descent into unprovoked military aggression. Many hundreds of people in Washington, in government and particularly in the media, are now accessories after the fact, say 9/11 sceptics, and they should be jailed along with the Pentagon's torturers and whoever fabricated the false evidence that Iraq had nuclear weapons.

9/11 sceptics demand nothing less than a large-scale unfettered no-holds-barred criminal investigation into the 9/11 attacks, with no prior assumptions made. They do not want an Iran–Contra style "investigation" with a handful of villains sentenced to minimal terms in country-club style prisons (a limited hangout in CIA jargon). Whether inclined to believe the official 9/11 story or not, everyone who supports the rule of law should support this demand. Everyone who obstructs it should know that they risk the accusation of complicity in what is currently an unsolved mass murder.

Ian Henshall

1
The Cult
Launches

A TERRORIST ATROCITY

The official story of Flight 93 tells of four men who checked in at the United Airlines ticket counter at Boston Logan airport on 11 September 2001 bound for Los Angeles on United 93, a Boeing 757 airliner. Their Islamo-fascist kamikaze mission was led by Mohamed Atta, who coordinated things by mobile phone from his own take-off point at Boston's Logan airport.

Two of the men checked bags into the hold, two did not. The name of one of them, Haznawi, caused his bags to be specially screened for explosives before being loaded. No CCTV recorded the four passing through security, but staff later recalled nothing suspicious. Thirty-seven passengers boarded Flight 93 between 7:39 and 7:48 a.m. The four men took their seats in first class.

Heavy traffic delayed the 8:00 a.m. take-off until 8:42. The first rogue plane hit the World Trade Center moments later, and another at 9:03, but no warning went to Flight 93. At about 9:10, United Airlines imposed a nationwide ground stop. Still no warning went to Flight 93. Only at 9:23–9:24 did the pilot receive a message sent on his own initiative by a United dispatcher saying: "Beware any cockpit intrusion –

United Airlines Flight 93
(UA 93)
Newark to San Francisco

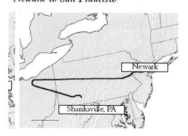

8:42	Takeoff
9:24	Flight 93 receives warning from UA about possible cockpit intrusion
9:27	Last routine radio communication
9:28	Likely takeover
9:34	Herndon Command Center advises FAA headquarters that UA 93 is hijacked
9:36	Flight attendant notifies UA of hijacking; UA attempts to contact the cockpit
9:41	Transponder is turned off
9:57	Passenger revolt begins
10:03:11	Flight 93 crashes in field in Shanksville, PA
10:07	Cleveland Center advises NEADS of UA 93 hijacking
10:15	UA headquarters aware that Flight 93 has crashed in PA; Washington Center advises NEADS that Flight 93 has crashed in PA

The 9/11 Commission's published timeline for Flight 93 appeared to make sense. However, it failed to mention that Deena Burnett alerted the FBI to the airliner's hijacking at 9:27 a.m., in addition to a flight attendant notifying United Airlines at 9:36. Both these calls were made while the plane's transponder still gave its identity, location and altitude. The US Air Force had four armed jet-fighters in the air at the time. If neither the FBI nor United informed the US Air Force, they were grossly negligent and heads should have rolled. If the air force was informed and did not act, commanders should have been court-martialled. But there were no known sackings as a result of the failure to intercept Flight 93, indicating that an intercept did in fact take place but had to be covered up.

Full-sized versions of all the pictures in this book can be seen at:
www.911dossier.co.uk

CREDIT: 9/11 Commission report

Two a/c [aircraft] hit World Trade Center." After flying normally for forty-five minutes the pilot, Capt. Jason Dahl, replied at 9:27: "Ed, confirm latest mssg, plz – Jason."

At 9:28, United 93 dropped 700 feet from cruising altitude of 35,000 feet. Eleven seconds later, air-traffic controllers in Cleveland, Ohio, heard a voice saying "Mayday" amid sounds of physical struggle and thirty-five seconds later, a voice shouted: "Hey get out of here, get out of here – get out of here." The pilots transmitted no formal hijack alert.

On other stricken planes that morning there were four reported hijackers, but passengers on Flight 93 reported only three. "The operative likely intended to round out the team ... had been refused entry by a suspicious immigration inspector at Florida's Orlando International Airport in August," the 9/11 Commission reported. The Commission ruled out speculation that a hijacker, perhaps in uniform, had been allowed to use the cockpit jump seat from the outset of the flight, and named another first-class passenger, Ziad Jarrah, as the pilot. He had been a radical Moslem with Atta in Hamburg in the 1990s, and had accompanied Atta to a meeting with Osama Bin Laden in his Afghan mountain hideout, at which he volunteered to take on a suicide pilot mission in the USA. He agreed to pose as an innocent airline-pilot candidate at a training school in Florida. Accordingly, he associated with other hijackers both in the sunshine state and in Las Vegas, while maintaining an elaborate facade of family commitment, travelling in and out of the USA half a dozen times, phoning his parents in the Lebanon at least every ten days and his girlfriend in Germany almost every day.

Jarrah "remained seated and inconspicuous until after the cockpit was seized; and, once inside, he would not have been visible to the passengers," the Commission stated. At 9:32 air-traffic controllers heard a voice apparently telling passengers to sit down because "we have a bomb on board". The plane's autopilot then was adjusted to turn the plane round and head east instead of west. The cockpit voice recording indicated that someone apparently held captive in the cockpit gave resistance and was somehow silenced.

"Shortly thereafter, the passengers and flight crew began a series of calls from GTE airphones and cellular phones ... until the end of the flight." These calls brought the news of the WTC crashes to Flight 93 in the air. Call recipients said passengers told them that the hijackers did not mind them making calls, although at 9:39 air-traffic controllers heard a second pilot announcement mentioning a bomb. People reported passengers giving varied information, including some details of the hijackers' weaponry, crimes and items of dress.

Out of about 30 phone calls, "five described the intent of passengers and surviving crew members to revolt against the hijackers. According to one call, they voted on whether to rush the terrorists in an attempt to retake the plane," the 9/11 Commission reported. One caller was said to have ended her message with the words: "Everyone's running up to first class. I've got to go. Bye." The cockpit recording captured the sounds of an apparent passenger assault through the cockpit door, and some relatives listening to the recording later claimed they recognized voices in the distant tumult.

The plane rolled to right and left, and pitched up and down, and there were sounds of continuing struggle outside the cockpit. A voice in the cockpit asked: "Is that it? Shall we finish it off?" Among the other cries outside, someone yelled: "Roll it!" For a further two minutes, the cockpit voices discussed ditching the plane. At 10:03, with the cockpit voices shouting repeatedly in Arabic "Allah is the greatest, Allah is the greatest," the plane headed down, banking hard right and rolling on to its back, hitting an empty field near Shanksville, Pennsylvania, at its top speed of 580 miles per hour. It exploded upon impact, setting fire to the nearby woods and spraying tiny body parts and other debris into the trees and up into the sky to float to earth as far as eight miles away. At the same time, the whole aircraft vanished into the friable soil of the reclaimed open-pit mine leaving only scattered shards of metal mingled with the earth. Neither engine was retrieved from the crater: only a part of one engine was found about a mile away.

The US Air Force never heard that Flight 93 had been hijacked until 10:07 a.m., after the United Airlines Boeing 757 had gone down, so of course they were unable to intercept it and communicate with the rogue pilots. They certainly did not have any opportunity to shoot it down.

A DEFINING MOMENT IN HISTORY

Nine days after the events of 11 September 2001, George W. Bush solemnly addressed a packed Congress. He did not declare war on a rival state, in the way that the USA had solemnly declared war on Japan in the wake of that country's "surprise" attack on Pearl Harbor. He declared war on an asymmetrical war-making method. He declared "war on terror".

There was no uniformed enemy to fight, but, as commander-in-chief of the US armed forces in a time of war, Bush put himself legally in a position to impose martial law, unleash the secret state with a licence to imprison, torture and kill at will, monitor all telephone calls, suspend habeas corpus and the Posse Comitatus Act, cancel important terms of the US Constitution, and generally arrogate maximum power into his office.[1]

However, before getting round to this unconventional declaration of abstract war, he had something even more important to announce. Taking precedence over declaring war was his endorsement of the reports that heroic passengers of United Flight 93 had fought back against ruthless foreign hijackers. Bush reserved his opening words for praising "the courage of passengers who rushed terrorists to save others on the ground. Passengers like an exceptional man named Todd Beamer." And he asked: "Would you please help me welcome his wife Lisa Beamer here tonight?"[2]

Thus the Flight 93 warrior cult was officially launched into orbit over America from the highest pad in the country nine days after 9/11.[3] In due course, Bush told Tom Brokaw on NBC Evening News he thought the disappearance of Flight 93 was a "defining moment" in American history.[4]

However, among the people, who had not yet caught on to the cult, there were widespread patriotic suspicions that the supposedly mighty US Air Force, proven so embarrassingly impotent against three rogue airliners, had succeeded in shooting down the fourth, Flight 93. The masses expected nothing less from the commanders of space. Naturally this view was not patriotic but subversive in the eyes of the heroism-spinners. The worrying suspicion of a shootdown was particularly strong in Pennsylvania, where eyewitnesses had seen debris falling from the sky at a distance of eight miles from the impact crater.

Even the FBI initially shared the suspicions, as their agents admitted at the site of the aircraft's disappearance in the Allegheny mountains. But the reports from grief-stricken relatives of heroic resistance aboard Flight 93, heavily promoted on TV news, soon caused the FBI investigation to be redirected. The mass media newsdesks at first reported the possibility of a shootdown, but then they, too, dropped the topic, and penetrating questions that should have been put to Rumsfeld, Cheney,

Ashcroft or Bush, were instead put to a group of "phone-call recipients" temporarily deranged by shock, grief and delusions of grandeur reflected on them from their superhero relatives. Before long, Flight 93 was an altar to heroism and any talk of a shootdown was heresy.[5]

BEREAVED AIR-CREW REPORTED CALLS

The first reports from the bereaved of phone calls from Flight 93 had started with two women who either were, or had been, members of airline cabin crew, one of them with United Airlines itself, the operator of Flight 93. The women's status as trained airline personnel gave their reports credibility. Reports of phone calls from passengers were hard to believe because calls from passengers on the other three planes had been scarce to non-existent. However, in the panic prevailing at the time no one except a small senior group knew this relevant fact.

The two women appeared together citing heroic resistance aboard Flight 93 at the top of CNN's special 9/11 coverage on 12 September and again on NBC Evening News on 13 September. No other call recipients appeared with them. Deena Burnett, who had received the first call and immediately alerted the FBI, was a keen Republican who had formerly been a Delta Airlines flight attendant, Delta being based in the Bush state of Texas. She said her husband had mentioned intending to take action against the hijackers. Alice Hoglan, also a keen Bush supporter, was currently employed as a flight attendant with Chicago-based United Airlines.[6] She said her son had called her from United 93 at 9:42 a.m. and told her that three hijackers had taken over the plane and he intended to join a passenger revolt.

For most of the daytime TV news coverage on 12 September, Alice Hoglan was the only phone-call recipient who gave witness to a passenger revolt, appearing seven times on CNN, six on ABC, three on NBC, and once on CBS.[7] Her son, Mark Bingham, had been a corporate PR man and a keen Republican, who had helped sponsor a benefit dinner for Senator John McCain's presidential candidacy in 2000. Bingham's biography rapidly followed his mother's huge exposure on news TV, reciting his physical prowess and bully-boy abilities.[8]

In the meantime, more reports of phone calls from the plane to other homes had followed those of the two airline staffers, coming from traumatized families in various states of alarm, shock and grief. The phone calls had hit the relatives' and friends' households when they were already reeling from the TV news of an all-out "attack on America" at the World Trade Center and the fresh crash at the Pentagon. Although other call recipients would face the US media horde in the ensuing days, it was United Airlines employee Alice Hoglan who was everywhere on 12 September, citing the passenger revolt her son had reported. Of course, by normal journalistic ethics, all the bereaved should have been left in privacy and dignity to recover themselves.

BIBLICAL DIMENSION

The conversations with the doomed on Flight 93 that the families and friends reported, and that were expertly shaped by media managers over the next few days into an organized storming of the cockpit, had a religious significance that reverberated among the 40 million evangelical Christians in the so-called "red" states, where the appointed regime of George W. Bush had its most fervent support.[9]

Many of the fundamentalists, who believed that the Holy Bible contained the divine truth as revealed by God himself, had experienced terrifying intuitions of an approaching Armageddon during the events of 9/11. "Armageddon", deriving from ancient Hebrew, referred to the Megiddo mountains in the Holy Land, which the prophet of the Bible's Book of Revelations had predicted would be the scene of the final battle between the kings of the earth – or the forces of good and evil – at the end of the world.

Free of apocalyptic delusion, this effectively referred to the ongoing faith-based strife over a territory of the demolished Turkish Ottoman empire that contained Jerusalem, a particular city revered by three different religions. For Jews it was their ancestral capital, for Christians the place of martyrdom of their "redeemer", and for Moslems their third most holy city. It had become a flashpoint in the emerging struggle for the last great crude-oil deposits on earth.

For many Christians who interpreted the Bible literally, it was in accord with the prophecy that visions should appear in the skies, depicting conflict between good and evil, while mayhem broke out below. The callers on Flight 93 had been players in this god-like drama.

It was an evangelical Christian, Todd Beamer, who apparently had made the longest and most inspiring of the phone calls, reciting the Lord's Prayer and Psalm 23, and coining in tearful passion the army's recruitment slogan, "Let's Roll".

CARGO CULT

The twentieth-century Melanesian cargo cult was, in the words of an ethnologist, "an inexplicable and repetitive complex of delusions" that grew among an invaded people.[10] In the case of Flight 93's disappearance, similar social stresses were at work and similar "inexplicable and repetitive delusions" occurred. Americans had experienced, for the first time in their homeland, calamity from the sky. It had been delivered by airplanes. A unique cargo had been left behind in the form of a bundle of messages from above. About half of them had been delivered using cellphones. This American invention had appeared rather suddenly a few years earlier, but on Flight 93, cellphones came into their own. The sky-warriors brandished them like talismans to ward off the Evil One on high and confer with fellow Christians below.

IRRATIONALITY

The cargo cult took the cellphone calls from Flight 93 to heart, defying reason. Sober newscasters on national TV referred to the cellphone calls that had come from on high.[11] Print journalists constantly wrote about cellphone calls conducted at cruising altitude, although their common sense must have told them the calls were misattributed or at least open to question. The attribution of the Armageddon voices to magical cellphones continued right up to 2006.[12]

The cellphone obsession illustrated the deluded essence of the Flight 93 cult.[13] Cult members, while otherwise able to function normally in society, on the subject of Flight 93 lost the ability to distinguish between fact and fiction. Thus they believed against all reason that cellphone calls could reach earth from cruising altitude of six-and-a-half miles.

Reasoning was an ability that among evangelicals was already hampered by deluded biblical doctrines such as the virginity of Jesus's mother, the miracles performed by Jesus, and his resurrection in fully corporeal form after being tortured to death. In this peculiar area of consciousness, divine revelation,[14] although irrational, was *more* truthful than fact. When conveyed into transcript, it became scripture,[15] and when raised to that status, it could assert anything and be believed.

For example, adherents of the Flight 93 cult perceived:

- clear meaning in the nonsense of the Flight 93 cockpit voice recording as discovered, deciphered, translated, transcribed and interpreted for them by a government eager to exorcise the widespread suspicion of a shootdown;

- truth in the reported content of cellphone calls that could not have happened;

- truth in the delusional images depicted in movies that regularly "reconstructed" the Flight 93 events year after year, for the same purpose.

Irrationality is doubly dangerous in that most dangerous of creatures the human being, and particularly when it spreads virus-like in a human crowd. Collective delusions can occur, with group visions and lethal actings-out. In this mental climate, debate becomes confused with heresy.

Accordingly, any reasoned questioning of the cult's delusional beliefs soon merited the most extreme response, such as denunciations, expulsions, death threats. Among many others, the actress Susan Sarandon reported in 2006 that she had received a flood of death threats for opposing the USA's invasion of Iraq that had relied for much of its inspiration on the Flight 93 cult.[16] The lethality of the passions involved needed no further illustration than the estimated number of civilian deaths arising from the invasion and occupation of Iraq. A scientific study that showed up to 100,000, even reaching 200,000, civilian deaths were regularly denounced and eliminated from the public record by cultists.[17] For the deluded members, it was perfectly acceptable that fighters in Iraq should believe that they were avenging 9/11 when none of the alleged 9/11 hijackers had come from that country. By the same twisted logic, any talk of a shootdown of Flight 93, however patriotically inspired, was to be crushed.[18]

CULT PRIESTS

The emergence of the Flight 93 cult suited the warmongers. By eagerly fostering it, they succeeded in evading the early questioning of the administration about a shootdown. (The early questions were just stonewalled until they went away.[19]) Within hours of Flight 93's disappearance a parade of Congressional bigwigs paved the way for Bush's elevation of the sect. Each day a more important dignitary visited the Shanksville "crash" site and recited the heroism script, thereby encouraging the newly-grieving and therefore impressionable relatives.

- Within 24 hours, US Rep. John P. Murtha, a Pentagon insider, said the rogue pilot's target "had not been a reclaimed strip mine" (referring to the impact site he was visiting). "Somebody made a heroic effort to keep the plane from hitting a populated area," and it had not been a US fighter-pilot.

- Senator Arlen Specter of Pennsylvania, who as a chief counsel for the Warren Commission's investigation into the assassination of President Kennedy had authored the establishment cover-up "single-bullet" theory, proposed a Medal of Freedom for the rebel passengers, filling the shattered relatives and friends with false reflected grandeur and fertilizing their imaginations.

- His fellow Pennsylvania senator, Rick Santorum, a member of the Senate Armed Services committee for seven years, presented workers at the site with a flag that had flown over the US Capitol, and praised the rebel passengers as heroes, further ballooning the relatives' delusions about their telephone calls.

■ On 15 September, Pennsylvania Governor Tom Ridge, a close friend of Bush, claimed before a memorial service that, by fighting back, the passengers and crew had "*undoubtedly* saved hundreds, if not thousands, of lives".[20] [Emphasis added.] Ridge went on to become founding director of Bush's huge new Department of Homeland Security, and he regularly went on the TV news making alarmist statements like: "Every family in America should prepare itself for a terrorist attack."[21]

By then the relatives and friends were not only deranged by grief but deluded by visions of the superhuman achievement of their loved ones.

WORD SPREADING

On 8 November 2001, Bush the "War President", who had taken office intending to avenge his father in Iraq, stamped the Great Seal's authority on the phone-call scriptures by citing Todd Beamer's "last known words" and making them the last words of his presidential war-making speech: "We will no doubt face new challenges, but we have our marching orders. My fellow Americans, let's roll."[22]

"Let's Roll" became the Flight 93 cult's war-making slogan.

General Motors and the Pentagon, twin anchors of the carbon-guzzling economy, echoed the Commander-in Chief. The car-maker came up with an advertising campaign for fuel-hungry sports utility vehicles under the slogan "Keep America Rolling". The Pentagon launched a fast-track project to repair its headquarters building,

US navy personnel, heading towards an unprovoked attack on Iraq, formed themselves into the Flight 93 war-making slogan that emerged from a Pentagon-linked corporation in the wake of 9/11. One of their pilots took off and photographed them from the sky for this promotional picture. Years later, over 80 percent of forces occupying Iraq believed they were avenging Iraq's sponsorship of the 9/11 events.

CREDIT: US war industry promotional image

damaged on its north side during the 9/11 events, and the politicals branded the worksite with the motto "Let's Roll".[23]

"Let's Roll" badges started appearing on militia uniforms, vehicles and airplanes, and the catchphrase formed the basis of the Pentagon's recruitment campaign for the Iraq war, falsely linking Beamer's presumed heroism to the Bush military and 9/11 to Saddam Hussein.[24]

FIRST DRAFT OF SCRIPTURE

On 3 December 2001, the official story of Flight 93 was written down in full. It crystallized the cult narrative and annihilated once and for all any talk of a shootdown. The *Washington Post*, deemed by sceptics to be the voice of the CIA, was the publisher. *Newsweek*, a division of the *Post* with 21 million readers in 190 countries, was the organ. Millions more would read the *Newsweek* story at online MSNBC, owned by the Bush-funding Microsoft Corporation and the arms-making megacorporation General Electric.

Much of the collating and assembly of the data had been done in the preceding weeks by the *Post-Gazette* corporate news monopoly in Pittsburgh, a city that had briefly believed itself a 9/11 target, and in the region of which the stricken plane had disappeared. *Post-Gazette* reporters had assiduously contacted the bereaved to glean from them every last detail of telephone conversations conducted at the extreme edge of sanity when Armageddon seemed to threaten the whole country, with tens of thousands believed dead and up to twenty-two airliners hijacked.

Rumours had spread among the bewildered and captive passengers and crew on the doomed aircraft, prompted by the pilot's reported "we have a bomb on board" announcement. The phone-call recipients on the ground, already stressed by fear and worry, further modified the rumours started above. The media then completed the distortion in writing down the scripture.

Newsweek adopted the language of cult-scripture, rooting for American faith, righteous pugnacity and revenge. They rehearsed in full what they called the "ancient litany" (the Lord's Prayer) that the evangelistic football-player Todd Beamer had reportedly intoned along with the Verizon/GTE Airfone operator. (The *Post-Gazette* appeared to have added Psalm 23 – perhaps just for good measure.) They lip-curlingly quoted from the terrorist instruction manual that the bogeyman Mohamed Atta had obligingly placed in his baggage for the FBI somehow to find and eagerly translate. They depicted the Christian passengers as the first 9/11 Crusaders, casting federal law aside and storming the cockpit to prevent another suicide attack. They described them tasting victory just as the airliner crashed, a fantasy that later had to be corrected by the 9/11 Commission (only to reappear in movies in 2006). Of the strong evidence for a shootdown, which included available air force F-16 fighter planes, an eight-mile wide debris field upwind, a missing jet engine and the absence of a tailplane at the impact site, the journalists made no mention.

SELLING THE VERIZON CALL

As an account of an airliner's inexplicable disappearance, the *Newsweek* account was useless. It focused instead on wringing out the juicy human drama imagined on board, drawing principally on an unsubstantiated phone-call report arising from inside the Pentagon-linked Verizon Corporation. Economy-class passenger Todd Beamer was reported by a supervising operator named Lisa Jefferson to have used an Airfone to call the operator, apparently in an agitated and tearful state. The entire account of the unrecorded call came from Ms. Jefferson. Part of *Newsweek*'s account of it went as follows:

> "Lisa," he said suddenly. "Yes?" responded Jefferson. "That's my wife," said Beamer. "Well, that's my name, too, Todd," said Jefferson. "Oh, my God," said Beamer. "I don't think we're going to get out of this thing. I'm going to have to go out on faith." Jefferson tried to comfort him. "Todd," she said, "you don't know that." Beamer asked her to promise to call his wife if he didn't make it home. He told her about his little boys and the new baby on the way.

Such single-sourced hearsay from an unrecorded call had nothing to do with the plane's perplexing disappearance. It was an evasion of the hard questions that needed putting to the officials in charge of the Pentagon, many of them known to be signatories of a radical document calling for US world domination by force of arms and mentioning the need for a "new Pearl Harbor" as a triggering pretext.[25]

The official story propounded by *Newsweek* and MSNBC online and their amen-corner shamelessly promoted the Flight 93 cargo cult while ignoring important matters of state, such as how the alleged hijacking had been carried out, why the plane had been lost, and what part the US Air Force had played in its end. Not least, it ignored obvious questions raised in particular by the Beamer telephone call: why no one had recorded it and why his wife did not know for four days that he had called. Above all, in that regard, it did not inquire whether Lisa Jefferson was an evangelical Christian, and thus a suggestible recruit for the cargo cult.

Jefferson, the telephone operators' supervisor, received a Verizon Excellence Award for her Flight 93 performance on 2 April 2002. A company boss said: "With calm reassurance, she provided comfort to Todd Beamer during the last moments of his life and, at the same time, gathered important information to assist law enforcement officials. She also faithfully delivered Mr Beamer's final messages to his widow and two small children." An excellence award might seem inappropriate. Jefferson had not secured a recording of Beamer's call. She had not gone through the questions in her GTE distress-call manual with a cabin crew-member but instead had questioned an ignorant, tearful passenger in tourist class. She had not connected the agitated man to his wife.[26] Nor had she informed his wife subsequently of the call as she had promised and as her boss claimed she had.[27]

Jefferson's evidence would never have influenced a court. It was single-sourced hearsay, and there was no recording of the call. For spooks inside a sprawling empire of wires like Verizon, rigging up a phone call to Jefferson's headset would have been simple. She had no idea what Beamer's voice sounded like, and she would never hear it again to judge whether he had been speaking to her. She proved her deluded membership of the Flight 93 cult when she told NBC Evening News on 11 September 2002, that she believed she had been "chosen" by God to take Beamer's call.[28]

The *Newsweek* article set the pitch and defined the tone for the media chorus around Flight 93. The phone calls were to be the holy notation. Their recipients were to be the channels of the divine music, the callers were the muses, up there with Saint Cecilia on high. All would be representatives of the crowd, the ordinary become extraordinary who, when summoned, rose to the occasion, donned a uniform and marched out to fight the good fight. Above all, there was to be no place in this soaring cantata for ugly discordant notes such as "debris-field", "shootdown", "missile" or "F-16".

LAUNCH TO THE LITERATE

LET'S ROLL

What the cult chorale needed was a lead singer, a fair soprano with a lilting sob. Step forward Lisa Beamer. Propelled into an orbit of fame by the US President, she became a media darling, favoured and pampered by the TV controllers and the shadowy figures behind them in the control rooms. Although other voices of the bereaved were raised, calling for a peaceful resolution of the Middle East crisis

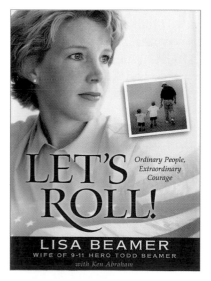

The flag-draped 2002 cover of Lisa Beamer's book with Ken Abraham. The publisher issued one million hardback copies on the first anniversary of 9/11.

CREDIT: Publicity shot

and demanding an immediate public inquiry into the 9/11 events, they were swamped by the adoration of Lisa Beamer.

It didn't matter that Mrs Beamer had never received a phone call from Flight 93. She was there to sell her husband's recruitment slogan: "Let's Roll".

Blonde and girlishly even-featured, with two model children conceived in wedlock and pregnant with another, the heartbroken but valiant widow appeared on top-rated TV shows such as NBC's *Dateline*, on which she said: "You know, in the Lord's Prayer, it asks us to forgive our trespasses as we forgive those who trespass against us. [Todd] was forgiving those people for what they were doing, the most horrible thing you could ever do to someone." She made similar devotional and imaginative comments tearfully on *Good Morning America*, *Dateline*, *Larry King Live* and *Oprah* (which she attended via the host's jet) among others.

She had her first taste of literary prestige when she signed a preface to a rushed-out evangelical hardback called *A Reason for Hope in a Time of Tragedy*.[29] *People* magazine named her one of the "25 Most Intriguing People of 2001".[30] She received sackfuls of mail. War veterans sent her their medals. Pilgrim-like, she retraced her husband's fatal journey in the company of TV cameras. Her family Christmas was shared nationally on CNN with Larry King. A staunch ally of the White House, she keenly advocated the federal government's $7 billion victim compensation scheme and had herself photographed unveiling a "Let's Roll" decal on the side of one of the USAF F-16 jet fighters that had played such an ambiguous role on the day her husband had died. She sought to have "Let's Roll" trademarked. She signed a six-figure book deal which, along with her seven-figure compensation cheque, made her a rich woman. If she ever had doubts about the authenticity of her husband's telephone call, as hinted in her subsequent book, these tokens must have banished them.

On 21 February, Mrs Beamer invited top-rated TV anchor Diane Sawyer into her New Jersey home, in Sawyer's words "to share, for the first time, her most intimate gift". The episode of *Good Morning America* featured video from the delivery room and shots of the newest Beamer child, Morgan Kay, back at home with her brothers. The next night Mrs Beamer and Morgan were guests on *Larry King Live*.

Dissenting voices were raised. "In recent months anyone who surfs the news programs has been subjected to Lisa Beamer's teary face on every outlet worth mentioning," wrote a sceptic, reflecting the obstinately secular segment of American opinion.[31] He said she had acquired a personal media representative and at least two outside PR guns, and granted over 200 interviews to the media. This overexposure of private grief led to "genuine instances of heroism and sacrifice becom[ing] nothing more than veiled warnings, inducements to the rest of us to keep our mouths shut and rally round the flag".

In August 2002, just in time for the anniversary, Mrs Beamer published her inspirational book, entitled – predictably – *Let's Roll!*. The publisher, Tyndale, had done brisk business with a series of barmy novels about life on earth after the return of Jesus Christ. The Left Behind books had sold in their millions to deluded evangelists who liked to entertain the idea that a second coming was just around the corner, after Armageddon had wiped out all the sinners.[32]

Tyndale bet the farm on Lisa Beamer. The publisher issued a staggering one million copies in hardback and Lisa was rolling in more ways than one. Hers was one of the biggest single book print-order since a Chicago publisher had printed millions of Korans for the US-backed Taliban insurgents in the 1980s.

On the one-year anniversary, as US television piped its first Flight 93 dramatization, she plugged her 500-ton mountain of books in a series of prerecorded devotional spots for ABC, NBC, Fox and CNN. The title went straight on to the *New York Times* best-seller list, but brought a number of negative reviews from readers. One typical online comment by Lukas Manneun from Washington, DC, said bitterly: "In a tribute to the free market and the opportunistic nature of human behavior, Lisa Beamer shows Americans big and small how to snatch a dollar out of the jaws of tragedy. If only she had a written a good book in the process."

THE GHOSTWRITER

Lisa Beamer's book was a transparent excuse by the White House to propagate the cult scripture. The tearful widow's private life as a homemaker was merely the Christian stuffing. The meat was in the blow-by-blow narrative of Islamic hijackings, recounted in a voice-of-God mode that alternated bizarrely with Mrs Beamer's homely reminiscences of Christian life with Todd. There was no way Lisa had penned this part of the account, which read uncannily like the first forty pages of the equally best-selling 9/11 Commission report that emerged from the hand of Commission director Philip Zelikow two years, fifteen million dollars and sixty lawyers later.

The voice of Lisa Beamer's alter ego belonged to a hack ghostwriter named Ken Abraham, who seemed to have received his lengthy, official-toned narrative straight from an oracle among the politicals in the Pentagon. The sprawling headquarters of the Department of Defense was an institution he knew well, having visited the previous year when writing another widow's book, this time about the crash of golfer Payne Stewart's executive jet.

The crash book was relevant experience for anyone considering Abrahams for Lisa Beamer's book. Stewart had been co-owner of a jet which had apparently undergone a very rare and sudden pressurization failure. The plane had gone off course while en route from Florida to Texas and collided with a pasture in the north-central part of South Dakota after flying for four hours, apparently on autopilot and ostensibly running out of fuel. South Dakota Governor Bill Janklow had said at the scene of the crash that investigators would find little to examine as "very few pieces of this tragedy are larger than a couple square inches".[33]

At the request of the Federal Aviation Authority (FAA), the Pentagon had swiftly scrambled US Air Force F-16 and F-15 fighters, which followed the jet and reported seeing no activity on board. They got close enough to look into the windows and see the frost inside. As the Lear 35 eerily raced across a half a dozen states, Stewart's Australian-born wife, Tracey, had followed the drama on CNN, trying to reach her husband on his cellphone. Like Lisa Beamer, she had then worked with Ken Abraham to produce a best-seller.

After 9/11, sceptics had immediately cited the Payne Stewart case for the way it radically contrasted with the US Air Force's performance against the hijacked airliners. On a word from the FAA, the duty airbases in Florida had rushed supersonic jet fighters up to 43,000 feet to intercept Stewart's rogue executive jet and, if it threatened to crash on a populated area, to shoot it down.

Before getting into Pentagon-related texts, Ken Abraham had tilled the vineyards of the Lord in evangelistic literature. Of his many Bible-bashing titles (*Hot Trax Devotions for Guys*), the latest had been the most racy: books written about criminal televangelist Jim Bakker, or edited for the overweight apocalypse-preacher John Hagee (*The Beginning of the End*, *From Daniel to Doomsday: The Countdown Has Begun*, *Jerusalem Countdown*).

DOUBTS REVEALED

If Lisa Beamer was mainly a passenger on her own book, there were some tell tale passages in which she made her presence felt. When she became involved peripherally in the action and she had a news story to tell, Ken Abraham's ghosted text was unable to conceal signs of tension.

There was the ordeal of the absent call from above. Todd had left Lisa to find out about the disappearance of Flight 93 on the news like everyone else. In their hour of need, as Armageddon threatened and the minutes ticked by, he had made her endure an awful silence. Her family and friends and various Christian ministers had rushed to support her as she lay semi-catatonic in a darkened room fearing the worst.

When she heard about the other calls that had come in from Flight 93, she was very upset that Todd had not called her. Inevitably, she thought of his detested cellphone, which represented everything corporate about her workaholic and frequently absent husband. "Todd was a gadget nut who carried two cellular phones with him constantly – I nearly had to wrestle those phone out of his hands every time we went on vacation ... if Todd was ... in any trouble, he'd call," she fumed, raising a bone of contention that had always marred their relationship.[34]

United Airlines rep Nick Leonard called her Friday night, four days later, with the astonishing news. Todd *had* called. "The FBI has been keeping the information private," Leonard told her, "until they've had the opportunity to review the material. But now they've released it. I have a written summary of the call."

Strangely, Lisa Beamer soon learned that the FBI had not kept the call so secret after all. Larry Ellison, boss of Oracle, the computer company Todd worked for, had spun the story of Todd the hero aboard Flight 93 on Thursday, before anyone else knew of Todd's phone call. Even more strangely, the Verizon Corporation, owners of GTE Airfone, for some unknown reason and quite contrary to convention, had *not* recorded the call.

In other words, the circumstances surrounding Todd's call were for more suspicious than President Bush's dramatic declaration had suggested. In what way could the FBI need to investigate such a phone call? What did Larry Ellison have to do with it? The very next night he was on television calling for the introduction of a national ID card, something his company would be very interested in supplying to the Bush government at enormous cost.[35] United Airlines only revealed after four working days the phone call Lisa Jefferson had promised to report to Lisa Beamer immediately.

Lisa Beamer's strong conviction that Todd would have called her, and that she'd heard about his call to Verizon a bit late dissipated a little after her telephone interview the following Saturday with the Verizon supervisor, founding Flight 93 cult-member Lisa Jefferson. The latter explained that Beamer had not wished to speak to her out of concern for her pregnancy, but the widow was not conceding much: "He *may* have been concerned about our unborn baby had I gotten *too* upset. So I wasn't *too* surprised to learn from Lisa that he had considered calling me and had chosen against it." [Emphasis added.]

In this excuse for Todd's failure to call, the widow sounds unconvinced; nor does she persuade the reader. It's not as though Todd had performed earthly transgressions, such as crashing the car or gambling the house away. He might have thought of her pregnant condition under such circumstances, and avoided calling to prevent her getting upset and having a miscarriage. But what he is reported to have said – the praying, the psalming – shows that he was preparing to meet his maker and that he knew this was his last phone call on earth.

Todd Beamer needed to say goodbye to his life-partner and mother of his children, exchange a few last tender words with her, and share a prayer to the God they both ardently believed in. It does not ring true that he would cut his life-partner out of his last few minutes in this world, and choose instead to converse intimately for more than fifteen minutes with a complete stranger. Lisa must have seethed when she heard her namesake, a lifer with the telephone company, recounting her husband's tragic last thoughts, and him with *two* cellphones in his pocket. She was far too decent to put it in print, but frankly it must have been a slap in the teeth for her and the kids. If Todd Beamer really did this, he was far from being a golden hero of legend.

Lisa was so doggedly loyal that she was ready to speculate unconvincingly on why so many calls had come from Flight 93, even though heroic Todd had not called her. "Some people have speculated that the terrorists actually wanted passengers to call, to increase the fright they felt they were inflicting . . ." "Speculated" was the operative word, since only one passenger call had come from all the other stricken flights,[36] and none at all from passengers on the fullest airliner, Flight 11, carrying about ninety-two people. Furthermore, telephone operatives would have been able to locate the lost aircraft using cellphone call data if calls were getting through, so the alleged hijackers were doubly unlikely to have encouraged such connections.[37]

More tension showed through Mrs Beamer's text when it came to the evangelical content of Verizon's unrecorded call, as it was recounted by the devout Lisa Jefferson to Mrs Beamer. Faced with this woman recounting the intimate exchanges she claimed to have had with Todd, Lisa Beamer became quite sceptical. "I'd *never before* heard of Todd reciting the Lord's Prayer in pressure situations," she told her ghost-writer crisply. "Interestingly, Psalm 23 *wasn't a mantra Todd recited* often." [Emphasis added.] Very interestingly, indeed.

Mrs Beamer confirmed that Lisa Jefferson had promised Todd she would tell his pregnant wife about the call.[38] She noted down that her husband had "told about family, made her promise to call me".[39] Lisa was far too well behaved to say so, but she made it clear in her narrative that this was something Jefferson had not done. Instead, United Airlines had informed her by phone four working days later, at nine in the evening, when the FBI had finished doing whatever policemen had to do with an unrecorded telephone call.

Perhaps Lisa Jefferson's broken promise had confirmed for the widow that there was something fishy about the unrecorded, unwit-nessed phone call reported from inside a megacorporation that was working closely with the US government, including the Pentagon. However, her doubts would have been swamped by media coverage that feverishly cited supporting evidence like the Lord's Prayer that was printed on Todd's bookmark, or the Bible classes that he had recently been attending.

In Mrs Beamer's account, the believability of Verizon's report of Todd's call wobbled momentarily and then was restored when it came to the wonderful phrase he had coined and Ms Jefferson had "over-heard" over his dangling phone line. The Let's Roll slogan was "all Todd", she reassured her readers. Her attachment to Let's Roll was understandable because the catchphrase had become a valuable prop-erty. "Everyone from mouse-pad sellers to fireworks makers was filing applications"[40] and practical Lisa had called the lawyers and set up a charitable children's foundation to capture the earnings. She refused many proposals, but allowed Wal-Mart to use it (in their employee-motivation programme) as well as Florida State University's 2002 foot-ball team[41] and, of course, her patrons at the Pentagon and their friends, the British producers of the first Flight 93 movie – which didn't mention a shootdown.

There's one more passage in her book where Mrs Beamer was unable to disguise a measure of scepticism about the events surrounding the demise of Flight 93 and of her late husband. With other bereaved persons, she visited the crash site in a thinly populated area situated thirty miles from the nearest movie theatre. Like everyone else, includ-ing the mass media, she had to stay about a quarter of a mile away from the impact crater. She dutifully believed the Pentagon and the FBI when they told her the whole airliner had disappeared into the ground, along with the wings and the tail. Nevertheless, she was unable to disguise her complete bewilderment, approaching disbelief.

> The federal authorities wouldn't allow us to get too close to the actual spot where the plane had struck the ground. I didn't see a single piece of airplane anywhere. The authorities said that they had found a few engine parts, one large piece in a pond about half a mile away, and some small fragments about the size of a notebook. Other

than that, the plane had totally disintegrated. Tiny pieces of plane debris were embedded in the trees surrounding the site. More than 400 rescue workers had combed the area searching for fragments or anything that could identify victims. Little could be found... Anything that remained of Flight 93 was buried deep in the ground.[42]

The "deep in the ground" explanation seems tacked on, as if Ken Abraham had appended it as a sort of explanation for the absence of almost all trace of the aircraft. There was no word about where the

GOVERNMENT EXHIBIT P200057 01-455-A   M-CSP-00009957

The Pentagon, the FBI and a lone eyewitness said the intact United Airlines Boeing 757 plunged at full speed into friable soil at a reclaimed open-pit mine near Shanksville, Pennsylvania. The earth engulfed the whole 64-ton aircraft, including its wings, tail and all persons aboard. The plane accordioned down to 30 feet in length underground. Sceptics suggested that the eight-mile debris field indicated the plane had been shot down and only part, if any, of it had hit the crater. They also questioned claims that a passport and a bandana were retrieved from the impact site.

CREDIT: US federal government evidence photo

wings and tail had gone, and Mrs Beamer's account contained a hint of the unspeakable suspicion of a shootdown by the US Air Force that her entire career as a White House sanctioned media celebrity had been intended to extinguish.

AMONG THE HEROES

HarperCollins, the major book publisher owned on behalf of a list of bankers by the born-again immigrant Rupert Murdoch, beat Mrs Beamer to it by a month when it brought out the "definitive" story of Flight 93 by a *New York Times* sports reporter called Jere Longman.[43] He apparently interviewed "hundreds" of people to write his book, and, as the title *Among the Heroes* implied, the main intention of it seemed to be to bring the passenger martyrdom story to life by pumping relatives and friends for information additional to the surprisingly detailed telephone-call reports they had given to the media at the height of their shock and grief in the days after 9/11.[44]

Longman's account was written close enough to the events to retain vestiges of the suspicions that had surrounded the crash in the early days. Although he faithfully traced the official story through his narrative, his investigations nevertheless led him to a courageous conclusion: "Many crucial questions about the final minutes of the flight remain unanswered." It was a statement that did not quite chime with the evangelical cult's delusional beliefs – or with the line taken by the politicals at the Pentagon.

In another break with the official account, Longman recorded the words of the first man on the Shanksville scene, Lee Purbaugh, a scrap-metal worker who apparently had been hired only the previous day. "The only claimant to have eyewitnessed the 'crash' ran to the site and wondered where the plane was. 'It was unbelievable,' Purbaugh said. 'Something that big had scattered that quick. *There was nothing there.*'"[45] [Emphasis added.] If putting the word 'crash' in inverted commas were not bad enough, Longman actually referred to the official story as Pentagon "claims", which must have furrowed a few brows around the E-ring.

If this conclusion, so similar to Lisa Beamer's, was not awkward enough, Longman went even further: "The Pentagon claimed that 'the fuselage accordioned on itself more than thirty feet into the porous, backfilled ground.' No mention of the wings or tail . . . Pennsylvania state troopers said that they had seen no piece of the plane larger than a phone book . . ."

Then, in quoting Somerset County coroner Wallace Miller, Longman wrote the unwritable: "If you didn't know, you would have *thought no one was on the plane* . . . You would have thought they *dropped them off somewhere*."[46] [Emphasis added.] Miller's wisecrack demonstrated that the Pennsylvania hinterland seethed with sceptics.

Sadly, Longman's early glimpses of a much more perplexing air disaster with a possibly sinister dimension were buried in the avalanche of media-driven war making excitement that followed, much of it deceptive reports of weapons of mass destruction in Iraq.

Saddled with his "heroes" brief, Longman did not explore the peculiar circumstances of the downing of Flight 93. He did not publish a map of the debris field, which would have shown plane debris on the ground a full eight miles upwind. He did not investigate the excavation of the Shanksville site during and after the FBI's period of control. Nor did he mention either the various planes eyewitnesses saw overhead around the time of the impact, or the F-16 fighters that were aloft and available. All these elements he left out, perhaps because they pointed so blatantly towards the possibility of a shootdown, a possibility that the mass media and even the FBI initially had entertained but soon dropped.

BINGHAM, GLICK, BURNETT, JEFFERSON

A stream of also-ran books followed the two blockbusters of 2002.

The gay world played its part in the cult on 15 September 2002, coming up with a book by *The Advocate*'s Jon Barrett on Mark Bingham, the gay rugby-player who was supposed to have joined the rebels. It was based primarily on material given to the author by his mother, Alice Hoglan, who "instilled in him a belief that he could be anything", according to the book's sleeve-notes. She had campaigned energetically on 12 September, appearing many times on TV news, reporting that her son had been a hero. Alice Hoglan also happened to be employed at the time by United Airlines, and she later gave a five-minute interview on CNN in which she backed President Bush all the way. To this book there was another Christian angle. Earlier, author Jon Barrett had edited a delusional reader for teenagers entitled *Faith: Stories of Belief and Spirituality*.[47]

After the United States got bogged down in Iraq, bookshops kept the cult's martyr narrative on the boil when Lyz Glick, another of the Flight 93 widows, followed with a hagiography of her late husband in 2004. *Publisher's Weekly* said of it: "Out of her grief, Lyz has produced this beautiful book memorializing her husband, who became a media hero for his role in the probable attack on the hijackers." The "probable" cannot have gone down too well with the Glicks, who were fully deluded members of the cult, having reported Jeremy Glick's call as having been made on a cellphone, as reported by CNN and, originally, the *Pittsburgh Post-Gazette*. Indeed, Lyz Glick hardly needed a telephone to speak to her husband because, as the book's blurb put it, her letters

A biography of Mark Bingham came from gay journal *The Advocate*. Its description of him on the cover as "a man who fought back on September 11th" came exclusively from a brief telephone call reported by his doting mother, a Bush fan who worked for United Airlines and was all over the TV news on September 12th promoting her son as a hero.

CREDIT: Promotional image

urged daughter Emmy to "listen for what Lyz can still hear when the wind is right: her father's voice".

Another widow, Deena Burnett, the former Delta Airlines flight attendant, co-wrote a book published in early 2006 about "everyday heroes" called *Fighting Back: Living Life Beyond Ourselves*. She had revealed her political colours. She was the homemaker whose husband supposedly made as many as four telephone calls to her from Flight 93, the first reportedly by cellphone at an altitude of over six miles. Displaying her cult membership, Mrs Burnett strongly insisted on the call having come from a cellphone. In the election year 2004, she delivered a statement of Christian faith to massed delegates at the heavily guarded Republican National Convention in New York, preceding even superhero former NY mayor Giuliani, thereby bearing witness for the cult, and encouraging thousands to take the message home across the nation and disseminate it to others. She also demonstrated that, like fellow airline staffer Alice Hoglan who had also been an early witness to the phone calls, she was a keen devotee of President Bush. Fox news broadcast her speech, whereas it had not covered speeches by the bereaved at the Democratic party convention, nor the national anthem.[48]

As the cult's sponsors fought mounting public bitterness against the bloody Iraq occupation, and the commander-in-chief's popularity plunged, Lisa Jefferson joined the literary world in 2006 with a memoir ghostwritten for her by the evangelical anchorwoman of her hometown Chicago's CBS news-radio station. It was published by Moody's, an imprint whose motto is: Proclaiming the Gospel of Christ and a Biblical Worldview.

Given the title *Called* (double entendre intended),[49] the book told the story of Jefferson seeing "her life transformed, simply by answering Todd Beamer's call. Jefferson sends a stirring challenge to all of us – whether it comes during quiet obscurity or international adversity, we must be prepared to answer God's call."[50]

Perhaps Ms Jefferson was trying to calm a guilty conscience with this devotional work published five years after the events. Privately, she must have known that she had not done the things her boss said at the Verizon excellence award ceremony that she had done. Possibly hidden secret-state minders wished to consolidate her story against

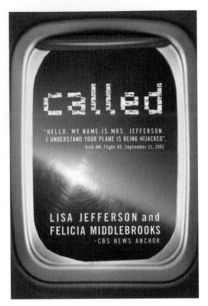

Lisa Jefferson's 2006 book was pure cult lore, promoting the divine inspiration of Todd Beamer's suspect call. It was subtitled with lengthy factual data, as if to assert the authenticity of what was a single-sourced and unrecorded report, surrounded by corporate misinformation about the call to Lisa Beamer. Jefferson's employer, Verizon, was at the time a US government contractor in the amount of $1.4 billion. The book's publication coincided with the intensive campaign to launch an assault on Iran.

CREDIT: Promotional image

the irritatingly persistent sceptics. Perhaps the evangelical memoir had nothing to do with either motive, but it did place the sole source of the Beamer call squarely within the cult.

LAUNCH TO THE MASSES

"No one in this world has ever lost money by underestimating the intelligence of the great masses of the plain people. Nor has anyone ever lost public office thereby." H. L. Mencken's memorable lines must have been in the minds of the powerful and hidden figures who agreed to endorse the Crusader legend of Flight 93 in order to crush widespread rumours of a shootdown by the US Air Force and recruit for war.

The string of made-for-TV and feature movies that presented the Flight 93 legend without referring to a shootdown started in 2002 and climaxed with *three* in rapid succession in late 2005 and early 2006, as if in preparation for a new assault on Iran. Because they are cult artefacts that posed as fact while being riddled with fiction, they rank among the poorest-quality films ever made. They garnered respectful, even rave, reviews from corporate house-critics, who were not about to be banished from future corporate screening junkets by referring to widespread suspicions of a shootdown. All of them came packaged in fervent attestations of exhaustive research by the producers. These claims, too, were ardently endorsed by the media choir. In fact, the films so completely failed to investigate their subject that they resembled little more than the propaganda that used to issue from the offices of the totalitarian Nazi and Soviet studios in Europe.

LET'S ROLL: THE STORY OF FLIGHT 93

Let's Roll: The Story of Flight 93 was a pure cult object. It ignored the evidence and made no mention of any shootdown. Directed by an unknown UK director, Chris Oxley, it followed word-for-word the line of the Pentagon politicals that Ken Abraham had stenographed into Lisa Beamer's book. In it, the bereaved friends and relatives sat

Chris Oxley's cult movie faithfully depicted the hijackers at the controls of Flight 93, although no eyewitness evidence placed them there, and the cockpit voice recording of them made little sense. They were also shown wearing the red bandanas recounted by the grieving relatives, although green is the Islamic colour, and red is worn by the notorious Los Angeles street gang, the Cripps, which was much better known to Hollywood executives. Four years later, prosecutors in a 2006 court case produced a photograph of an intact and laundered bandana supposedly found at the site of the aircraft's mysterious disappearance, although the hijackers who would have worn them were presumably crushed to bloody pulp.

Credits: Movie publicity release/US evidence photo

around sharing their delusions about what might have occurred, and the director intercut his dramatization, featuring numerous cellphone calls at cruising altitude. The reported speech spoken by unknown actors into their clasped handsets was stilted and unconvincing. The whole effort was suffused with telepathy, as cult members conducted their seance and Oxley channelled Ken Abraham. The result looked as if Oxley had visited the oracle alongside the ghostwriter.

It was a one-hour movie made for TV, produced by Granada and shown on Britain's main commercial channel and around the world.

Let's Roll elicited only the mawkish response that could be expected of its material. In a down-page review, the *Guardian*'s critic Nancy Banks-Smith wrote, for example: "Mobile phones [cellphones] made an extraordinary difference. Flight crew, passengers and their families were closely in touch for more than half an hour. They repeated: 'I love you. I love you,' as a falling spider throws out lines of silk to save itself." Neither the drama nor the producers, Granada TV, bothered to explain how cellphone calls at cruising altitude were possible that day, when, according to Alexa Graf, the spokesman for AT&T in 2001, they could only occur by fluke at best, or to ask why so few came from the other stricken flights, particularly Flight 11.

THE HAMBURG CELL

The Hamburg Cell, directed by Antonia Bird, was a 2004 TV movie produced by the UK's Channel 4 and Mentorn Films. It came with the predictable stamps of authenticity all over it. Every Flight 93 film was ostensibly so true to its subject that you might as well have been watching life itself unfolding. True to cult beliefs, this one ignored much of the evidence, named Ziad Jarrah as the suicide pilot, and left out the shootdown suspicions.

"It's based on two years of extensive research by screenwriter Alice Pearman," the *Daily Telegraph* raved. Alice Pearman had produced prime-time *Panorama* news documentaries for the BBC. Her role as a purveyor of TV news reality, blending into her role as a propagator of illusion, closely paralleled the career of Paul Greengrass, who was supposed to be touting his Flight 93 script around Hollywood when Pearman was up to her neck in her German research.

"She examined trial transcripts and investigation files; interviewed people who knew the hijackers [*sic*]; amassed vast amounts of material. Together with co-writer Ronan Bennett, she then whittled it down to a narrative about how Ziad Jarrah, a secular Muslim student from Lebanon, was recruited into the al-Qaeda cell based in Hamburg, and became one of the pilots who carried out the hijackings of 11 September 2001. 'There is nothing in the film that hasn't been documented,' says Bird. 'I can't think of a single incident in the film that has not come from evidence or research.' "[51]

Her sales pitch was instantly discredited by a sharp-witted reviewer, who pointed out that "they inexplicably have Atta and company prepare Swiss Army knives instead of box cutters".[52] So much for the vast amounts of researched material.

The trade critics around the film's 2004/2005 winter launch were at pains to point out how sensitively handled the topic was. Jarrah's fiancée would have begged to differ, had she not been driven into a witness protection programme and forced to change her identity, address and career. Jarrah's mother would also have disagreed: she had listened to the rogue pilot's voice on the air-traffic control recordings and not recognized it.

Jarrah seems to have flirted with beards and veils and militancy when he was twenty-one and newly residing in Germany as a student. But he also indulged in cannabis-smoking and attended many parties. The idea that he rushed off to Afghanistan for three weeks with other radicals, ostensibly to join up to fight for the Islamic Chechens against Russia, and instead signed up with Osama Bin Laden to become a sleeper in the USA, came straight out of the USA's post-9/11 torture gulag, from informers who claimed to have known him.

Torture evidence is worthless and also, in this case, nonsensical. Bush had claimed that al-Qaeda sent its agents to "hide" in target countries. The FBI director had denounced their fiendishly complex "deception". UK Chancellor Gordon Brown (arguing for ID cards) in 2006 cited a 9/11 hijacker who had "30 identities". Ziad Jarrah had not hidden, had deceived no one, and had taken no known supplementary identities. His conversion from a fun-loving graduate of Catholic schools, fluent in French, English and German, devoted to his common-law wife, never failing to contact his family every ten days or so, to a demented Islamic radical signing up with Osama Bin Laden in the Afghan mountains, and then turning back into a decent, regular fellow in Florida was unconvincing. The idea that he would have collaborated with a mentally unstable character like Zacarias Moussaoui was implausible. He might just as plausibly have been engaged in dealing hashish.

The *Telegraph*'s critic acknowledged that in following the FBI scenario *The Hamburg Cell* was illogical, even baffling.

"As portrayed by Karim Saleh, Jarrah always remains something of an enigma," the *Telegraph* critic wrote. "There is no scene where we see him deciding to go to the mosque for the first time; no single incident that makes sense of his involvement with al-Qaeda. There are no easy answers here to explain his psychological motivations." Here was more discredit being heaped on Alice Pearman's "extensive research".

Director Antonia Bird was totally contradictory. She claimed not to interpret Jarrah, but at the same time to be certain he had been a suicide pilot. "We were determined to stick to the facts and not put our own interpretations on their lives, particularly Jarrah's," she told the paper. "We don't know. Nobody knows. We only know how long it took him to get involved, where he got involved, *and what he ended up doing* – and that's what we show. It's something people will have to think about and decide for themselves." [Emphasis added.] We've already seen that the film erroneously portrayed its hijackers preparing weaponry that did not accord with the White House story. It further portrayed Jarrah making a suspicious decision to switch his field of study to aeronautical engineering under the influence of his sinister radical comrades in Hamburg. He actually decided to change his course, not after meeting the radicals, but well before he had any contact with them. Moreover, Jarrah's apparent fundamentalism started to appear, not in Hamburg, but after a visit to his secular roots in the Lebanon. He was just twenty-one years old at the time.[53]

The Hamburg Cell opened with Jarrah the fundamentalist making the sinister "I love you – I love you – I love you – and rings off" phone call that the mass media emphasized. Sadly, the 9/11 Commission decided that this call never happened. Instead, Jarrah made a normal call. "In the early morning hours of September 11, Jarrah made on final call to [Aysal] Senguen from his hotel ... The conversation was brief and, according to Senguen, not unusual."[54] More bad news for Ms Pearman.

Then there's the letter sent on 11 August with the wrong address. It included the lines: "I did not escape from you but I did what I was supposed to do and you should be very proud of me ... Remember always who you are and what you are. Head up. The victors never have their heads down!" Jarrah's fiancée denied that it was the confession the mass media made it out to be. She said that lines, written in German between two non-native speakers and taken to refer obliquely to the 9/11 plot, were simply about the upcoming wedding they planned and his decision to defy his family and take flying lessons, a dream since childhood.

The *Los Angeles Times* reported that Jarrah did not go to prayers and had no connection with Atta in Hamburg, and that his flight-school comrades completely disbelieved the allegation that he was a hijacker.[55]

The newspaper reported a different story after the trial in Germany of one of the Hamburg radicals, upon which much of the research for *The Hamburg Cell* was based. This version, far from endorsing the official theme of secrecy and subversion, however, depicted a large band of outspoken men keen on growing beards and being militant. "The evidence presents a new view of the Hamburg cell. So public were the beliefs of the hijackers and their associates that the often-stated notion that they were a cell of secret 'sleeper agents' of the al-Qaeda terrorist network seems almost opposite the truth." The newspaper failed to observe that all the attention-seeking might have been deliberate, if some of those involved were double-agents, as opinion polls suggested was the belief of about 100 million Americans.

THE FLIGHT THAT FOUGHT BACK

By 2005, the occupation of Iraq was going badly for the Crusaders. The dusky Moslem devils remained unruly, and, in the absence of the required popularity, the US commander-in-chief's re-election was going to have to be rigged using electronic voting machines that left no paper record for a recount.[56] Recruitment figures were sagging, and the periods of service for the National Guard members who garrisoned Iraq were being arbitrarily extended.

The Flight 93 cult had been a great recruitment tool for the warmongers, and hidden wire-pullers evidently decided to wheel it out again in preparation for the planned assault on Iran. An astonishing *three* movies were to come out. Of course, these productions did not occur by public demand, but by the decision of the men behind the scenes, corporate TV management being entirely despotic and containing not a single element of democracy in its entire structure. Heavily trailed ahead of time, the dramas would appear on TV viewers' screens worldwide, and might be branded a huge success whether they succeeded or not, because the TV audience had no idea how audiences were measured. Since advertising space would not be sold on the first of the movies, Madison Avenue monitoring would not apply.

Naturally, the first film of the sequence, *The Flight That Fought Back*, to be shown on the Discovery TV channel, would not depict a perplexing transportation crash involving a possible shootdown by the US Air Force. That had nothing to do with what the producers or the Pentagon

The cover-blurb of the 2005 cult movie *The Flight That Fought Back* repeated the belief that the plane had been seized by operatives who had planned their mission for two years, although two of the alleged hijackers reportedly had checked baggage into the hold, an action that invited special security screening and that any well-planned mission would have avoided in order to reduce risk-taking to the minimum.

CREDIT: Promotional image

politicals wanted. They were after a semi-divine revelation of stalwart courage in the face of maniacal Islam. Above all, it would be so authentic that nobody would ever again dare bleat the word "shoot-down" again. And the authenticity would be delivered by those who had been in touch with the heroes by phone, the indomitable friends and relatives of the elect.

The result was the closest thing to a remake of *Let's Roll* that could have happened without actually dragging out Chris Oxley again. It was another British production, and this time the producers made great play of the Pentagon's assistance, as if Department of Defense politicals had never heard of Flight 93 before, nor worked closely with Chris Oxley and Antonia Bird on earlier productions.

The US Discovery Channel first aired it, commercial-free, on the fourth anniversary, and played it later in the UK and around the world for its cumulative 1.4 billion worldwide subscribers, or about one-fifth of the earth's human population.

Coming from "The acme, the Rolls-Royce, of documentary film makers," as the *Wall Street Journal* had called Discovery, if this did not blast those shootdown rumours off the historical record, then nothing would.

Producer Phil Craig issued a line of sales talk that matched Paul Greengrass and Antonia Bird for glib cant. His movie was a "full and accurate reconstruction" of the flight. It "incorporate[d] the best possible research available, including actual voice recordings from passengers and crew members". (There was no mention of why it had taken the Pentagon four years to find such tapes.) His movie included "interviews with family members, some of whom describe what they heard in actual conversations with people on board the flight". If anyone in corporate media land detected a blatant rehash of Oxley's 2002 effort, we didn't hear about it.

"With a compassionate commitment to painting the most accurate picture of what happened aboard Flight 93, we were given unprecedented access to recordings that have never before been aired on television," Craig said with an unsavoury mixture of piety and bragging.[57] "In order to present the most accurate depiction possible, we conducted in-depth research, exhausted all resources, and uncovered rarely heard eyewitness accounts. Also, for the first time, we learn more about Ziad Jarrah, one of Flight 93's hijackers, by interviewing those who trained him to fight and fly."

Craig displayed the typical cultist's (or TV producer's) contempt for reality. He did not refer to Jarrah as an *alleged* hijacker. He did not mention that Jarrah's martial arts training had no bearing on the supposed hijacking, because no one on the plane ever saw him, in the cabin, at the controls, or anywhere else, let alone dishing out lethal rabbit-punches to those around him. He did not admit that he was parroting the official line on Jarrah, first plugged by the *Post-Gazette* only seven weeks after the events.[58]

The programme "featur[ed] the widest range of interviews with family members yet assembled, including many whose stories have never before been told," Craig claimed. In other words, the distressed and bereaved had been included in the cult in larger numbers than ever before.

His film would be seance fiction, structured exactly like Oxley's 2002 film, featuring an action narrative interpersed with "some family members shar[ing] their personal beliefs about how their loved ones might have spent their last moments". "Personal beliefs" was another term for speculation, which was another word for pure fantasy. It did not matter that cultist Jere Longman, after interviewing hundreds of those involved, had said the last minutes of Flight 93 remained a mystery. Nor would the US Air Force feature anywhere in the movie, particularly at the controls of F-16s, firing heat-seeking missiles at the Boeing 757's six-tonne Pratt & Whitney jet engines and blasting them to bits so that only one fragment could be found on the ground.

When the film was piped into a billion homes, the house-critics raved, but the *New York Times*'s unblinkered TV critic, Ned Martel, immediately nailed the movie's director, David Goodison, as a seriously misguided rip-off artist: "The creepy elements are the narration by Kiefer Sutherland, the split-screen storytelling, the elapsed-time read-out. These are signature innovations of Fox's "24", a series that has long played on twenty-first-century fears of sudden mass destruction. Ripping them off for this production seems seriously misguided."[59]

Discovery's Christian viewers were a bit disgusted to see Todd

Beamer, an enshrined saint of the cult, depicted as a weeping lurker, muttering prayers and not taking part in the assault on the cockpit, which instead was led by a homosexual and a woman, a recognizable piece of prevailing British political correctitude. Many were puzzled, too, that Lisa Beamer did not appear among the testifying relatives. Was the Beamer call being downplayed by the Pentagon politicals now, because Verizon somehow had failed to record it?

And what about those passenger-recording revelations? No one seemed to notice. The film elicited only seven comments from viewers on the mainstream Internet Movie Database (IMDB),[60] one of them by regular contributor Francis Huddy of the UK: "Of course, the 'reconstruction' side of the film, for all we know, may be absolute rubbish. Do cell phones really function from thousands of feet in the air, at 500 m.p.h.? Was the plane shot down by a US Air Force fighter? We may never know. . . This is no forensic reconstruction of what probably happened on Flight 93, just a fairy tale of what many would like to have seen happen based on spurious cell phone calls made to friends and relatives on the ground and links between the cockpit and airspace control." *Ouch!*

Ian Henshall[61] contacted the producers about their account when they were researching it, mentioning the widespread doubts about cellphones being usable at cruising altitude. The producers seemed more excited about the Pentagon providing them with extracts of the passenger recordings, and they duly treated the cellphone calls as gospel, as required by the ruling delusions of the cult's membership.

In their timeline, the producers listed one of the few authentic-sounding cellphone calls from Flight 93. At 10:01 a.m., "passenger Andrew Garcia makes a call to his wife, Dorothy. He only has time to say 'Dorothy' before he is cut off." A duration of less than one second was the authentic sign of a cellphone call made not quite near enough to ground level. However, as so often in these cult accounts, the timeline crucially did not state whether the call was made by cellphone or Airfone. Since the producers had received "unprecedented access to recordings", they should have been able to provide such details. The research that had "exhausted all resources" had not stretched that far.

Perhaps in exchange for the recordings that politicals had so help-fully provided, the most recent revision of the Pentagon's story stood proud in this production's support materials. "10:00 a.m. Three F-16 fighter jets scrambled from Langley Air Force Base in response to earlier attacks arrive over Washington around this time," the text stated. "The pilots are still unaware that Flight 93 has even been hijacked." This central claim of NORAD and the 9/11 Commission, repeated like a mantra throughout the Commission report, had been convincingly destroyed by sceptical analysis.[62] Moreover, the first eyewitness at the impact site said "there was nothing there", but according to the producers of this movie, the Pentagon was ignorant of Flight 93 from beginning to end and certainly never shot it down.

In the USA, *The Flight That Fought Back* was duly announced to have been the Discovery Channel's highest-rated programme of the year that far, and the third highest-rated of all time. As always, the announcement came from the very same management that had been responsible for piping it to the masses in the first place.[63]

FLIGHT 93: THE MOVIE

The intensive media campaign to save the government from shoot-down suspicions and to prepare the public for an assault on Iran continued four months later on the Arts and Entertainment (A&E) Network, and was viewable in more than 130 countries by over 230 million TV households. Called *Flight 93: The Movie*, the drama was another excruciatingly bad production, this time directed by a known Pentagon hack.

It was the first production to go all the way and tell the cult hero legend without the supporting fantasies of the relatives and friends. It launched in February 2006, with A&E claiming (like Discovery) that it had been a hit with the masses. Soon it entered rental distribution channels as an instant DVD for those among the 86 million US homes supplied by A&E who might have missed the frequently repeated TV broadcasts.

Signs of the manipulative nature of this dramatization were evident in the evolving DVD cover design. The earlier version, preserved on the internet, showed Flight 93 plunging undamaged towards the ground. The cover headlines rotely reiterated the core cult scripture that "four terrorists" had been on board, although the reports of passenger calls only cited three and there was no firm evidence of a fourth.

In the second version of the cover, the producers inserted the image of an eyewitness to the impending crash of the totally intact airliner. But the most mysterious aspect of the covers was that they both portrayed the plane in its fatal nosedive right way up, instead of upside down as the 9/11 Commission insisted it had been, presumably basing their version on data retrieved from the black boxes. How could a film that had been so carefully researched have made such a glaring error? Contempt for fact was a sign of the cult, except when it came to exposing evidence in court, when the story suddenly changed.

A & E's TV drama commited a further travesty by portraying one of the alleged hijackers wearing a bomb-belt. There was no evidence of a bomb-belt on Flight 93; not from the reported passenger calls, not from the flight deck recorder, not from the impact site. Its existence in this movie was a fabrication conjured up from the strife-riven streets of Israel, Afghanistan and Iraq and fantasized aboard Flight 93. That a movie made for 86 million US households and hundreds of millions beyond should present hallucination as fact is a classic sign of cultish delusional behaviour. It was also skilled political manipulation of public opinion. The Hollywood oracle, *Variety*, called it "a restrained and impressive achievement".[64]

In another false scene, the movie depicted an alleged hijacker brutalizing a flight attendant who was an older woman. There was no evidence for the scene. That the brutality was highly provocative seemed to have meant nothing to the reckless producers. The predictable result was the

Coming five years after the events, the Fox production of Flight 93 for A&E introduced a new element, a full bomb-belt, that the producers imagined had been smuggled through airport security, thus demonstrating their status as high-priests of the Flight 93 cargo-cult delusion.

CREDIT: Promotional image

worst kind of sentiment expressed by another viewer on the IMDB: "The next time I see an Islamic extremist I'm gonna slam my elbow into his greasy grill."[65]

The producers had the gall to fanfare this flight of fiction with a motto in capital letters:

BASED ON FULLY ANNOTATED
FACTS FROM THE PUBLIC RECORD

And what was the industry's verdict on this movie? *Hollywood Reporter* wrote on 30 January 2006 that it "refuse[d] to stray far from what can be substantiated." You have to wonder how "far" *complete untruth* is from what can be substantiated. The so-called critic was no doubt copying from notes thoughtfully provided by Fox.

Some questions were asked, however. For example, the film portrayed the alleged hijackers entering the pilots' cockpit, something about which nothing at all was known. Indeed the method of seizing the controls of all the aircraft involved that day remained an utter mystery, and no formal alerts had been given by any of the eight pilots, something that the official story always skipped over.

Did this bother the producers? Apparently not at all. The film's screenwriter, Nevin Schreiner, in a letter to the *Washington Post* wrote: "According to our pilot sources, access to the cockpit is normally gained through flight attendants giving a coded knock, which is recognized by pilots and acknowledged by their providing entry. We assumed the hijackers used this method to enter the cockpit." After causing mayhem in first class, possibly committing bloody murder and causing the screaming and shouting overheard by relatives on the phone, the hijackers *politely knocked on the cockpit door*?

For these cult-member producers, it was fine to make a ludicrous assumption, and depict as "fully annotated" something that had bewildered and worried rational people all over the world for five years.

The film was accepted by and ran on the A&E Network, which also owned the History Channel and the Biography Channel. In the light of this manipulative film drama, one could only wonder what version of history and biography A&E delivered to US homes and to hundreds of millions more overseas.

Three images from three different Flight 93 propaganda movies released within six months of each other played up the central point: ordinary Americans had struck back at wicked Islamists. The theme had been launched by Congress warmakers and sent into orbit by the US President. It had a double purpose: to recruit support for invasion of the Middle East, and to demolish the obstinate popular view that the US military had shot down Flight 93. The three movies were released in 2005/2006 as President Bush's popularity nosedived.

CREDITS: A&E publicity shot/Discovery Channel publicity shot/*United 93* publicity shot

The film, in spite of its fakery, was not reported to be a flop by the hidden figures who piped it. Like *The Flight That Fought Back*, it was allegedly very successful. Reportedly, more people watched the programme than any other in the twenty-plus year history of the A&E Network. But the viewer comments on the mainstream IMDB website amounted to a grand total of nine.

The A&E Network was a joint venture of the Hearst Corporation, ABC, Inc., and NBC Universal. A&E had apparently won lots of awards. "The keys to our success have been our *quality products*," said the corporate website. "Today, A&E continues its commitment to *high ethical values* and to creating a workplace where employees are encouraged to strive for *professional excellence*." [Emphasis added.]

And whom did this corporation with high ethical values choose to direct their movie about the extremely sensitive subject of Flight 93? Why, they selected none other than Peter Markle, who had earlier directed a made-for-TV drama called *Saving Jessica Lynch*, of which one reviewer wrote: "[It] might as well have been released by the Department of Defense for PR purposes."[66]

Markle's film was such a debauchery of the facts that it became a case-study for propaganda in those few progressive university media departments that survived in Bush's USA.

In commissioning their Flight 93 film, A&E obviously knew that Markle had been part of one of the most disgraceful episodes in modern

US media history, when the Pentagon had tried to fashion Jessica Lynch into an icon for the US-led Iraq invasion.

The story was "one of the most stunning pieces of news management ever conceived," commented the BBC.[67] In an authoritative documentary, rejected *in toto* by the Pentagon, John Kampfner showed that the entire Lynch legend had been a fabrication from beginning to end.

The disgraceful episode, and Markle's movie rushed out to back it up seven months later, supported the sceptics' case that the US corporate war machine similarly rigged the events of 9/11 and the media coverage of it in order to manipulate public opinion against Islam and in favour of the USA's armed occupation of the Middle East.

UNITED 93

The first two movies of the 2005/2006 campaign to revive allied warmaking morale launched as three American states prepared impeachment proceedings against the Commander-in-Chief. The third movie, *United 93*, got its US launch amidst the lurid excitement of a political show trial that the Bush regime conducted against Zacarias Moussaoui (the trial itself also had a timing element: it was intended to influence the coming autumn elections).

The movie was the first to attract a director of calibre. Paul Greengrass was a hard-nosed ex-TV newsman from Cheam, Surrey, with a salesman's gift of the gab enhanced by a Cambridge University education. Following ten years in TV news, he had taken up a fifteen-year second career and established an enviable reputation for fly-on-the-wall film-making that escaped controversy while handling sensitive topics.

His first fiction feature had been an anti-war treatment of the Falklands conflict, made in 1989. In 2002, he'd made a drama about the so-called Bloody Sunday riot in Ireland's disputed London-Derry that, by subtly fudging issues at key moments, had cleverly contrived not to take sides. He wrote a respected script about the hideous Omagh bombing in Northern Ireland that was filmed in 2003. At the time, he occupied a position near the creative peak of the UK television industry as a maker of films that mirrored the reality of news stories.

United 93, the third British-made movie about Flight 93, had a lie planted smack on the front of its promotional material. The blurb stated: "Four planes were hijacked. Three of them reached their target. This is the story of the fourth." The picture showed a Boeing 757, evidently meant to be Flight 93, taking off against a background of the smoking Twin Towers. Sadly, the towers were set on fire several minutes after United 93 had flown away.

CREDIT: Promotional image

His tragic fall into the deluded Flight 93 cult occurred in the same year, and seemed to be the result of a Faustian pact between him and Universal Studios. It looked as if Universal boss Ron Meyer had offered Greengrass a sure-fire hit movie with an enormous budget if he would just do them another little favour afterwards. All he had to do was make yet another Flight 93 movie, this time directed at the sceptical young who attended cinemas. This distinguished British talent, who had been passionately anti-war, would join the Crusaders who had supernatural knowledge of what had happened in the mysterious transportation disaster. His style of film-making would finally fix the Flight 93 legend.

Universal Studios was owned by NBC Universal, which also owned NBC TV and NBC TV news, which was all owned by General Electric, media giant and major weapons contractor. Reportedly, General Electric had donated $1.1 million to George Bush for his 2000 election grab.[68]

Universal asserted that there had been no Faustian pact. They claimed that quite the opposite was the case: they said Greengrass had originally proposed what they termed his own script of a Flight 93 film. Universal had begged him to direct the $80 million *Bourne Supremacy* without any conditions and only had agreed to film "his" movie later.[69] But it's hard to reconcile the final script with Greengrass's track record as the director of films that take controversial and difficult positions. Perhaps the shadowy power-mongers running the TV/movie world had indeed not required their Flight 93 movie pound-of-flesh at that point, but timed for 2006, when an assault on Iran was planned. Perhaps they further knew that the Moussaoui lynching trial was to be staged in 2006 to help prepare the way for the new war (and the election victory needed for it). Whatever they knew, they scheduled the US launch for 28 April that year, just as the Moussaoui trial reached its climax on the TV news and war-makers were agitating for an unprovoked nuclear assault on Iran.

All Greengrass's films hitherto had been low-budget pictures in the UK. The temptation of an $80 million ticket for the proffered Hollywood feature must have been strong, even if it meant agreeing to put his name subsequently to a delusion. In 2006, it emerged that he had signed for a *second* feature in the Robert Ludlum blockbuster series, doubling his Universal budgets to some $160 million and propelling him solidly into the Hollywood elite. This figure represented an estimated ten times more money than he had ever received to make all the previous films in his career. Such an opportunity must have influenced his decision to make United 93 or he would not be a fallible human being. Every man had his price, as they knew only too well in Hollywood.

Greengrass's job was to stamp the Flight 93 events with his brand of tough authenticity, goading young cinema audiences into believing that this was the way it really happened and no other, even though, as the *Hollywood Reporter*'s film critic courageously noted in reviewing his picture: "No one really knows what happened on United 93."[70]

The real point of United 93 remained the same as all the other Flight 93 movies. Rumours about a US Air Force shootdown were still whizzing around the internet and 9/11 Truth meetings, and had even been glimpsed momentarily on US mainstream television being expounded by a prominent TV actor, Charlie Sheen. They had to be eradicated once and for all. Billions had watched the cult's faith-based travesties directed by second-raters on television, now moviegoers had to receive a dose of hard-hitting "reality" from Greengrass.

The movie would be produced at England's Pinewood-Shepperton Studios, which happened to be operated by the chairman of the BBC, Michael Grade. The team of Meyer, Grade and Greengrass would finally smash the shootdown rumours and get the dubious public on side for crushing Islam.

Greengrass employed sixty military air-traffic controllers and other industry people as actors for the utmost authenticity, and built an elaborate set using a recycled Boeing 757 for perfect accuracy, although significantly half of his 111-minute film would be set in government and military offices. In those locations, Greengrass would rubber-stamp the official story, with bewildered air-traffic controllers failing to understand messages or contact the air force, and the military scrambling impotently to build a response plan. Official incompetence would be the theme, although no one was fired and the principal players had been promoted. Naturally there would be no mention of the war-games scheduled for that day.

With the film ready to launch, Universal's commercial greed almost felled them at the first fence. The studio announced that 10 percent of the movie's gross income would be given to a United 93 charity – but only on the film's first *weekend*. A few independent critics thought the offer demeaned the memory of those on board and insulted their relatives by its pettiness. "Something is truly, soul-sickeningly rotten here and no amount of soberly enlightened testaments, fire-and-brimstone political punditry, or gaseous pronouncements to the contrary can distract from it," wrote Keith Uhlich of *Slant* magazine. With first-weekend earnings of $11.6 million, Universal nevertheless stumped up more than $1 million in conscience money.

The producers made great play of the fact that the relatives supported their film, except of course that nobody contacted the relatives of those who were supposed to have performed the hijacking. Even if the film-makers had wanted to contact them, the alleged hijackers' identities were unknown and, in the case of Jarrah, his family indignantly protested his innocence. The bias involved in the families' endorsement was thus exposed.

The razzmatazz around a Hollywood production promised to deepen and widen the gap between those who cared about what happened in the perplexing air disaster and those who imagined they knew. A foretaste came with a statement by Gordon Felt, brother of passenger Edward Felt, quoted in the film's publicity.[71] "It is never easy to relive the events of 9/11," he was quoted saying, "yet I support 'United 93' as a tribute to the heroism of my brother and the thirty-nine other passengers and crew who collectively chose to say 'no' on that fateful day."

The endorsement was typical cult delusion. No one knew that Ed Felt had made the call. The anonymous caller, who was only tentatively identified by officials as Ed Felt, was believed purely on circumstantial evidence to have been hiding in one of the plane's toilets, either at the front or at the back. He had apparently made a barely plausible and panicky 9-1-1 cellphone call, the recording of which has not been released, in which he allegedly screamed "We're being hijacked" about half-an-hour after the hijack reportedly had taken place. He was supposed to be addressing an emergency services operator for whom the media had reported two different names, take your choice. He hardly qualified as either a hero or one who chose to say "no".

It was not pleasant to see commercial film producers exploiting their clients' illusions as stamps of authenticity on a propaganda movie.

The Moussaoui show trial duly garnered the movie priceless free publicity on the TV news around the world as newscasters plugged it time and time again in connection with the unhinged court ravings of a mentally ill man who had been in prison during 9/11 and who was bent on receiving a death sentence and thereby becoming a martyr.

THE MAKING OF A TRAVESTY

Greengrass described his film, produced by hitherto reputable Working Title Films, as "a meticulous re-enactment" of what had happened, as if such a thing were possible given the paucity of available evidence. He said he was basing the action on "two dozen" passenger phone calls and the cockpit voice recorder, but he had no compunctions at all about using a Pentagon-authorized prop, a bomb-belt, thereby mimicking the Pentagon propagandist Peter Markle's travesty, made in Vancouver at almost the same time. By such methods, in the words of an independent

Like *Flight 93*, A&E's simultaneously made movie, Greengrass's version of the legend showed one of the hijackers donning an elaborate bomb-belt that could never have been smuggled aboard an airliner through security checks at Newark airport. The evidence did not even call for a real bomb. Rumours of a bomb aboard the airliner arose from the pilot's reported excuse for changing course, a supposed bomb, which was announced to the passengers and overheard by air-traffic control due to a pilot error.

Credit: Working Title Films publicity shot

critic, "the film show[ed] its contrived and utterly offensive dramatic hand, one reliant on passing off conjecture as proven truth."[72]

The entire avowed basis of Greengrass's film project was largely conjecture, because neither the calls nor the recording formed an adequate record on which a reputable director could base a docudrama.

- Evidence showed that the story of the band of enraged passengers storming the pilots' cockpit to bring the plane down before it could reach its 9/11 target was nearly all supposition.

- The number and identities of the hijackers remained questionable.

- The phone calls were hearsay, reported by relatives in acute nervous and emotional distress, suffering totally inappropriate pressure from the government and the media to produce evidence supporting the official line and deny a shootdown.

- The cockpit voice recording was incoherent, and parts of it could as easily have supported a recording of sexual intercourse as an argument over the controls of an airborne airliner. One of the rogue pilots was even supposed to have said in Arabic at 9:45 a.m: "Tell them to talk to the pilot. Bring the pilot back," when according to the official story the pilots lay on the floor with their throats cut.[73]

The airline said the hijackers sat as follows: "Ziad Jarrah took seat 1B, first-row aisle, the nearest seat to the cockpit. Ahmed Alhaznawi, Saeed

Alghamdi and Ahmed Alnami sat in 3C, 3D and 6B, the last row of first class."[74] But the BBC reported later that Saeed Alghamdi was still alive.[75] His driving licence and car registration showed his address as 10 Radford Blvd., on the US Navy's Pensacola base in Florida.[76] Another report showed Ahmed Alnami to be alive.[77] Jarrah's identity was hotly contested.[78] None of the identities was certain, but five years later, those were the names on the cast list of Greengrass's movie (complete with their biographies, in the film's promotional press-pack).

The in-flight passenger phone calls that Mr Greengrass cited only mentioned three hijackers, although Bush's 9/11 Commission said there were four, and the other rogue flights were supposed to have had five each. The more than thirty passenger phone calls that were eagerly and imaginatively reported in the US media never mentioned a fourth hijacker on Flight 93. This anomaly had not yet been explained, and Greengrass simply ignored it, showing Jarrah sneaking into the cockpit unobserved.

Where did the mystery pilot come from and how did he take over? Some people had pointed to the planted reports of uniforms in Mohamed Atta's suitcase, itself probably planted. But President Bush's 9/11 Commission firmly discounted speculation that a hijacker in uniform ingratiated himself into the company of the airline pilots before the flight started.[79] So the calls left three hijackers and no pilot, which did not make much of a movie.

The only sign of a qualified pilot on Flight 93 was the scorched, but not *too* scorched, visa and the intact passport-photo page of Ziad Jarrah that reportedly were found[80] by an FBI searcher combing the eight-mile-wide debris area, although Jarrah's body and cabin luggage presumably got immolated in the crater near Shanksville. Even if genuine and not planted, the pictures might have depicted a forged identity. For example, US district attorney Patrick J. Fitzgerald told the 9/11 Commission on 16 June 2004 that "[the hijackers] who did not have American citizenship were provided with stolen passports, altered passports (often obtained from fighters who'd since been killed) and passports obtained through bribery and fraud". In February 2006, UK Chancellor Gordon Brown, calling[81] for tougher anti-terrorist measures asserted that: "One 11 September hijacker used thirty false identities to obtain credit cards and

$250,000." Even Jere Longman, author of *Among the Heroes*, wrote measuredly: "With Jarrah *apparently* at the controls". [Emphasis added.]

The 9/11 Commission and Paul Greengrass nevertheless followed the party line by putting at the controls of the rogue aircraft an invented fourth hijacker, Jarrah, who had a pilot's licence attached to his name. They further included him on the hijacker cast list.

Like the previous cult movies, United 93 pivoted on a passenger revolt that led to the aircraft being ditched in mid-mission, thereby saving from attack a presumed Washington, DC, target. The passengers were depicted as the first Crusaders against Islam, because, in contrast to all the passengers on other stricken flights that day, they had learned about the 9/11 events from phone calls to the ground. Like all good Crusaders and Pentagon recruits to war in the Middle East, they killed Moslems (a gratifying and purely imaginative thrill provided at the end of the movie).

The first cut of United 93, which Universal showed to some industry reviewers, had originally ended with a sign-off caption stating:

AMERICA'S WAR ON TERROR HAD BEGUN

But at the last minute Universal evidently deemed this caption too partisan-sounding with Bush's ratings plunging to the levels of Richard Nixon when he was ejected from office.[82] They cynically changed the Bush terror slogan into a sober dedication to the victims.

PHONE CALLS

The phone calls the passengers and the recipients claimed came from Flight 93 were hotly contested by sceptics, and there was nothing "meticulous" at all about the information available on the issue. According to the 9/11 Commission and the media accounts gleaned from call recipients, some callers definitely used cellphones. Others definitely used the GTE Airfones fitted to the backs of the aircraft seats by United (but not by American on Flight 11).

Claimed cellular caller Tom Burnett reportedly called four times,[83] mentioning a gun (or guns) on board and predicting a rebellion. According to his wife Deena, who had worked for Texas-based

Delta airlines, "[The first call] was Tom, calling from the plane on the cellphone he had nearly lost in a sporting goods store two days earlier."[84] Explaining how he was able to make the ten-second call during a hijacker takeover without being prevented, Deena told the FBI he had an earpiece and speaking cord, so he could have made the call unnoticed.[85] His next call was on an Airfone. His third call, according to Longman, was by cellphone again, and his fourth Longman failed to identify by type, as often conveniently occurred in the cult texts.

Deduced cellular caller Mark Bingham's call failed after only a few moments, and his friends and family promptly tried to call him back. That would suggest they called his cellphone number, unless Bingham had both "an Airfone Activation number to activate the phone to receive calls"[86] and the time to explain it to them. Longman says he called by Airfone.

Cellular caller Jeremy Glick used a cellphone according to the original CNN/AP passenger list, which said: "Glick ... called his wife, Lyz, and in-laws in New York on a cellphone to tell them the plane had been hijacked." The *Pittsburgh Post-Gazette*, which covered Flight 93 on 13 September originally endorsed the cellphone version, but six weeks later on 28 November the story had changed and he "picked up a GTE Airfone just before 9:30 a.m. and called his in-laws in the Catskills". The call supposedly lasted twenty minutes, but strangely Glick said nothing about how the hijacking had been done, nor who the pilot was.

Non-cellular caller Todd Beamer's phone call to a Verizon operator perhaps could not be reported as a cellular call, because its content was to emerge from inside the Verizon corporation. It had to be reported as an Airfone operator call, even though Beamer was a gadget nut who carried two cellphones. Todd Beamer never spoke to his wife, and seemed happy to speak to a stranger instead, even though his reported tears and prayers showed he knew he was nearing the end of his life. Nor did Lisa Jefferson, the supervisor who failed to record the call, patch his last call through to his home number where his wife, a pregnant homemaker, anxiously waited.

Cellular caller Marion Britton at 09:41 a.m. called long-time friend Fred Fiumano, "from whom she had borrowed a cellphone". That's from the *Post-Gazette*, on 22 September. Longman wrote: "Marion gave Fiumano a phone number. Write it down, she said. Her cellphone was not working. She gave him the [cellphone] number of another passenger." She used "a borrowed phone", which must have been a cellular one.

Cellular caller flight-attendant CeeCee Lyles called her husband twice, apparently both times by cellphone. On the second occasion, her husband "looked at the . . . caller ID on the phone".

Cellular caller flight-attendant Sandy Bradshaw called her husband, Phil, using a cellphone. That's what he told their home-town North Carolina *News-Record* just ten days later, on 21 September.

Cellular caller Elizabeth Wainio told her stepmother that the passenger next to her had loaned her a cellphone, according to MSNBC on 22 September.

Cellular caller the anonymous voice known as Edward Felt had no choice but to use a cellphone because he was supposed to have made a last-minute seventy-second emergency call while supposedly hiding in one of the toilets.

Note that there are nine cellphone callers mentioned here, with fair-to-solid contemporary back-up from the callers or callees that they actually made cellphone calls. Now move forward to the trial of Zacarias Moussaoui in 2006, and magically the number of cellphone calls had collapsed to just *two*.[87]

It's not surprising that these cellular phone calls, being impossible, five years later were being drastically downplayed, after having been plastered all over the news coverage for years with no protest from the FBI. But the 9/11 Commission, itself relying on FBI investigation files, confirmed on Page 12 of its report that passengers and flight crew "used GTE airphones and cellular phones". The insistence on impossible cellphone calls was repeated in 2006 by the A&E Network when it stated on its website: "By 9:58, most cellphone calls had ended." Greengrass's movie also depicted passengers using cellphones.

Cellphones don't work at five or six miles of altitude. That's why airlines were only introducing pico-cell technology to enable them to do so in 2006/7.

Even the "Felt" call, ostensibly made at low altitude at top speed, was extremely unlikely to succeed and, even if it did, could never last the claimed sixty seconds.[88] The call in which the caller managed to say only "Dorothy" sounded more authentic.

The sceptic website 911Research pointed out that "there are reports of thirteen cellphone calls from Flight 93 passengers, but only zero or one from passengers on any of the other flights. If passengers on Flight 93 were able to complete so many cellphone calls, why were they so rare on the other flights?"[89]

We could look elsewhere in the 9/11 events for a pointer to a solution of this puzzle. Barbara Olson, the CNN-TV pundit, made the only reported cellphone calls from Flight 77 as it supposedly sped towards the Pentagon that day. Such was the original assertion of her husband or his political aides. He was US Solicitor-General and seated at his desk in the Justice Department when the calls purportedly came in.[90] In an interview with a foreign newspaper several months later (the conservative UK *Daily Telegraph*), Mr Olson changed his story and said his late wife made both collect [reverse-charge] calls by Airfone. American Airlines confirmed in 2004 that (unlike United on Flight 93) it did *not* equip with Airfones the Boeing 757 used for Flight 77. So the Solicitor-General was mistaken about the call. But why mention Airfones suddenly? Was he attempting to avoid a billing paperchase?[91]

The real import of the Olson call became clear the day after 9/11, when the White House attributed the alleged 9/11 hijackings to boxcutters. This came as a result of the "cardboard cutters" mentioned in the reported Olson call, which had emerged from the Department of Justice, headquarters of the FBI. Although regulations clashed, such knives were arguably allowable on board US scheduled flights at that time, and United and American airlines thus escaped huge class-action suits for neglect, although a few 9/11 cases are ongoing at time of writing and the airlines were accused of illegal collusion.[92] Far from suffering an economic impact as a result of supposedly allowing an arsenal (including Hollywood's bomb-belts) on to Flight 93, United joined other airlines in profiting from substantial federal compensation payments from its White House friends. Both American Airlines and United contributed to the Bush campaigns in 2000 and 2004.

Putting aside the technology of the phone calls, there was no validity in their content, either. Reported speech was weirdly stilted and abbreviated. The cult scripture provided unspeakable lines for a movie director and his actors:

- ■ "It's bad news. I need you to be happy."
- ■ "Ted, what can I do? What can I tell the pilot?"[93]
- ■ "We've been hijacked. He had an Islamic book."
- ■ "It's getting very bad on the plane . . . the plane is making jerky movements."[94]

Citing Greengrass's own words, independent critic Cole Smithey commented: "[Greengrass's] 'clear' gaze doesn't extend to quoting the 'actual' air phone dialogue, perhaps because he couldn't compensate for its inherent falseness."[95]

In fact, the content of the phone calls was pure hearsay spun by the gung-ho media, ever in search of a juicy story with which to distract viewers from their suspicions of a shootdown.

The Pentagon's recruitment slogan for Iraq was particularly suspect. "Let's Roll" had reputedly been overheard at the Verizon customer center down a receiver left dangling. A *Newsweek* article of 3 December 2001 turned the dangling phone into cult scripture nearly three months after the events, and the writers astutely adopted a guessing pose on the call's origin. "Todd Beamer may have been having trouble with his credit card, or he may just have punched 0 into the Airfone," it said, quoting corporate sources. Coincidentally or not, the confusion again conveniently avoided a billing paperchase in the event of an independent inquiry such as by a grand jury.

It just so happened that at the time of the 9/11 events, Verizon was the contractor for installing a major high-security telecoms package across the entire DC government apparatus, including the Department of Defense. "WITS2001 is Verizon's largest and most complex government contract, valued at up to $1.4 billion over a term of four years plus four one-year options" is how Verizon's website described the deal. Look for a mention of that in Greengrass's "meticulous re-enactment", made for the Bush-supporting General Electric corporation.

Bush, when he declared "war on terror" in Congress on 20 September 2001, in his opening remarks praised "the courage of passengers who rushed terrorists to save others on the ground. Passengers like an exceptional man named Todd Beamer". But Beamer's single-sourced call was suspect.

The content in the other calls was third- or fourth-hand hearsay, dubiously committed to memory by relatives or friends in a state of alarm, shock and grief. Details of the hijackers, their fashion statements and weapons almost certainly originally arose from panicky rumours among the passengers, who reportedly had been banished to the rear of the plane's two cabins. Such passed-down rumours the call recipients further corrupted and embroidered in later discussions among themselves. The final corruption occurred when cynical media managers, answering to well-briefed bosses, arranged the so-called evidence in the required way, so as to extinguish all thought of a plane shootdown.

THE TAPE

Nor did the cockpit voice recording cited by Greengrass offer reliable evidence. There seemed to be two versions of it:

Version One: played by the FBI to passengers' relatives on 18 April 2002, concluded with the calm voice of a male passenger apparently at the controls.

Version Two: heard by the 9/11 Commission, concluded with hijackers deciding to ditch the plane and shouting religious mottoes.

Obviously, the US Air Force could not be found to have shot down an airliner that had just been saved by righteous American citizens, as in Version One, so when the relatives appeared on *The Larry King Show* on 13 February 2006, one of them asserted that they had heard Version Two, the 9/11 Commission's, which was the safe one published for the Moussaoui trial.

These two conflicting versions of what was ostensibly one tape had never been explained, and the published transcript had only confused the issue, because it showed the plane crashing at 10:03 a.m., when for years it was held in media reports that cited seismic studies to have crashed at 10:06 a.m. It was hard to avoid suspicions of evidence tampering. Possibly the positive-ending Version One might have indicated manipulation of the passenger relatives. The negative ending

Version Two supported the 9/11 Commission's plane-crash line. It remained suspicious that there were two reported versions of a supposed single tape, with three minutes possibly missing, perhaps to avoid evidence of a shootdown.

Setting aside the conflicting climaxes, the tape as briefed by the FBI on 23 March 2002, to *New York Times* sports reporter Jere Longman, was not much use for establishing anything other than the possibility of evidence tampering. Longman, who went on to author the pivotal cult text *Among the Heroes*, admitted that the loop-tape covering the "last" thirty-one minutes did not:

- cover the alleged hijackers getting into the cockpit;
- reveal how they did it or whether they killed the two airline pilots;
- make it clear whether the passenger team was able to get into the cockpit;
- show whether the rogue pilots had crashed the Boeing 757 deliberately, or lost control of it, or anything else.

So much for Greengrass's "reconstruction" using the tape.

SHOOTDOWN 1

The Flight 93 heroic legend, and Greengrass's film drama, pivoted on the passengers ganging up and saving a Washington, DC, target by causing their airliner to crash-land. But all the evidence pointed to the airliner having exploded in mid-air. Debris fell from the sky, eyewitnesses had said. Officials had found nothing bigger than briefcase-size shards, and had only reluctantly responded to reports that debris had fallen across an eight-mile-wide area.

The Evidence

- One of the two engines could not be found anywhere at the impact site. A heat-seeking missile would hit the engine.

▨ Only a one-tonne piece of the other six-tonne engine fell to the ground, landing a mile from the impact site.

▨ The ostensible crash site was devoid of aircraft debris unlike all other impact sites, such as a similar one in Cyprus on 14 August 2005,[96] in which an airliner hit the side of a mountain at high speed and disintegrated into small pieces, but nevertheless left its entire tailplane intact.

▨ Marina operator John Fleegle told ABC Evening News on 13 September 2001 that part of Flight 93's fuselage had been found at Indian Lake, three miles from the impact crater.

▨ Fragmented debris fell against the wind up to eight miles away.

▨ Many eyewitness reports attest to the aircraft experiencing difficulties as it came down.

▨ There was evidence that the US Air Force and the 9/11 Commission changed the timeline to rule out a shootdown or other downing of the aircraft. (See caption to timeline on page 2 and Chapter 2, Deception: The USAF Never Knew.)

Heat-seeking missiles might have destroyed one or both of the jet engines. It was the US secret service that operated the missile defences of the White House and flew auxiliary jet fighters out of Andrews Air Force base, a few minutes away by supersonic jet. Perhaps that agency pressed the button. There had been reports of a sonic boom over Pennsylvania, and the secret state had vast resources comparable at least to the scale of the economy of Russia. Of course, the 9/11 Commission claimed that the armed forces had known nothing about Flight 93 until it crashed, but the noted California dissident author David Ray Griffin denounced the claim as "a bare-faced lie", and produced convincing back-up evidence.

With Goodison, Markle and Greengrass brought in as hammers to drive home the official version, a strong body of intellectuals contesting it, and about 100 million Americans pretty sceptical, Americans were deeply divided. Burns Weston, a US professor of law, said that Americans now had "a disparity between official 9/11 'spin' and independently researched 9/11 fact so glaring as to suggest the possibility of a constitu-

tional crisis unlike anything our country has ever known". The heavy-duty 'spin' on the Greengrass film was set to aggravate the crisis.
To accept its premise, the public had to:

- swallow the story that booming Newark International airport, where Flight 93 originated, had no CCTV camera surveillance with which to record hijackers passing through security equipped with a complete bomb-belt and gas-masks;

- accept that CCTV also was lacking at Boston Logan airport, where ostensible mission ringleader Mohamed Atta was supposed to have met nine other plotters, while little Portland jetport in Maine, by contrast, conveniently could and did covertly take pictures of the bogeyman for the world to see;

- believe that United Airlines and federal air-traffic controllers, although aware of the first multiple hijackings in US history, nevertheless lost Flight 93, but at the last minute knew precisely where to look for it;

- believe that they failed to call in the US Air Force, although the military originally said it knew all about the hijackings, and the FBI (and probably secret service) knew of the first passenger call from Flight 93;

- allow that neither of Flight 93's pilots gave the hijack alarm when their aircraft was supposedly taken over by hijackers brandishing knives, guns, gas-sprays and a bomb-belt, although passengers gave no description of any actual seizure of the cockpit by the three hijackers they reportedly saw.[97] (The 9/11 Commission retailed reports of other airborne pilots overhearing "screaming" and of ground-control hearing voices shouting "Get out of here" and "Mayday", but these events, while indicating a hijacking, did not constitute the formal alarm that would have legally obliged the FAA to alert the USAF. The military, therefore, retained its plausible deniability. This again suggested lawyers at work.);

- accept that the rogue pilot (whom no one aboard reported seeing) erroneously flipped a switch that patched his "stay calm/bomb aboard/returning to airport" announcement, apparently meant for passengers, through to air-traffic control instead and therefore conveniently on to the record. We are to believe he made this blunder in spite of his having "trained for two years", practised on simulators, and having "back in the Florida apartment he'd left four days earlier . . . set up a full-size cardboard replica – three panels in all – of the cockpit of the airplane";[98]

■ believe that, although the USAF had known for 40 minutes that a second aircraft had hit Manhattan, hijackers nevertheless felt confident enough of the air force's continuing unreadiness to U-turn and commence a thirty-minute flight towards America's most heavily defended buildings;

■ accept that they formally requested a change of course that was duly authorized by air-traffic control;

■ believe, perhaps most unconvincingly of all, that the passengers beat on the cockpit door and even bashed it with a drinks trolley when among their number were at least two cabin staff (CeeCee Lyles and Sandy Bradshaw) who should each have had the knowledge required to unlock it.

Paul Greengrass said on his website that he hoped his film "made some things clearer about 9/11 and dispelled a few myths and confusions, and that the audience understood that the debate that took place on the plane speaks to us today".

It would have been fascinating to know what "myths and confusions" Greengrass intended to dispel with his "meticulous re-enactment" that so closely followed the Bush government's line and that of the recruiting officers at the Pentagon. To what debate was he referring? Debate about 9/11 had been vigorously suppressed and Greengrass's pious wish was pure cant.

As Greengrass's film prepared to launch, Universal's website forum was jammed with outraged postings that denounced the movie as an exploitative travesty and nothing more than war-making propaganda. On launch day 28 April, Universal cancelled all United 93 postings with the following words: "We apologize for the removal of the message boards – due to technical difficulties all previous threads have been inadvertantly [*sic*] deleted. We invite you to renew your dialog and discuss your thoughts on the film."

Remarkably, the movie industry's house organ, *Variety*, found a conscience and detected signs of distortion: "Even with its copious research, the film departs from prior accounts in several subtle and not-so-subtle ways, reminding us (as does a closing disclaimer) that this recreation is just that – based on the best available evidence, with inferences and composites constructed for dramatic effect," wrote Brian Lowry.[99]

The greatest distortion of all came with a comparison of the cult film's budget of $18 million with the budget of the 9/11 Commission – $15 million.[100] But the biggest omission of the movie was its complete neglect to describe the failure of United Airlines to take measures to save Flight 93 from destruction by warning its pilots or other staff about the other hijackings. According to the 9/11 Commission, the company took none.[101]

2
The Deception

SECRECY

There was to be no crash investigation of the normal kind after Flight 93 disappeared. "Flight 93's crash is considered a criminal act, and that makes all the difference. The FBI is in charge of the investigation, and everything, even the most minute details, are being kept under strict lock and key," a news report said at the time.[1]

The National Transportation Safety Board (NTSB), which had investigated all US aeronautical crashes for thirty-three years, could not investigate this one except peripherally. Nor could it investigate the cockpit voice recorder, kept under FBI control. The deaths of the passengers and crew were murder, not accident.

But who was the perpetrator? It was widely believed at the time that the plane in question had been either blown up or shot down, or both.

A Reuters report immediately following the attacks said: "Pentagon officials vigorously denied initial reports that a military fighter had shot down the United Airlines [93] jet."[2] But, at the outset, the FBI did not rule out a shootdown. Questioned about it two days after the events, agents at the impact site said they were keeping an open mind.

"SHANKSVILLE, Pa. (Reuters) – Federal investigators said on Thursday they could not rule out the possibility that a United Airlines jetliner that crashed in rural western Pennsylvania during this week's attacks on New York and the Pentagon was shot down.

'We have not ruled out that,' FBI agent Bill Crowley told a news conference when asked about reports that a US fighter jet may have fired on the hijacked Boeing 757. 'We haven't ruled out anything yet'."[3] Later, Crowley retracted his statement.

So how exactly was it determined that the disappearance of Flight 93 involved a crime and, if so, what kind of crime and perpetrated by whom?

Three other aircraft had impacted prominent buildings, evidently deliberately. Clearly, crime had been involved in those cases. However, in the case of Flight 93, no target had been hit, the aircraft had disappeared, and the debris evidence indicated *prima facie* that the aircraft had somehow broken up in the sky. It might have been a crime, it might have been an accident.

We know what the authorities decided, but it's important to consider the reasoning, because it involved a choice between two very different procedures. If the disappearance of Flight 93 definitely involved a crime, then the FBI would investigate. If it involved an accident, or there was doubt either way, the NTSB would take the case. The department of justice knew that the NTSB's approach would be vastly different from the FBI's.

DECEPTION: THE TWA 800 CASE

Compare TWA Flight 800, a case of similar weight and importance that had occurred four years earlier. A Boeing 747, it crashed into the Atlantic Ocean off the coast of Long Island on 17 July 1996, killing all 230 aboard, more than five times as many as were on Flight 93. Certain parties claimed that the plane had not crashed because of mechanical failure but because it had been hit by a missile, probably fired by a US military source or by right-wing militiamen using stolen military missiles.

Sceptics suspected a crime, but the FBI was keen to prove them mistaken. The President's re-election was involved. The National

CIA Animation

The entire government apparatus was brought to bear on the TWA 800 disaster in order to prove that the jumbo jet had not been shot down. Instead of defining it as a crime and handing the case to the FBI, the government assigned it to the National Transportation Safety Board, which conducted the most thorough investigation in its history. The CIA got involved, as the animation shown here demonstrates.

CREDIT: US Government image

Transportation Safety Board (NTSB) went to remarkable lengths to recover the plane and reconstruct it in order to find out what had really happened. They discovered it was all caused by an obscure design fault that nobody had known about.

According to NTSB chair Jim Hall, his staff worked with the Coast Guard, the Navy, the FBI, NOAA, and many other state and federal agencies with the encouragement and support of the White House and Congress in providing the resources needed to conduct what became the most extensive, complex and expensive investigation in the Safety Board's thirty-three-year history.[4]

"From the beginning, the scope and dimensions of this investigation have been extraordinary," Hall reported. "The salvage effort, organized by the Navy, one of the largest diver-assisted salvage operations ever conducted, extended from July to November, 1996. The Navy divers worked in very difficult and dangerous conditions and, for a time, their efforts had to be halted because of the onset of the Atlantic hurricane season.

"When the diving operations were completed, there followed months of work by contracted fishing trollers that scoured hundreds of miles of the ocean floor.

"In the end, we recovered the remains of all 230 victims, and more than 95 percent of the aircraft," Hall said. "The reconstruction of the 93-foot segment of the fuselage, including the center wing fuel tank, was unique both in size and scope. More than 30 people worked meticulously for many months to sort through innumerable pieces of wreckage and assemble the wreckage in an effort to better understand what happened to Flight 800."

Hall said the investigation also included the most extensive radar data study in the board's history, including a review of *several hundred thousand radar returns* from nine radar locations in five states. The investigative team had also spent a great deal of time organizing and *carefully analysing the summaries of witness interviews* that the Federal Bureau of Investigation provided to the board. [Emphasis added.]

In other words, the appropriate investigative agency for an aircraft crash conducted a very thorough investigation, working closely with the FBI, to see if there had been a crime involved and, if so, what kind of crime.

DECEPTION AT THE SHANKSVILLE SITE

It's worth comparing the outlay of time, money and effort expended on investigating TWA 800, supported by numerous state and federal agencies, including the White House and Congress, with the attention given to the disappearance of Flight 93.

According to John Carlin of the *Independent*, FBI agents left the roughly sixty-four square-mile debris and impact area after thirteen days. That allowed just one day to cover on average five square miles. The *The New York Times* reporter Jere Longman reported that the agency had failed to conduct a rigorous crime-scene search of the whole area, and only reluctantly investigated the reports of debris and human remains lying eight miles away. The bureau ignored eyewitness reports of burning debris falling from the sky and dismissed accounts of a white jet circling low over the area after Flight 93 had gone down. So far as we know, they made no recovery of the Boeing 757 and no reconstruction of it. The reconstruction of TWA 800 had been photographed and published, but any reconstruction of Flight 93 that took place never reached the light of day.

In the course of their investigation, the FBI claimed to have found the aircraft's black boxes in the impact crater. However, even though according to their preliminary scenario all the victims and perpetrators were deceased, and release of the data could not affect the outcome, the bureau adamantly refused to release a transcript of the cockpit voice recording, because they were investigating a "twentieth hijacker", still alive, the mentally ill Zacarias Moussaoui, who would eventually face a death-sentence show trial in 2006. Although FBI agents briefed certain reporters about the "tape" (it was actually retrieved from a memory-chip), eventually played a thirty-minute recording to relatives under heavy security, and released snippets over time, they never formally released the whole thing until the Moussaoui trial judge ordered all the transcripts released. The contents left people none the wiser, and even raised suspicions that they had been orchestrated. (See Appendix.)

We can envisage a very different investigation of Flight 93, carried out by the NTSB on the scale of its TWA 800 case, going as follows:

- excavate the empty impact site deeply to see if a fuselage was indeed buried there and if so recover it;

- conduct a search for the missing tail and wings;

- search sixty-four square miles to forensic standards;

- collect all aircraft parts and painstakingly reassemble them to determine the cause of crash;

- inspect engine parts for serial numbers and match them with those of Flight 11;

- conduct a laboratory analysis for traces of the tell-tale chemicals left by a missile impact, or the type of torn metal and chemical traces that would indicate a bomb blast;

- conduct tests on the passenger remains to see if they were gassed or otherwise drugged, as passengers on Flight 11 had been, and the 9/11 Commission speculated they all had been;[5]

- investigate reports of cellphone calls, conduct experiments to see if they were feasible at cruising altitude at the bearings where records showed them to have occurred; compare call reports from relatives with phone bills and determine validity;

- trace the rogue pilot announcements overheard by ATC.

- conduct a thorough analysis of the radar data along the whole of the aircraft's alleged flight route.

However, the White House and Congress, who had been helpful in the TWA 800 case, showed a notable lack of zeal in tracking down the evidence when it came to Flight 93, although the FBI returned several boxes of belongings they found.

What did occur as a result of the FBI investigation was that the cockpit recording gave a boost to the story of passenger heroism. The *New York Times* reported on 22 September 2001: "A desperate and wild struggle took place aboard the hijacked United Airlines Flight 93 before it crashed in southwestern Pennsylvania, according to the plane's cockpit voice recorder."

However, this seemed to have been the result of initial excitement. Later, the tape as briefed by the FBI on 23 March 2002, to Jere Longman, was not much use for establishing anything. It did not make clear whether there was a passenger revolt, whether passengers got into the cockpit, or whether the rogue pilots crashed the Boeing 757 deliberately, lost control of it, or anything else. A relative who listened to the tape on 12 April 2002 described it as "bizarre" . Longman's courageous verdict was that "many crucial questions about the final minutes of the flight remain unanswered".[6]

DECEPTION: THE USAF NEVER KNEW

A report in the *Independent* newspaper on 20 September 2001, the day the US President declared war, ran as follows (excerpted):

America's defence establishment has disclosed that it ordered its fighter jets to intercept all the passenger aircraft hijacked in last week's attacks on New York and Washington ... The data made clear that military intelligence was aware of the hijackings – and possibly the suicidal nature of their mission – before any of the aircraft had hit their targets.

Three years later, however, when the 9/11 Commission published its report, the military's line had changed radically. Now, the USAF had never heard of Flight 93. "NEADS [the USAF's northeastern HQ at Griffiss Air Force Base, near Rome] first received a call about United 93 from the military liaison at Cleveland Center [air-traffic control]

No matter how many bodies were supposed to have been reclaimed at the Shanksville site, or how many eyewitnesses said they had seen a Boeing 757 go down, hard-core sceptics still found an irresistible resemblance between the smoke cloud generated by the apparent crash of Flight 93 (left) and the smoke cloud emitted by a bomb dropped from the air, as in this shot of a so-called Taliban village in Afghanistan being exterminated by US navy aircraft on 9 November 2001 in revenge for 9/11 and Flight 93.

CREDITS: Val Mclatchey/US Navy

at 10:07. Unaware that the aircraft had already crashed, Cleveland passed to NEADS the aircraft's last known latitude and longitude. NEADS was never able to locate United 93 on radar because it was already in the ground."[7]

The report underlined its surprising finding: "At 10:17, the Command Center advised headquarters of its conclusion that United 93 had indeed crashed. Despite the discussion about military assistance, no one from FAA headquarters requested military assistance regarding United 93. Nor did any manager at FAA headquarters pass any of the information it had about United 93 to the military."

So, instead of being armed with foreknowledge and ordering intercepts of all the rogue planes, as it had admitted in documents released just after the events (see above), three years later it seemed the USAF hadn't heard of Flight 93 until after it had disappeared.

But the FAA air-traffic controllers in Cleveland knew as early as 9:28 that something was badly amiss because, according to the Commission's report, the person at the screen in Cleveland heard "sounds of possible screaming" from the plane and noticed that Flight 93 had descended by

700 feet. Although they did nothing at that time, four minutes later, they heard an unidentified voice saying to persons unknown: "We have a bomb on board," and finally notified their supervisor, who in turn notified FAA command center in Herndon, Virginia.

When Cleveland later checked with Herndon about involving the USAF, the Commission report claimed, Herndon "told Cleveland that FAA personnel well above them in the chain of command had to make the decision to seek military assistance and were working on the issue."[8]

Between forty-five minutes and an hour earlier, two rogue airliners had hit the World Trade Center, and yet senior officials at FAA headquarters still had to discuss whether another rogue airliner with a bomb on board was an important enough matter for bothering the military. This was enough to stretch anyone's credulity, and yet apparently they still had not made up their minds when the following exchange took place:

> Command Center: Uh, do we want to think, uh, about scrambling aircraft?
>
> FAA Headquarters: Oh, God, I don't know.
>
> Command Center: Uh, that's a decision somebody's gonna have to make probably in the next ten minutes.

Evidently they decided that they should *not* bother the military, because fourteen minutes later, at 10:03, when Flight 93 seemed to have disappeared in Pennsylvania, the report said: "No one from FAA headquarters [had yet] requested military assistance regarding United 93." In other words, the 9/11 Commission portrayed the FAA as hopelessly incompetent. Strangely, no one was known to have lost their job or even to have been reprimanded as a result of this allegedly pathetic performance. At about the same time, the FAA made a smooth job of landing rapidly more than 4,000 aircraft, all the planes in the US skies, in an unprecedented operation that it initiated and for which it received praise from the Commission.

Of course, there were teleconferences going on among the high-ups at which the military could have learned the rogue status of Flight 93 and its bomb aboard. The 9/11 Commission could not deny that fact, nor assert that the teleconferences had started too late. Instead, the

Commission chose to argue that *all* the teleconferences *were so useless* that none of them could convey to the USAF the basic information that Flight 93 was rogue with a bomb aboard. Its summary statement said: "The FAA, the White House, and the Defense Department each initiated a multiagency teleconference before 9:30. [But] none of these teleconferences . . . *included the right officials* from both the FAA and the Defense Department." [Emphasis added.]

The National Military Command Center Teleconference

The 9/11 Commission claimed that Pentagon operators were unable to reach the FAA by phone. However, the Commission admitted that the operators were able to reach everyone else. Furthermore, the FAA's Laura Brown seemed to have her own information about when this teleconference began – which suggested that the operators *did* reach the FAA.

The FAA's Teleconference

The officer at the Pentagon (National Military Command Center) was reported saying that "the information [about Flight 93] was of little value" so he did not pay attention. However, the FAA had another phone-line to the military command. Laura Brown's evidence given to the Commission (a memo written at the time) showed that besides the phone bridge set up by the FAA with the Pentagon, the "Air Force liaison to the FAA . . . established contact with NORAD (North American Air Defense Command) on a separate line". So even if no one at the Pentagon was interested, the USAF still would have received the information. Her memo said, moreover, that "[t]he FAA shared real-time information . . . about . . . all the flights of interest," and the Commission itself agreed that by 9:34, FAA headquarters knew about the hijacking of Flight 93, so it was a "flight of interest". The Commission's claim was, therefore, flatly contradicted by this memo, which was read into the Commission's record.[9]

The White House Videoconference

The 9/11 Commission claimed that it did not know what figure from the Department of Defense was involved in the White House videolink.

However, it generalized (see above) that "the right people" were not involved in all the videoconferences, which was why they were useless. But there was no way they could know this, if they did not know who from Defense was involved in the White House videoconference.

Anyway, it would have been perfectly easy to find out who was involved, because Richard Clarke, who coordinated the videoconference, wrote in his book *Against All Enemies* that Secretary of Defense Donald Rumsfeld was present, along with General Richard Myers, Acting Chair of the Joint Chiefs of Staff, and Jane Garvey, top official of the FAA. There were *no righter* people who could have participated.

Clarke wrote that at about 9:35, Jane Garvey reported on a number of "potential hijacks", which included "United 93 over Pennsylvania". Therefore, more than twenty-five minutes before Flight 93 went down, according to Clarke, both Myers and Rumsfeld heard from the head of the FAA that Flight 93 was considered a potential hijack.

Sceptical author David Ray Griffin commented on this analysis: "The Commission's tales about FAA incompetence and worthless teleconferences are ... directly contradicted by Laura Brown's memo and Richard Clarke's book. Their combined testimony implies that the Commission's main claim – that '[b]y the time the military learned about the flight, it had crashed' – is a bald-faced lie."[10]

It seems more likely the the *Independent* had it right in the first place, and military intelligence was aware of the hijackings – and possibly the suicidal nature of their mission – before any of the aircraft had hit their targets.

DECEPTION: EARLY CELLPHONE CALL ESTABLISHED A CRIME

If there was deception involved in Flight 93's disappearance, it would be vital to establish early that a crime had been committed in the downing of the aircraft, so that the FBI could validly conduct a strictly criminal investigation and not the National Transportation Safety Board, which would conduct a much more extensive inquiry, possibly finding evidence of a shootdown.

Flight 93 could never be acknowledged to have broken up in the air or crashed by accident, or the NTSB would be called in. Therefore the first cellphone call from on board the aircraft had much more than human-interest importance. It was the key to determining that there had been a crime aboard Flight 93, which would both allow a shoot-down order and cancel out the NTSB.

Tom Burnett's call at 9:27 a.m., reported by his wife, Deena, fitted tidily into this scenario, because the moment there was hijack activity, he phoned and instructed his wife to call the authorities. She called the emergency number, 9-1-1, and the FBI promptly monitored the call.

If his timely instruction was just a coincidence, and a common-sense thing for a practical man to say under the circumstances, it still remained for the FBI to explain why it did not alert the US Air Force, which claimed that it heard about Flight 93 a full forty minutes later at 10:07 a.m., after it had disappeared. If there was an official lie here, it would be a clear indication of something amiss with the downing of Flight 93, as widely suspected in Pennsylvania at the time.

The general knowledge at the bureau of Flight 93 being another hijack was confirmed by a Newark, New Jersey, flight controller named Greg Callaghan, who remembered talking about Flight 93 on the phone to an FBI agent (unnamed) at 9:41 a.m.[11] The agent reportedly told him: "We suspect that this aircraft has now been taken over by hostile forces." But still no call apparently went to the US Air Force.

There are plenty of reports that put the flight-plan change closer to 10:00 a.m., but many reports also said it was five minutes before Callaghan spoke to the FBI agent, revealed that those controlling the aircraft had filed a new flight plan (for Reagan airport in Washington, DC) and got it confirmed – inexplicable unless there was official complicity of some kind.[12] Any hint of something so unthinkable never appeared in the scenarios of the Flight 93 movies, although about 100 million Americans thought the government had known about the attack plans, and the passengers in their phone calls never said how the hijacking was done, nor did they describe seeing a fourth hijacker, always presumed officially to be the pilot.

Deena Burnett, who was at home with their three daughters, said she and her husband spoke for about one minute. Meanwhile, on the ground, the air-traffic controller heard "possible screaming" sounds on her headset at 9:28, so Mr Burnett appears to have called at the very time the hijacking was taking place. But there's a problem. Mr Burnett was in first class, with a ring-side view, yet he did not describe the central criminal act: the actual hijacking, and nor did any of the other first-class callers.

Deena was impressively clear-headed at this early hour. "She noted the precise time for each call to the couple's California home: 6:27, 6:34, 6:45 and 6:54 a.m. [Pacific Standard Time]."[13] She claimed she scribbled notes on a shopping list in her kitchen as she spoke, and later transcribed the content of the calls from memory. Deena's transcription, noted on the Tom Burnett family foundation website, went as follows:

Deena: Hello.
Tom: Deena.
Deena: Tom, are you OK?
Tom: No, I'm not. I'm on an airplane that has been hijacked.
Deena: Hijacked?
Tom: Yes. They just knifed a guy.
Deena: A passenger?
Tom: Yes.
Deena: Where are you? Are you in the air?
Tom: Yes, yes, just listen. Our airplane has been hijacked. It's United Flight 93 from Newark to San Francisco. We are in the air. The hijackers have already knifed a guy, one of them has a gun, they are telling us there is a bomb on board, please call the authorities.

He hung up.[14]

DECEPTION: THE VANISHING GUN

Deena immediately called 9-1-1, the emergency number, and got herself recorded saying: "They just knifed a passenger and there are guns on the plane." She insisted later that her husband gave her the information. "He told me one of the hijackers had a gun. He wouldn't have made it up. Tom grew up around guns. He was an avid hunter and we have guns in our home. If he said there was a gun on board, there was."[15]

There was strong motivation for the government to suppress such a report. If a gun had been smuggled on to Flight 93, United Airlines could have faced ruinous lawsuits. Extra motivation for denying a gun report came from failures in FAA security as far back as 1998, when the Administration's undercover teams had easily smuggled guns and bombs aboard airliners at various airports across the country.

Only, if there was no gun, why did Tom Burnett refer to one?

The 9/11 Commission wrote: "One recipient of a call from the aircraft recounted specifically asking her caller whether the hijackers had guns. The passenger replied that he did not see one. No evidence of firearms or of their identifiable remains was found at the aircraft's crash site, and the cockpit voice recorder gives no indication of a gun being fired or mentioned at any time. We believe that if the hijackers had possessed a gun, they would have used it in the flight's last minutes as the passengers fought back."[16]

However, there remained one scenario by which a gun might have been aboard the plane legally, and that was if it was held by an authorized air marshal or other security-cleared agent, permitted to carry a weapon through airport security, or to enter a plane by another route. This would have put a different complexion on the case, one that the 9/11 Commission never contemplated, and the Flight 93 films could not imagine depicting, because it would suggest that the takeover of the aircraft was carried out by black-ops personnel, or even foreign-flag agents with security clearance.

It seemed unlikely that Tom Burnett was simply handing down a rumour, because his was the first call, and he had a ringside seat during the plane's seizure (although he never described it). On the other rogue flights, one other report of a gun had surfaced. An FAA memorandum written in the immediate wake of 9/11 said that a flight attendant aboard Flight 11 had reported that a hijacker had shot first-class passenger Daniel Lewin with one bullet. This document was described as erroneous by the FAA, a verdict endorsed by the 9/11 Commission. Lewin, an Israeli computer millionaire, had had a history in military special operations. He might have had security clearance and pulled a gun. Either that or, as Burnett said, one of the hijackers already had a gun.

These oddities offered a fleeting glimpse of the hidden world of clandestine struggle that sceptics knew existed and that might have been concealed behind the cover-ups.

There's the problem of the bomb Burnett mentioned, too. That's the one that they portrayed as an elaborate bomb-belt in the Flight 93 movies. Again, the government (and United Airlines) would not want the smuggling aboard of such a thing to be exposed. Reportedly, nobody could account for it. If it exploded, a rigorous air-safety investigation should have revealed tell-tale chemical traces on the airplane debris or discovered by laboratory tests that it caused the mysterious empty crater. If it was unexploded, a genuine forensic search of the vast site should have recovered it. If the bomb did not exist, and was nothing more than a bluff by crazed fanatics who had siezed the plane, Tom Burnett would be proved right. In his 6:45 a.m. (9:45 a.m. EDT) call, Deena recorded him saying: "What is the probability of their having a bomb on board? I don't think they have one. I think they're just telling us that for crowd control." Peter Markle and Paul Greengrass should have read this line and thrown out their bomb-belt travesties.

DECEPTION:
THE IMPOSSIBLE CELLPHONE CALL

There were further concerns around the kind of phone that Burnett utilized to make his call.

Many media reports carried words to this effect: "9:27: Tom Burnett calls his wife, Deena, using a cellphone."[17]

What could have made Deena so certain her husband pulled off this miraculous call with his cellphone while his aircraft was at six miles of altitude and climbing, and while a hijacking was taking place? She had an apparently persuasive reason. "Deena wonders if the call might have been before the cockpit was taken over, because he spoke quickly and quietly as if he was being watched. He also had a headset like phone operators use, so he could have made the call unnoticed."[18]

But the altitude was all wrong for cellphones. The transponder message that regularly indicated to air-traffic controllers the plane's identity and altitude did not disappear until 9:41 a.m., so the air-traffic controller was still watching Flight 93 in real time, tracking towards Pennsylvania. According to the official story, the controller heard "possible screaming" sounds on her headset at 9:28, and noted on her radar screen that Flight 93 had just dropped 700 feet below normal cruising altitude of six and a half miles, so we know that the cellphone call alleged to have occurred at 9:27 was so unlikely as to be all but impossible. It was another year before bankrupt US airlines started spending their precious money on testing the pico-cell technology that promised to make cellphone calls at normal cruising altitude routinely feasible.[19]

The plane was not flying low (under 8,000 feet, or 1.5 miles), where sometimes a fluky connection could be made for a moment or two, for example during take-off or landing. In fact, after the brief drop, Flight 93 *increased* its altitude. "Between 9:34 and 9:38, the controller observed United 93 climbing to 40,700 feet and immediately moved several aircraft out of its way," Commission staff reported.[20] Furthermore, the semi-official Flight Explorer route map showed Flight 93 maintaining cruising altitude all the way.

Mrs Burnett was a former Delta Airlines flight attendant, and a Christian. As a married homemaker, she took part in a team. She followed instructions. She was also a Republican who gave a plucky heart-rending speech at the 2004 Convention, couched in religious terms. She was not about to invent a cellphone call.

But there was one possible inconsistency in her character, as presented to us in the media record. Although the Flight 93 tape hearings were supposed to be conducted under court-ordered provisions of the strictest confidentiality, the mass-media clarioned Deena's impressions afterwards: "The FBI played the half-hour flight-deck tape in April [2002] for her and seventy other relatives of the forty crew members and passengers killed in the crash. When she heard her husband's voice, Deena immediately locked eyes with her mother-in-law, Beverly Burnett, and they held hands and wept. 'We had not heard his voice in eight months at that point and just immediately began to cry,' Deena says."[21]

This depiction of Deena Burnett as impulsive, emotional and liable to burst into tears contrasted sharply with the way she had been portrayed at the time of her doomed husband's last phone calls: cool, collected, eye on the clock, pen at the ready.

Reporters noted that she was still carrying around her transcripts a year after the events. That might be a hint of a guilty conscience. Possibly, she had not been quite so efficient as she'd portrayed herself. Perhaps in her shock and grief she had become muddled and blurted out "guns" to the 9-1-1 operator when Tom had never mentioned them. When the bigwigs started making her husband out as a hero who saved thousands of lives she'd had to stick to the story. She'd networked with other call recipients. She heard about other cellphone calls and assumed Tom had used his. Perhaps all the stories became blended over time. That's how group delusions begin.

There's the hint of an explanation in this extract from a mainstream sermon in a mainstream church about Jesus's resurrection:

> That one little story element – eating the piece of broiled fish – is the key to the whole thing. On one level, it's a simple demonstration that the Risen Jesus is *real*, he's not a ghost, he's not a hallucination, he's not a shadowy remnant of his former self, he's not a collective memory that the disciples somehow share. The Risen Jesus is *really there*; his hand doesn't pass through the table or the fish or the disciples, but can be touched and held and they can feel the strength in his grip; he isn't just a memory from the past, but he can say new things to them and interact with them and share their meal with them. On one level, eating the fish is a simple demonstration that Jesus is not an apparition, that he is bodily alive.[22]

If this was how Christians imagined dead people, as souls that they somehow could conjure back to life, perhaps one married to the first Crusader believed in her shock and grief that she could raise her husband from the dead by her witness. Or perhaps, if she extolled his virtues and sang his praises, she might expedite his journey to Heaven to sit at the right hand of God.

Or perhaps she received a phone call, the details of which she noted down all wrong in her panic and distress and reported to 9-1-1 in a muddle, getting the weapons mixed up and somehow believing a cellphone call could work at cruising altitude. That might be why she clung to her scrawled notes a year later, taking them with her everywhere. All the call recipients probably were similarly muddled, being in a state of shock and fear, and immediately being summoned to live up to a national legend in the making.

Deena Burnett seemed to be a model witness, but the call she so carefully noted was a mess in every way except one: it instructed Deena to alert the authorities. That alert plausibly made the FBI the first agency to be informed of a crime aboard Flight 93 and secured the ensuing disappearance of the airliner as a crime scene and not a transportation accident. This might have suited anyone wishing to manipulate the events from behind the scenes and to avoid an NSTB investigation, but it also posed a problem: it meant a major federal agency, the FBI, and their governing department, Justice, knew at least thirty-six minutes before it disappeared that Flight 93 had gone rogue. It is not credible that the FBI would have failed to tip off the US Air Force, which had four armed supersonic jet fighters in the sky at the time. This knowledge effectively destroyed the US Air Force's story that it knew nothing about Flight 93 until 10:07 a.m., after it had disappeared. If the air force was lying, it certainly had something to hide.

DECEPTION: FLIGHT DATA RECORDINGS

In other air crashes, the flight data recorders were handled openly, with crash investigators discussing the progress of their inquiries with news reporters. For example, in the EgyptAir Flight 990 crash of 1999, in which the relief co-pilot was suspected of deliberately ditching the plane and killing all 217 people aboard, the cockpit voice recorder (CVR) revealed him muttering a religious invocation in Arabic. "The phrase 'I put my faith in God's hands' was uttered 'multiple times'," sources told CNN.[23] There was public debate about the phrase's meaning and whether or not it had benign implications. The sources "emphasize that the voice recorder information, by itself, is not conclusive," CNN added. Also, the collation of the cockpit voices with the flight data was important, to build a picture of what happened aboard. "Two pilots and two engineers from EgyptAir left Washington for

A cockpit voice recorder with its "pinger" attached. The CVR is installed close to the tail of the plane. At the Flight 93 impact site, there was no tailplane visible, but the CVR was reportedly recovered from the crater.

CREDIT: Promotional image

Seattle, where data from the flight recorder will be used in a Boeing simulator to recreate the final moments of the flight."

The NTSB later published the CVR transcript prefaced with the following caution: "The transcription of a CVR tape is not a precise science but is the best product possible from an NTSB group investigative effort. The transcript, or parts thereof, if taken out of context, could be misleading. The attached CVR transcript should be viewed as an accident investigation tool to be used in conjunction with other evidence."[24] Furthermore, intra-cockpit and air–ground communication were differentiated, and a range of levels of sound quality and comprehensibility were indicated. In addition, the four channels of audio involved were named, and the quality of their content gauged.

In the case of the Flight 93 CVR, none of the above measures and cautions were included. In other words, for Paul Greengrass to claim that he had made "a meticulous re-enactment" based on the CVR was both unscientific and tendentious.

DECEPTION:
TAMPERING WITH THE RECORDING

For about three years there were two crash times in circulation: 10:06, the seismically measured time, and 10:03, the time given by flight data and the one the 9/11 Commission settled upon in the end. Media stories dealt with this by explanations such as the following: "[Aviation experts] said it could mean that the FBI and other government agencies either failed to properly synchronize the times, or there were other problems in the retrieving or handling of the tape from the so-called "black box" recovered from the wreckage at Shanksville, Pennsylvania. Or, experts speculated, it could mean there was a major on-board electrical failure on the plane three minutes before Flight 93 crashed, causing the recorder to quit working."[25]

Sceptics, however, believed the digitally stored recording might have been tampered with. There were two motives: one to destroy a record of a shootdown of the airliner, the other to manipulate reaction to the record.

To cover up the shootdown, the last minutes of the recording could simply be left as white sound, while the voices could be jumbled up or blanked out and various perplexing remarks ignored, such as: "Inform them, and tell him to talk to the pilot. Bring the pilot back," supposed to have been said in Arabic at 9.45 a.m. Or the repetition in English of "sit" or "sit down" or "down" on average every four seconds over a period of three minutes, when the cockpit only contained two seats, one for each pilot.

To manipulate the public's response, relatives and friends of the passengers could be brought on side by being led to believe that their loved ones had very nearly wrested control of the aircraft from the wicked hijackers. This involved the calm voice that Alice Hoglan distinctly heard in 2002, saying: "Pull it up." "She said the English voice toward the end of the recording was so distinct that she believes it's evident the speaker was inside the cockpit," CBS reported.[26] Strangely, those words did not appear in the transcript released by the Department of Justice at the 2006 Moussaoui trial.

The tape and transcript she witnessed apparently ended without Islamic fanatics shouting religious mottoes. For example: "the relatives

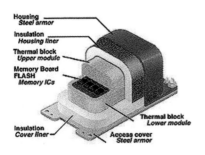

A CVR does not contain any "tape recordings", since its memory is on integrated circuit boards. However, digital data could be transferred to other media and remastered or doctored in that form.

CREDIT: Promotional image

of Flight 93 passengers who heard the cockpit tape April 18 at a Princeton hotel said government officials laid out a timetable for the crash in a briefing and in a transcript that accompanied the recording. Relatives later reported they heard sounds of an on-board struggle beginning at 9:58 a.m., but there was a final 'rushing sound' at 10:03, and the tape fell silent." The transcript released in 2006 ended with men shouting praises to Allah. Where had they been in 2002?

The news report continued: "Vaughan Hoglan, the uncle of passenger Mark Bingham, said by phone from California that near the end there were shouts of 'pull up, pull up,' but the end of the tape 'is inferred – there's no impact'[27]." Again, the words 'pull up, pull up' did not appear in the 2006 transcript. (See Appendix.)

Nor was it clear which lines of the transcript Deena Burnett was referring to when she emerged from the CVR replay session and said: "We had not heard his voice in eight months." The microphones only recorded what went on in the cockpit, and her husband had presumably not entered the cockpit – or had he?

Even the shouts of religious mottoes in Arabic appeared to have been doctored. For example, in 2004 a news report said of the recording: "The airplane rolled onto its back, and *one of the hijackers* began shouting, 'Allah is the greatest. Allah is the greatest.'"[28] In early 2006, this had turned into: "In its final plunge, *the hijackers* shout over and over in Arabic: 'Allah is the greatest! Allah is the greatest!'"[29] [Emphasis added]. In the 2006 transcript, the motto was repeated ten times at the end.

The clash between the blatant evidence of a shootdown around the impact site and the military's lies about never hearing about Flight 93, on the one hand, and the hints of changes in the content of the cockpit voice recording and the oddities around some of the passenger calls, on the other, suggested that there had been official deception, intended to wipe out the popular belief that a shootdown had occurred.

3
The Hijackers

THE "OPERATIONAL LEADER" MOHAMED ATTA

Atta was the chief bogeyman of the 9/11 events, the pilot of Flight 11, and ostensibly operational leader of the alleged Flight 93 hijackers. Police established his identity within an hour of Flight 11 hitting the World Trade Center's North Tower, when they found his bags held back at Boston Logan airport.

Hundreds of security personnel flooded the airport, totally emptying it and closing down operations. The bags checked through to Los Angeles by Atta from Portland, Maine, initially identified by their way-tag number, were in due course opened, revealing a treasure trove of incriminating possessions. It reportedly included:

1. a hand-held electronic flight computer, often described as a must for flight training;

2. a simulator procedures manual for Boeing 757 and 767 aircraft;

3. two videotapes relating to "air tours" of the Boeing 757 and 747 aircraft;

4. a slide-rule flight calculator;

5. a copy of the Koran;[1]

6. a handwritten document in Arabic entitled "In the name of God all mighty, Death Certificate". It instructed that "When I die, I want the people who will inherit my possessions to do the following";[2]

7. a suicide-killer's handbook that Atta was supposed to have authored, which Arabic speaker and Lebanon resident Robert Fisk later described as "very, very odd"[3] (copies of the handwritten document appeared at the crash sites or motels of a couple of the other gang members and featured prominently in press and TV reports at the time[4]);

8. United Airlines uniforms (they later turned into counter-disinformation about a wedding suit, and illustrated the more far-out oddities that cropped up in the 9/11 data);

9. the *pièce de résistance* that came to light in spring 2006, with the announcement by a retired FBI agent that Atta had left a master-list of his accomplices' names, targets and personal data neatly folded into his bag.[5]

This was a daunting array of technical know-how and religio-legal mumbo-jumbo. The kamikaze pilot clearly had been Atta and he was a Moslem fanatic.

Computer-mad Americans were nonplussed when FBI chief Mueller appeared before the exclusive Commonwealth Club in San Francisco and announced that "the hijackers had no computers, no laptops, and no storage media of any kind."[6] The year was 2001, the computer revolution had happened and laptop computers were already in common use, particularly by frequent flyers like Atta. It came as a surprise that although an estimated $400,000 to $500,000 had been spent on the mission, it had not been possible to provide the high-flying, jet-setting operatives with a few laptops, or even just one for the "operational leader" himself.

It became even harder to understand when papers revealed that an FBI legal officer in Minneapolis, Colleen Rowley, in advance of the 9/11 events, had attempted to seize the documents of a supposed twentieth hijacker, the mentally ill Zacarias Moussaoui, which were stored – er, *on his laptop computer.*[7]

Of course, if Atta had been depicted as a nerdy type with a laptop, he could never have plausibly carried a treasure trove of damning evidence in his bags. This is the initial evidence of official deception around Atta's luggage.

Further suspicions were raised by the sporadic contemporary media reports of airline uniforms being found in the bags. This element of the story only caught on properly in the Flight 93 legend to explain the mystery pilot who was never seen but somehow appeared at the controls. However, Bush's 9/11 Commission demolished it, and even the later Flight 93 movies, based almost entirely on fantasy, didn't use a uniformed hijacker to conduct the airliner's seizure.[8] How, then, did the reports of uniforms in Atta's luggage arise except through false reports planted in the corporate media? And why would they be planted, and by what agency?

THE CONNECTING FLIGHT

Atta checked his treasure trove of incriminating materials through to Los Angeles after driving 150 miles from Boston to Portland, Maine the day before 9/11, and on the morning of the events taking a connecting flight from Portland jetport back to Boston Logan airport. The 9/11 Commission said he took the connecting flight "for reasons that remain unknown".

> No physical, documentary, or analytical evidence provides a convincing explanation of why Atta and Omari drove to Portland, Maine, from Boston on the morning of September 10, only to return to Logan on Flight 5930 on the morning of September 11.[9]

For sceptics, by contrast, it seemed obvious that Atta had gone to Portland jetport, the nearest direct connection to Boston, in order to check through his baggage so that it could plausibly be held off Flight 11 from Boston Logan airport. The only way the contents of his bags could be revealed was if they were held off Flight 11, and the

CREDIT: Internet image

Atta's connecting flight to Boston Logan at 6:00 a.m. on 9/11 was 150 miles. The 9/11 Commission found his trip inexplicable. Sceptics said he went to Portland with only one purpose: to plant baggage that could later be "found" at Boston after Flight 11 crashed. The contents were an elaborate hijack kit, complete with a terrorist handbook and a list of accomplices and their targets. Portland was the nearest airport for a connecting flight, because flights from Manchester, New Hampshire, went to Boston via distant Philadelphia.

most credible way for them to be held off was if they came to Boston on a late connecting flight.

Atta therefore had no choice but to take the otherwise inexplicable risk of going to the nearest airport with a connecting flight, selecting the latest possible connection on the day of his ostensible mission, and checking baggage through to Flight 11 so that it could be held off and opened after Flight 11 crashed.

For sceptics, that explained the inexplicable flight: Mohamed Atta, the "linchpin" of the 9/11 events, had driven to Portland for the sole purpose of planting incriminating baggage in the hold of a connecting flight.

FAKED EVIDENCE PLACED ATTA IN PORTLAND

To validate the evidence in the baggage, Atta had to be placed in Portland taking a connecting flight, and indeed the only CCTV pictures of Atta showed him in Portland, and not in Boston. Unfortunately, a cursory examination of the photographic evidence that placed Atta in Portland overnight revealed that the date and time data on them were mostly false.

Prosecutors at the trial of Moussaoui in 2006 produced in evidence the uncropped images of Atta and his companion Abdulaziz al-Omari at a Jet Tech service station. These pictures had been circulated earlier

Jet Port Gas
9/10/01

Two of the images of Atta that purported to show him in Portland were suspect. The Jet Tech gas station shot taken the previous night (above left) showed the wrong date, 11–10–01. The airport security images (above right) showed two different clock times. The FBI website showed the Jet Tech pictures cut down (left), presumably to hide the incorrect date.

by the FBI in cropped-down form to hide the incorrect date. The revealed CCTV image from Jet Tech showed Monday 11–10, when it should have shown 9–10.

CCTV images from Wal-Mart the same evening were also shown on the FBI website similarly cropped down to hide the date, although their originals did not appear in court.

There was something wrong, too, with the CCTV images ostensibly taken at Portland jetport next morning. They showed Atta and Omari passing through the security checkpoint at both 5:45 and 5:53 a.m. simultaneously. While rigged pictures showed Atta in Portland, there was no photographic evidence of his presence in the Boston area or at Boston Logan airport.

Why would the authorities fake evidence that Atta had been in Portland? And what did the deception say about him being the leader of the 9/11 mission and its supposed Flight 93 hijack team?

The motive for the deception would have been to validate Atta's baggage being held off in Boston. Its contents could then be used to identify the 9/11 operation as a foreign attack by Moslem extremists. Sociopathic US and UK transnational corporations[10] could then rake in thousands of billions of dollars in tax revenues building a war-making empire. Interestingly, abundant witness evidence placed Atta in Portland before 9/11, perhaps when the required pictures had been taken.

ATTA'S INCREDIBLE RISK

The 9/11 Commission told us that this "operational commander" took a last-minute connecting flight to Boston, but its report failed to observe that by taking such a flight he was risking his entire mission. Many common occurrences in air travel could have delayed him, particularly rush-hour congestion of the sort that held up Flight 93 for twenty-five minutes. If Atta really led it, such a delay would have destroyed the 9/11 operation.

A cautious planner working on a major guerilla mission would at least have had his operatives take an earlier flight to Boston Logan, the American Eagle departure at 5:30 a.m. Planning to take a last-minute connecting flight and barely turning up in time for it[11] did not fit the hijackers' image that the mass media presented in the wake of the events. For example, "Sen. Orrin Hatch, R-Utah, the top Republican on the Senate Judiciary Committee, said FBI and intelligence officials told him the attacks were 'well-planned over a number of years, planned by real pros and experts'."[12] Or another example: "Last Tuesday, American Airlines Flight 11 from Logan Airport in Boston showed just how slick, controlled, ruthless and professional his followers really were. Flight 11 was bin Laden's blueprint hijacking. It worked like a dream."[13]

Taking such a deranged risk would have felt more like a nightmare for the man known as Atta, if he had been an authentic "operational leader" and not a patsy.

MOTIVE FOR THE CONNECTING FLIGHT

The 9/11 Commission said the FBI could not provide a convincing explanation for Atta's connecting flight, although its PENTTBOM inquiry had been "the largest investigation ever conducted" and covered over half a million leads, conducted 165,000 interviews, processed 1.8 million tonnes of debris and lab-tested over 6,000 items. It seemed that, although the FBI asked plenty of questions in Portland next day, PENTTBOM never investigated the mystery of the connecting flight itself nor the handling of the suspects' baggage.[14] For example, the FBI in Portland failed to follow up evidence that Atta had earlier frequented the city, even though, after the mugshot was published, hundreds of people reported having seen him there.[15]

The mass media briefly wondered what could have been the powerful motive that made Atta, this apparently top-level operative, risk all on a connecting flight at that crucial time and offered feeble explanations that went along the lines of: "Going to Portland to board the connecting flight to Logan, investigators speculate, may have been designed so as not to draw attention to all 10 arriving at the Boston airport at nearly the same time."[16] The Associated Press (AP) news agency served up the same unconvincing explanation more than three years later.[17] But it was self evident that the men had gathered in two much smaller groups in different terminals, because the FBI said they had telephoned each other within the airport.

Even the US military's hidden al-Qaeda suspects, held somewhere incommunicado and inaccessible to the 9/11 Commission, could not be tortured into explaining Atta's connecting flight, perhaps because "Atta's" identity was unknown to them – as it was to the 9/11 Commission, something that the Able Danger revelations, detailed below, proved.[18] In fact, planting the baggage was the only explanation that made sense of Atta's inexplicable dawn flight.

CORPORATE MEDIA GAGGED

The puzzle of the 9/11 "ring-leader's" connecting flight, reported by Bush's official commission of inquiry, should have caused a storm of media interest, but journalists had been forbidden to ask questions. An example:

> In stories about al Qaeda and the September 11, 2001 attacks in the United States, we need not write that the group has been blamed

for carrying them out. *There is sufficient factual evidence*, including several statements from Osama bin Laden asserting responsibility, for us to write that al Qaeda carried out the attacks or for us to use similar formulations. [Emphasis added.]

Reuters news service so instructed its staff internally the month before the Commission published its report.[19] Sadly, Rex Tomb, Chief of Investigative Publicity for the FBI, when asked why there was no mention of 9/11 on Bin Laden's *Most Wanted* web page in 2006, said: "The reason why 9/11 is not mentioned on Usama Bin Laden's Most Wanted page is because the FBI has no hard evidence connecting Bin Laden to 9/11."[20] This admission made nonsense of the allegations from within the US gulag that Atta had accompanied the alleged Flight 93 pilot Ziad Jarrah to Bin Laden's cave in Afghanistan to enrol him as a suicide pilot.

The instructions from Reuters clearly discouraged staff from examining the more perplexing aspects of the case.

OMARI'S PASSPORT PLANTED

Further evidence of official deception around the held-off bags arose with Omari's disappearing luggage. A 2006 report quoted 9/11 Commission staff members saying Atta checked two bags and his companion Omari stood by.[21]

Sceptics wondered how to square this with Omari's passport being found in the held-back baggage at Boston.[22] According to the Commission staffers, Omari put no bags on the rack at Portland, and according to the police investigation his bags were never found by American Airlines staff at Boston Logan airport, only Atta's.[23] So where did Omari's passport come from? It must have been planted.

ATTA NEVER BOARDED

When "hundreds of investigators" invaded Boston Logan airport on 9/11,[24] they would have searched the baggage-handling area for any held-off bags. A special baggage stream handled bags whose owners had triggered the computerized passenger-screening system called CAPPS. Security staff used high-tech equipment to check these bags for explosives. Here, officers quite innocently could find the held-back bags that Atta had planted at Portland jetport. No conspirators were required in this scenario. If Atta had never boarded Flight 11, CAPPS procedure would have held his bags off automatically and everyone involved – security, baggage-handlers, police officers, airport staff – would be entirely unsuspecting, assuming like the US mass media that there had been a mistake.

Corporate media managers always referred casually to "a mix-up"[25] or mentioned that the bags "did not get onto"[26] the fated airliner. The AP wrote: "Atta's luggage ... was left behind."[27] Evidently, editors believed that Americans were so jaded about baggage delays that they needed no further explanation. Moreover, few air travellers understood the confidential CAPPS procedure that triggered a special screening behind the scenes.

However, there was outright deception by the corporate media. For example, the AP wrote at the time: "Amanullah Atta Mohamed's early flight from Portland, Maine, arrived at Logan International Airport, Boston, just in time for him to connect with American Airlines flight 11 to Los Angeles, but *too late for his luggage to be loaded.*"[28] This story got reiterated all over the world. It sounded convincing, except that it was false. The 9/11 Commission established that Atta's plane arrived *on time* and he'd had fifty-five minutes to make his connection. Of course, it never occurred to anyone that Atta might not have boarded his flight.

The unsuspecting officers would take the explosives-screened bags to a secure place and, after obtaining Judge Cohen's permission, cautiously open them.[29] Seeing the contents, the FBI agents' excitement apparently robbed them of all powers of professional reasoning. They accepted, for example, that Atta would have taken the giant risk of having his bags randomly opened at Portland jetport security to reveal a substantial and weighty Islamic hijacking kit, something that would have wrecked the whole mission if he'd been the genuine leader. But the authorities never released any photographs of Atta's bags and contents, perhaps to discourage copy-cat crimes.

9/11 COMMISSION HINT

None other than Bush's 9/11 Commission offered a hint that Atta "the operational leader" never boarded his flight. On the opening page of its report, in its *sole reference* to Atta's baggage, the Commission confirmed that Atta triggered CAPPS:

> When he checked in for his flight to Boston, Atta was selected by . . . CAPPS . . . The only consequence of Atta's selection by CAPPS was that his checked bags were held off the plane until it was confirmed that he had boarded the aircraft.[30]

Since his bags were not loaded, this was a page-one giveaway by members of Congress – not by "conspiracy theorists" – that Atta never boarded Flight 11. His specially handled bags were to be held off until he boarded. They were never loaded: therefore he never boarded.

If it was not CAPPS that automatically held off the bags because Atta had never boarded, we had to believe that baggage-handlers in the special security screening area intended to load the bags once Atta was reported to have boarded, but somehow blundered and – by a one-in-a-million chance – it was the bogeyman's bags that got held back. But in that far-fetched scenario, where was Omari's bag? The one that was supposed to have yielded his passport?

VIDEO SURVEILLANCE

One official conjecture around the Portland connecting flight was that the alleged terrorists thought the jetport might be a less effective choke-point. Surveillance might be absent and security lax. This weak explanation was still coming out in 2006. "Although they planned to hijack an American Airlines jet that would take off from Logan later that morning, investigators said they might have gone through Portland in the belief that airport security would be less stringent there."[31] These ignorant investigators must have thought their opponents were simpletons, like Zacarias Moussaoui or Richard Reid, because the situation was exactly the reverse. It was Boston

Logan that did not have video surveillance (unlike the humblest corner store). And CAPPS presumably applied at Portland, just like anywhere else where baggage could be checked on to a scheduled flight.

Atta had made repeated visits to Boston Logan, as his record at the parking lot showed. He also had ramp access, judging by the security clearance card that was reportedly found in the car he left at Logan and that the 9/11 Commission forgot about. He could easily have scouted the security checkpoints and boarding gates for tell-tale signs of video cameras.

In fact, the obvious motivation was precisely the reverse of the "investigators" dim-witted speculations. Atta knew there were cameras all over Portland, as there were all over the rest of Boston, even if they were not at its peculiar airport. He wore a distinctive single-striped black-and-white shirt that particularly stood out for cameras at the points he visited the night before (or much earlier, when he was seen around Portland by hundreds of eyewitnesses). In the morning, he turned up late at the jetport so that other passengers would not block his CCTV picture at the security checkpoint.

It remained a baffling aspect of the Atta affair that the FBI had plenty of visual evidence of his presence in Portland,[32] but none from Boston. A former high-level intelligence official told the US investigative journalist Seymour Hersh: "Whatever trail was left was left deliberately for the FBI to chase."[33] The trouble with this view was: why would criminals leave a trail in Portland if they wished to be linked to a crime originating in Boston?

This was yet further proof pointing to the luggage, because all the (officially faked) evidence came from Portland, establishing the possibility of checked-through luggage, and none from Boston Logan – not even pictures of the incriminating contents. The men were laying a trail, and it led to the luggage.

DID ATTA EVER BOARD FLIGHT 11?

The only thing that linked Atta to Boston Logan airport, apart from his booked airline ticket, was a three-minute cellphone call. But evidence for it was more tenuous and suspicious than it appeared in the media reports.[34]

FBI Director Mueller told the US Joint Intelligence Committee: "When Atta arrived at Logan Airport, he received a telephone call on his cellular telephone from a pay phone located inside Terminal 'C'. This call is believed to have originated from one of the Flight 175 hijackers who were waiting to board Flight 175 which was boarding in Terminal 'C'."[35] As Mueller admitted, this vague attribution of the call was just a belief.

Mueller also asserted that the alleged hijackers "hid their communications by using hundreds of different pay phones and mobile phones, coupled with hard-to-trace prepaid calling cards,"[36] but the FBI apparently *possessed* Atta's cellphone. Mueller told the committee: "A telephonic message on that same day *recovered from Atta's cellular telephone* has Ziad Jarrah referring to Atta as boss."[37] [Emphasis added.]

This astonishing claim raises two issues. First, the knowledge that Jarrah, the supposed suicide pilot of Flight 93, addressed Atta as "boss" must have come from the spoken content of the call. Unless taped records were being kept of all cellphone calls by the 110 million cellular subscribers in the USA at the time, this had to mean that Atta was under surveillance, with his phone calls being monitored and recorded, immediately *before* the events of 9/11.

Moreover, if Ziad Jarrah telephoned Atta that morning and called him boss, something had to be even more suspect about Mueller's evidence, because the evidence showed that Atta was not the operational leader of anything that day, only a patsy delivering baggage for a sting on Islam.

Secondly, where did the FBI get Atta's telephone? It should have been in his pocket, travelling to immolation on Flight 11. Here was a second clue that Atta never got on to Flight 11.

WAS ATTA BEING WATCHED?

The FBI had access to the content of Atta's calls before the events of 9/11, and possibly even held his cellphone afterwards. Could Atta have been under surveillance throughout? The answer was yes. "Starting in

2000, the CIA placed Atta under surveillance in Germany. He was trailed by CIA agents," according to Wikipedia, citing European press reports.[38] "Experts believe that the suspect remained under surveillance in the United States," the *Berliner Zeitung* reported.[39]

Rep. Curt Weldon confirmed in August 2005[40] that in early 2000, a few months before before Atta's alleged US arrival date on 3 June ,[41] a US Army military intelligence program, known as "Able Danger", identified a terrorist cell based in Brooklyn, New York, one of whose members was Atta, and recommended to their military superiors that the FBI be called in to "take out that cell".[42]

Also, there was the question of who else had Atta under surveillance. In this regard, Fox News had reported on the problems associated with foreign companies administering US residents' computerized phone billing (Amdocs) and processing their wiretaps (Comverse).[43]

THE PLANTER OF THE BAGGAGE

The identity of Mohamed Atta, elaborately constructed by the 9/11 Commission, disintegrated with the Pentagon whistleblowers' revelations.

Sceptics dimly discerned at least two Attas, possibly three, even four: one, the very serious, devout, mysogynistic, air-travel-hating archaeology student in Hamburg, of whom pictures existed. He was so diffident that he shrank before his own father.[44]

The other Atta was the party-going, cocaine-sniffing, airborne drug-pirating, hard-boozing, multiple-identity, even Hebrew-speaking Atta in Florida who was seen with his sexy stripper girlfriend among the clientele at one of the semi-legal offshore casino ships of convicted criminal lobbyist Jack Abramoff, as described by Florida researcher Daniel Hopsicker.[45] (Of that Atta, no pictures exist. Immediate questioning after 9/11 by teams of FBI agents and their contractors soon cleared up any evidence about him by removing it for forensic study.)

It's not clear whether the Pentagon's "Able Danger" computer investigators were following the electronic trail of a *third* individual using the Atta identity, who was based in Brooklyn. And was it a *fourth* who was a car-bomber, as we learned when the NBC's Kerry Sanders mentioned on TV's Evening News on 12 September "the presence of the name of *suspected car bomber* Mohamed Atta on a passenger list"? (Atta's name did not appear on passenger lists published later.)[46]

"[M]ore is known about Mohamed Atta than any of the other 9/11 hijackers," wrote the online encyclopedia Wikipedia,[47] and yet so little was known that this man called Atta seemed to have the magical power of appearing in two places at once. "There are reports that seem to contradict others, indicating that he was in two places at the same time. Some reports may be unreliable, and it is possible that more than one person used Atta's identity at various times."

Prague v. USA   A Czech journal *Respekt* recorded the dispute over whether Atta had visited Prague in March 2001 or whether he had been moving about the USA at that time.[48]

Iraq v. USA   *Newsweek* magazine reported on 17 December 2003: "A widely publicized Iraqi document that purports to show that September 11 hijacker Mohamed Atta visited Baghdad in the summer of 2001 is probably a fabrication that is contradicted by US law-enforcement records showing Atta was staying at cheap motels and apartments in the United States when the trip presumably would have taken place, according to US law-enforcement officials and FBI documents." (*Newsweek* did not attempt to explain who would be motivated to forge such a document.)

Philippines v. Germany v. USA   An example of triple confusion: "Atta is then [1999] reported to have been living in the Philippines, but is also reported to be living back in Germany. He may have travelled often between locations, or there may be some confusion between two different people. Some have speculated that another person was using Atta's passport in the Philippines at this time." [*Sun-Sentinel*, 28 September 2001] In addition, the Able Danger computerized surveillance put him in the USA in the course of that year.

So, not only did media reports show Atta in two or even three places at one time, the 9/11 legend itself popularly put him in Boston when he was actually 150 miles away in Portland, Maine.

Oddly, one source said Atta drove obsessively in the last thirty-four days of his known life, covering 4,200 miles in rented cars, or an average of 123 miles per day, risking a police interview the whole time.[49] If true, this would be further evidence that he was under covert protection.

RENTAL CAR: SUSPECTS NOT ON THE LIST

Atta ostensibly returned a rental vehicle to Pompano Beach on 9 September, but on the same day he was reportedly renting a blue Nissan Altima with Omari in Boston. "Using credit card receipts and telephone records, the FBI traced their whereabouts almost to the minute. Records show they rented a blue Nissan at an Alamo office in Boston on Sunday, Sept. 9th."[50]

The Nissan later turned out to have been rented in the names of a dead man and his brother. Sceptics couldn't help wondering how, in that case, FBI agents could use "credit card receipts and telephone records" to trace it to Atta.

When Atta left Boston, on either the 9th or 10th September, police presumed he drove the Nissan Altima. The dead man and his brother, Adnan Bukhari and Ameer Bukhari of Vero Beach, Florida, who had supposedly rented the vehicle, were early hijacker or collaborator suspects as a result of the trace but were exonerated two days later. This initial suspicion of the Bukharis clashed with the 2006 report that Atta had stashed a master-list of his collaborators in his baggage, opened by police on 11 September.

THE ATTA MYSTERY SOLVED

Since the whole official story rested on official releases, and the US government was extremely secretive about terrorist matters, even striking out twenty-eight pages from the report of its hand-picked 9/11 Commission,[51] why was the Portland connecting flight released to the media at all, with its rigged pictures, unless it had to be, in order to explain the baggage being opened? The baggage could only be opened if it survived the crash. And it could only survive if it was held off a late connecting flight. There had to be a connecting flight, the only one involved in the events, to explain the bags that were the only ones held back.

Since Atta was clearly a patsy who planted bags and ran, his role as "operational leader" of the Flight 93 suspects was discredited.

HOW FLIGHT 93 WENT ROGUE

If Atta was not who he seemed to be, the seizure of Flight 93 was equally elusive. Absolutely nothing was known about it in spite of all the books, articles, TV documentaries and feature films that pretended to know. Considering that the flight-deck recording began *after* the alleged hijackers supposedly took the controls, Lisa Beamer's account in her book was interesting:

> What *is certain* . . . is that the captain and copilot were yanked out of the cockpit. Passengers, including Todd, later reported seeing two people lying motionless on the floor near the cockpit, *possibly* with their throats cut.
>
> *No one is certain* how the terrorists got into the cockpit. Some *speculate* that they preyed on an older flight attendant, threatening to slit her throat if the pilots didn't come out of the cockpit. Or they *may* simply have broken through the thin door that separated the cockpit from the cabin. *Perhaps* they waited for an open door, then barged into the tight cockpit, slitting the throats of the pilots while they were still strapped in their seats.[52] [Emphasis added.]

Another thing that was certain: Lisa Beamer's account was the purest fantasy. The hearsay chain involved could be depicted as follows:

Eyewitnesses	At the front of first class
Todd Beamer	At the back of economy class
Lisa Jefferson	Inside Verizon Corp.
Lisa Beamer	At home
Ken Abraham	White House evangelical ghostwriter

Only in the Book of Revelations (or a "conspiracy theory" like Lisa Beamer's) could four degrees of separation be considered evidential, and not the stuff of legend and delusion. At least the White House ghostwriter was honest enough to describe imaginary accounts of how anyone got into the cockpit as speculation.

More credible are reports that neither the pilot's wife nor the coroner on the ground believed the pilots were murdered.[53] Also, the cockpit voice recording had one of the raiders asking for the pilot to be brought back into the cockpit, about fifteeen minutes after both pilots would have been dead on the floor according to Lisa Beamer. (See Appendix.)

Another problem: not one of the thirty-five phone calls reported from Flight 93 explained how the hijacking was carried out.

On 15 May 2002, the President's press officer, Ari Fleischer stated: "The people who committed the 9/11 events used *box cutters* and *plastic knives* to get around America's system of protecting against hijackings." Some of the passenger calls reportedly mentioned knives, which aren't quite the same thing. At 9:50 a.m. aboard Flight 93, flight attendant Sandy Bradshaw called her husband: "'Have you heard what's going on? My flight has been hijacked. My flight has been hijacked by three guys with knives,' she said. 'Who was flying the plane?' Phil asked his wife. 'I don't know who's flying the plane or where we are,' she said."[54]

But not all the callers mentioned knives. Alice Hoglan of San Francisco, one of the initiators of the reported phone calls from Flight 93, and a United Airlines flight attendant, "said her 31-year-old son, Mark Bingham, called her by air-phone 15 minutes before the Boeing 757 crashed and said the plane had been taken over by *three men* claiming to have a bomb."

"'The FBI asked us if we heard Mark mention anything besides a bomb. He made no mention of knives or box cutters or guns or any other weapons,' Hoglan said. 'He was forward in the aircraft, could probably be in full view of everything that was going on, probably saw what happened in the cockpit.'" Hoglan said this on NBC's *Today Show* according to a Reuters story datelined Shanksville.[55]

Probably, but not definitely. For some reason he said nothing to her about the crucial events in the cockpit.

The FBI collected fourteen knives or portions of knives at the Flight 93 crash site, but did not make publicity out of them, so they presumably were with luggage from the hold, as required by airline security regulations.[56]

Air-traffic control in Cleveland, Ohio, was supposed to have heard someone shout "Mayday" and sounds of screaming, but these could have come over the emergency wavelength from literally anywhere, including from the vast Pentagon empire. Calling "Mayday, Mayday" did constitute a formal emergency alert, but according to the 9/11 Commission the air-traffic controllers either couldn't understand it or were incapable of responding decisively.

"FAA guidance to controllers on hijack procedures assumed that the aircraft pilot would notify the controller of the hijack via radio communication or by 'squawking' a transponder code of '7500' – the universal code for a hijack in progress. Controllers would notify the Pentagon's National Military Command Center (NMCC) and to ask for a military 'escort aircraft' to follow the flight."[57] That was the procedure, but according to the air force, it didn't happen.

What counted was that the pilots did not give on-the-record hijack alerts that would have obliged the air-traffic controllers immediately to alert the USAF. Without a logged alert, the FAA could believably dither, while the Pentagon tried to maintain plausible deniability.

THE INTER-AGENCY EXERCISES THAT DAY

Could the air-traffic controllers have been confused by a live-fly military exercise going on at the time? That brought up another mystery around the unreported hijackings: official confusion apparently arising from the multiple exercises being conducted on an inter-agency basis by the military and by the New York Emergency Office with the Federal Emergency Management Agency on that day. Michael Kane of From the Wilderness website wrote:

> In May of 2001 [Vice-President Richard] Cheney was placed directly in charge of managing the "seamless integration" of all training exercises throughout the federal government and military agencies by presidential mandate.
>
> The morning of 9/11 began with multiple training exercises of war games and terror drills which Cheney, as mandated by the president,

was placed in charge of managing.

War games and terror drills included live-fly exercises with military aircraft posing as hijacked aircraft over the United States, as well as simulated exercises that placed "false blips" (radar injects indicating virtual planes) on FAA radar screens. One exercise titled NORTHERN VIGILANCE pulled Air Force fighters up into Canada simulating a Russian air attack, so there were very few fighters remaining on the east coast to respond.[58]

It also paralysed air-traffic controllers faced with unexpected noises coming over the emergency wavelength. They knew that such sounds did not necessarily emanate from United 93, but from any transmitter tuned to that separate wavelength.

How did foreign hijackers know about these exercises in advance?

Another aspect of the peculiar non-hijacking of Flight 93, was that the US Secret Service had been reported to monitor all air-traffic control screens. Michael C. Ruppert in *Crossing the Rubicon* wrote that, since May 2001, Dick Cheney had been running a completely separate chain of Command and Control via the Secret Service, which he said had the technology to see the same radar screens the FAA saw in real time.[59] The Secret Service also, Ruppert said, had the legal authority and technological capability to take supreme command in cases of national emergency. Dick Cheney was the acting Commander-in-Chief on 9/11. This would be near the heart of the secret state: a covert and separate political chain of command behind the scenes, outranking the top brass at the Pentagon. It's wonderful what a vast defense budget, capable of losing trillions[60] of dollars without anyone noticing, can achieve.[61]

THE FLIGHT PATH

Did terrorists change Flight 93's flight path?

This question opens up a minefield of speculation about professional and technical matters that the 9/11 Commission did not itself explore, preferring to rely on information provided by the Pentagon. Sceptics would have much preferred to view the results of a genuinely independent public investigation that was equipped to find out exactly what happened behind the scenes with Flight 93. For example, aeronautics experts believed that NORAD had special measures for contacting hijackers that it was not about to discuss with anyone, including members of Congress. These measures are necessarily excluded from analysis here. In the absence of a properly resourced and independent inquiry, there is only sketchy evidence about navigational matters regarding air traffic that day.

Planes were tracked by US commercial ventures such as Flight Explorer and Flytecomm. They published maps showing the course followed by any aeroplane tracked by air-traffic control.

First, looking at the map (see opposite), it's worth remembering that Flight 93 departed from Newark, which is only 30 miles south of the World Trade Center. The plane, if hijacked after take-off, could have flown into the Wall Street area within minutes, instead of flying for nearly fifty minutes in the wrong direction.

Notice, also, that Flight 93 made a diversion northwards soon after take-off. This happened to bring it close to another rogue plane, Flight 175, at 8:47 a.m. The two airliners were in close proximity just as Flight 175 turned its transponder off, robbing air-traffic control of identification and altitude data for the radar blip. This fitted in with a plane-swap scenario. For example, Flight 175 could have ducked under Flight 93's radar shadow and accompanied it unobserved to Cleveland or another airport in the region, and been replaced by a remote-controlled fake-up that slipped through a radar "hole" to the north. This resembled the scenario described in a purported declassified Pentagon document about provoking war with Cuba.[62] This was a scenario that was dealt with in 9/11 truth movement websites that we will return to below.

The Flight Explorer Map Itself: How Truthful Was It?

According to the tracked route, when the plane called Flight 93 turned around near Cleveland, it slowed down and climbed to more than 40,000 feet, then it sped up and came back down to 35,000 feet. It slowed down significantly until just before it disappeared, when it sped up again. Its fastest recorded speed was 509 knots, or 586 m.p.h., just after it turned around near Cleveland.

The new destination, DCA (Ronald Reagan Washington National Airport), got approval just as the plane made a sharp turn to the north

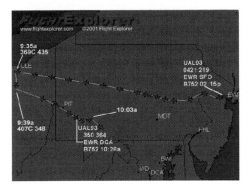

KEY:
"UAL93" = Airline + Flight no.
"350 440" = 35,000 ft, 440 knots
C = climbing
"EWR SFO = headed to San Francisco
"B752 2:15p" = Specific type of 757,
Estimated time of arrival 2:15

The Flight Explorer routemap showed Flight 93 initially veering northwards in the direction of Griffiss Air Force Base, regional HQ of the Air Force and a big radar research centre, where a major inter-agency exercise was being coordinated. On this vector it came close to Flight 175, another hijack victim. After 50 minutes aloft, the plane apparently made a U-turn near Cleveland airport, turning south and then southeast towards Washington, DC. The last swerves of the flight, in which it seems to have crashed in a westerly direction, are not shown in detail.

CREDIT. Flight Explorer, based on US government data

after passing Pittsburgh. The approval was peculiar, considering that it had to be granted by someone at FAA. An ABC news report by Peter Dizikes on 13 September said the station had learned that, shortly before the plane changed directions, someone in the cockpit had radioed in and asked the FAA for a new flight plan, with a final destination of Washington. Who in their right mind would grant such a request to a rogue airliner? This was at about 9:58 a.m., near the time someone aboard the plane reported an explosion and white smoke (and part of the World Trade Center collapsed). Most importantly, Flight Explorer showed that, once the plane reached cruising altitude, it never descended for its entire tracked flight. The map raised fundamental questions:

- How was it created without a transponder signal from Flight 93 on the last leg?
- Did Flight 93 really stay at cruising altitude until moments before it disappeared?
- If it did, how could the cellphone calls from Flight 93 ever have been credible to the authorities concerned?

And, concerning the change of course, why would the hijackers have filed for a change of destination to DCA long after it was obvious that the plane had gone rogue and represented an urgent danger to all other air traffic? How did they make this request and who granted it?

The 9/11 Commission was silent on these crucial issues, although the Flight Explorer company itself found this aspect of the course-change strange: on 9/11 they "learned that a United Airlines plane bound from Newark to San Francisco that crashed [*sic*] near Pittsburgh, Pa., at 10:10 a.m. [*sic*] had its flight path diverted. The flight was changed to arrive at Reagan National Airport, in Northern Virginia, [chief operating officer] Jeff Krawczyk said. 'When it got outside of Pittsburgh, it actually had a flight plan change to DCA,' said Krawczyk. 'We hardly ever get a flight plan change. Very unusual.'"[63]

"Whoever was ultimately in control of the plane, Flight 93 made a number of odd maneuvers in midair before it finally plunged to Earth. 'Halfway through its trip, around Weston, W.Va., it took some sharp turns, all within about two or three minutes,' said . . . Krawczyk . . . of Flight Explorer, a software firm that uses Federal Aviation Administration data to track flights."

"'It was going west, then took a turn to the north and then went west again,' Krawczyk said. Then the plane headed toward Kentucky and took a sharp turn south toward Washington, and around that time the FAA center in Cleveland lost contact with the flight, apparently because someone aboard had turned off its transponder, he said."[64]

The 9/11 Commission gave no answers. It did not mention Flight Explorer in its report, even though it was a division of Dimensions International, Inc., of Alexandria, Virginia, which "has successfully designed, developed and implemented a full spectrum of engineering solutions within the FAA, Departments of Defense, various civil agencies and the commercial sector since 1985". Not only did Flight Explorer work closely with the FAA and the Pentagon, but its sister company was Sentel Corp., part of the security and defence complex.[65]

Among all these ambiguities, the contorted route of the plane recorded on FAA radar remained completely unexplained, even by the transcript of the cockpit voice recording.

ZIAD JARRAH

The Ziad Jarrah case was a question of identity. It pointed towards the future world of total information awareness and police-state surveillance, because it looked like a clear case of identity theft, possibly by more than one party. And yet Bush's 9/11 Commission never mentioned the words "identity theft" anywhere in its door-stopper report, and never mentioned "identity" in connection with Ziad Jarrah.

The famous passenger phone calls from Flight 93, so numerous compared to the silence of those aboard Flight 11, talked of three hijackers aboard the airliner. It turned out that none of these alleged raiders had pilot training in their ID background. The US public needed a fourth hijacker who was qualified to fly an airliner across the nation, changing the autopilot setting, switching off the transponder, making announcements (faultily) to the cabin, obtaining official clearance for a new flight plan and otherwise making sense of the 120-ton rocket's bewildering array of controls.

This pilot was going to be Jarrah, and his absence from the passengers' view would have to be explained. The story would be that Jarrah evaded their view by sneaking from his front-row seat in first class after the cockpit had been seized, as recounted by the 9/11 Commission's dime-novel narrative. Sadly, this scenario was implausible because two of the other hijackers were busy dealing with the passengers and cabin-crew (according to a phone call from one of the cabin crew),[66] leaving only one to seize control of the cockpit from two ex-armed-forces pilots, which was implausible.

The only possible alternative version was that Jarrah joined the other hijacker in seizing the plane. But this also presented major problems. For example, in the space of one second the pilots could give a formal hijack alert that would automatically unleash the US Air Force. So each pilot had to be totally surprised in some way. The initial cries of "Get out of here, get out of here – get out of here" that air-traffic controllers overheard would indicate that the stealth and surprise were poorly executed, allowing the pilots crucial moments in which to either shout or key-in the alert. However, no such alert came in – unless it has been the subject of yet another official cover-up. Even if an alert did come in and was suppressed, the hijackers still had to subdue each pilot, unbuckle him and remove him from his seat without killing at least one of them, because a voice on the cockpit voice recorder at 9:45 a.m. asked for the pilot to be brought back in.[67] Above all, in this alternative scenario Jarrah would have been seen by the passengers.

DID HE ALWAYS FLY FIRST CLASS?

The real Ziad Jarrah may well have booked a ticket to San Francisco on United Airlines on 11 September 2001. He flew a lot more than most of us, being the well-looked-after son of a wealthy Lebanese civil servant. For example, he flew from his temporary home in the USA to Lebanon once in January 2001 and again in February 2001 to attend to family affairs. He told his devoted parents he might "drop by" his girlfriend in Germany, as if it were a taxi-ride away.[68] Although he currently lived in Florida, he had earlier lived in California, and he flew between the two, as he probably was doing on 9/11. He flew into the USA seven times during his student-visa period. A new Mercedes awaited him in the family garage when he had qualified as an airline pilot in the USA.[69]

Although it could be crucially important, it's not been made known whether Jarrah regularly flew first class or not. The alleged hijackers reportedly booked first class. Jarrah might have been in first class about his own business. He could afford it: his family sent him money whenever he asked, even when it was just "for fun".[70] Knowledge of his choice of class on his frequent earlier flights might have proved embarrassing to the official story, which was probably why Bush's 9/11 Commission overlooked the matter.

THE CALL

The website blurb of a CBC-TV *Fifth Estate* series programme called "The Pilot", aired on 10 October 2001, gives the following summary of Jarrah's actions on the fateful morning:

Jarrah calls [his fiancée] Aysel on the morning of 11 September and tells her three times that he loves her and hangs up. Jarrah boards United Airlines flight 93 from Newark to San Francisco. He and three others are seated in first class. Shortly after take-off, the hijackers changed the plane's flight path. Jarrah took controls [*sic*] of the airplane.

Sadly, as noted earlier, the 9/11 Commission decided that this call never happened. Instead, Jarrah made a normal call. "In the early morning hours of September 11, Jarrah made on final call to [Aysal] Sengün from his hotel. . . The conversation was brief and, according to Sengün, not unusual."[71] So the media hysteria was proven to be a deceptive, hate-mongering charade.

Sengün admitted that their relationship had become difficult during the Hamburg years. "She [told a German court] he had a very different view of Islam from her and became increasingly devout after moving to Hamburg in 1997. He had wanted her to cover up, but she said she wouldn't wear the veil for him, only for God."[72]

But this proved nothing, only that a young man only twenty-one years old and newly arrived in Europe had fallen under the influence of a group of radicals just as, for example, Pierre Elliott Trudeau, who went on to become the notable Prime Minister of Canada, flirted as a student with fascist subversives sympathetic to Vichy France in 1944.[73]

Even more damning than the blazoned phoney "I love you" phone call was the "suicide letter" that also got big coverage. The night before, Jarrah was supposed to have penned a last letter to Aysel, but the report of this was another of the 9/11 coincidences."A *month after* the hijackings, US authorities . . . *discovered* a letter written by Jarrah to his girlfriend in Germany and postmarked September 10. In the letter – which was *mistakenly addressed* and returned to the United States, where authorities *found* it – Jarrah told his girlfriend he had done his duty." [Emphasis added.]

"I have done what I had to do," he wrote in German, in handwriting that sloped in all directions. "You should be very proud. It is an honour, and you will see the result, and everyone will be happy."[74]

He could easily have been referring to his big commitment to becoming an airline pilot, which was how Sengün interpreted it. He signed the letter to his fiancée: *Ziad Jarrah*.

It was another of the fairy-tale aspects of the official narrative. This was the only signature to the events – and we were told he wrote the wrong address of his own lover, with whom he had lived, and with whom he spoke on the phone almost every day. Since American men handwrote letters so infrequently, this probably sounded credible to them. It also subscribed to the TV crime series fantasy that police "find" and "discover" things when everything they produce is supplied to them.

BOARDING THE PLANE

Presumably basing its information on United Airlines data,[75], the 9/11 Commission report gave the alleged hijackers' seat numbers but two of the identities were obviously stolen or forged.[76] If two of the alleged terrorists bore forged passports, obviously the other two could have had them too, and there are no CCTV photos to identify them visually.

It's odd, too, that: "Two checked bags, two did not." The alleged hijackers must have known about CAPPS, the computerized passenger-scanning system, which was public knowledge. Since the mid-90s, domestic flights had submitted all passengers to these checks, providing they checked baggage on to their flight. "The disclosure that some members of the suicide crews had triggered security measures differs sharply from previous portrayals of the hijackers as meticulous planners who craftily avoided all detection," the *Washington Post* wrote in a rare flash of perception.[77]

Getting selected by CAPPS could easily have led to a baggage scan at the very least, causing nail-biting delay, or a baggage inspection or even an interview, causing a passenger to miss the plane. A baggage inspection would have been particularly unwelcome if the hijackers had unwisely packed their plane-hijacking kits complete with a list of all the gang's names and missions, as Atta (their "operational leader") was supposed to have done in the case of his planted bags. A dedicated hijacker who had been planning his scheme for years would not wish to risk either possibility, both of which were triggered by checking luggage on to the plane. Moreover, the alleged hijackers were working as a team, supposedly coordinated by Atta with the help of a foreign intelligence service. Why did they all not avoid checking baggage on to the planes?

In the early days, when the FBI was still building its terrorist list (although the list by 2006 was supposed to have come whole from Atta's bags) the media was open about the lack of sure identification. A 15 September 2001 daily newspaper report (written on the 14th) from suspect-hotbed Florida said: "Investigators suspect that documents used by the Florida hijackers to enter the United States and enroll in flight schools were obtained using false identities at US consulates. The assumed identities could complicate the US investigation of possible terrorist affiliations."[78] As time went by, however, the FBI list remained unchanged and became scripture.

What about the DNA from Shanksville? Did that not provide cast-iron identification of everyone aboard?

That was something that only the Pentagon knew. Because the President defined the impacts as foreign attacks on 15 September, Pentagon medical examiners had received the 9/11 human remains, and it was they who conducted the laboratory tests.

In the 9/11 Commission's words: "The Department of Defense is the behemoth among federal agencies. With an annual budget larger than the gross domestic product of Russia, it is an empire."[79] It had more than 700 secure bases all over the world and a huge air force to service them with little public oversight. Just some of its spare planes in storage would have served most countries as a lavish air force.

This empire has not in fact revealed in so many words who boarded Flight 93. The official reference came from the Pentagon's medical office:

PENTAGON FLIGHT 93 DNA STATEMENT:
All but one of the passengers and crew were identified.[80]

Clearly this terse sentence had been processed through a department of asymmetrical war. Pentagon documents went through several levels of reviewers, each one examining and weighing the smallest comma, editing out fancy words until the document was uniformly dull. The process was called "coordination". It did not mention hijackers, only "all but one of the passengers and crew". This must have been the only

Pentagon document on earth that did not discriminate between the two. Either that, or the alleged hijackers were not included.

Before the 9/11 story fully crystallized into an al-Qaeda plot, "FBI director Robert Mueller . . . acknowledged that some of those behind last week's terror attacks may have stolen the identification of other people, and, according to at least one security expert, it may have been 'relatively easy' based on their level of sophistication."[81] Eight months after 9/11, and two years before the 9/11 Commission put its imprint on the official version, Mueller revealed the basic facts: "The hijackers . . . left no paper trail. In our investigation, we have not uncovered a single piece of paper – in the US or in Afghanistan – that mentioned any aspect of the September 11th plot. The hijackers had no computers, no laptops, and no storage media of any kind."[82] Four months after his speech, Ramzi Binalshibh was seized following a gunfight in Pakistan and his inquisition and torture (or possibly a chat over drinks beside a swimming pool) ostensibly provided the connections the FBI had lacked.[83]

In fact, the FBI's 14 September scriptural list of hijackers was a cobbled-together effort, as the following account of the insertion of Hani Hanjour into it attests. (Hanjour was the bad pilot[84] who, the 9/11 Commission decided, flew Flight 77 aerobatically into the side of the Pentagon, killing 125 civilian and military personnel and all aboard the Boeing 75 airliner. Although several CCTV cameras pointed at the scene, no footage of the airliner had ever been produced.)

FINDING THE PILOTS

In April 2006, a former FBI agent asserted that Atta's baggage had contained a complete list of all the names of the alleged hijacking gang.

> A former FBI agent and a former federal prosecutor who helped direct the New England investigation of the Sept. 11 attacks told *Newsday* that one bag found in Boston contained far more than what the commission report cited, including the names of the hijackers, their assignments and their al-Qaida connections.
>
> 'It had all these Arab-language papers that amounted to the Rosetta stone[85] of the investigation,' former FBI agent Warren

Flagg said. [A] former federal prosecutor, who declined to be identified publicly, supported Flagg's account.[86]

The ex-agent then delivered the whammy:

> 'How do you think the government was able to identify all 19 hijackers
> almost immediately after the attacks?' Flagg asked. 'They were identi-
> fied through those papers in the luggage. And that's how it was
> known so soon that al-Qaida was behind the hijackings.'

It had always been a problem for the FBI that it published a full list of
the suspects on 14 September, a list that never changed, even throughout the ensuing PENTTBOM investigation, the committee hearings
on Capitol Hill and the 9/11 Commission inquiry. Sceptics had wondered how they got the names so quickly, and came up with the CCTV
video of chief-suspect Atta equally rapidly.

Flagg's story was obviously meant to plug the gap. Unfortunately, it
conflicted with an episode that occurred before millions of TV viewers
on the morning of 14 September 2001 (three days after the list had
allegedly been found). With the TV-viewing masses wild to know who
had performed the hijackings, CNN interrupted an ongoing Rudy
Giuliani press conference to announce that there was breaking news
and went over to department of Justice correspondent Kelli Arena in
Washington, DC. "She has breaking news on the identities of those
eighteen hijackers," announced anchor Leon Harris.

Kelli Arena then read out the phonetically spelt versions of *nineteen*
names. Evidently she had only had time to jot them down in shorthand
from a hurried verbal briefing. She said the following:

> CNN managed to grab a list of the names of *the 18 suspected hijackers*
> that is supposed to be officially released by Justice sometime later
> today. I will do my best to read, to read the names, some are a bit
> unfamiliar. . . We are told by law enforcement sources that most of
> these names in some way connect in some way to indirectly or
> directly to Osama bin Laden. . . [Reads the first part of a list of names]
>   Continuing on, United Airlines *flight number 93*, Almad Alhanawi
> (ph), Almed Alnami (ph), Ziad Girad (ph) and Sayd Algamdi (ph).
> American Airlines *flight number 77*. Cammid Al-Madar, and *Mosear*

Caned (ph), Majar Mokhed (ph), Nawar Al Hazni (ph) and Salem Al Hazni (ph)... Again, this list not officially released yet by the Justice Department. We obtained this list of names through sources.[87] [Emphasis added.]

Arena said there were eighteen names, but actually read out nineteen, one of them phonetically Jarrah's, on the Flight 93 list.

Until early 2006, the presumption had been that the FBI had copied the Arabic names from the passenger manifests of United and American Airlines, which are always published without hijacker names, presumably to avoid granting any fame to mass murderers. The original airline passenger manifests have never been published, indicating perhaps a closing of ranks between corporations and pro-corporate government, although the publication of manifests is said to be illegal.

That presumption prevailed until Flagg's revelation.

The name that replaced *Mosear Caned* a few hours later on the FBI's printed nineteen-name list was "Hani Hanjour – believed to be a pilot". This substitute may have been a pilot, if a very poor one with uncertain licensing status, by all reports.[88] The blogger Xymphora commented on this name change:

> They needed a pilot on Flight 77, so they just picked another Arab-sounding name off the list, and then likely substituted the name of semi-plausible pilot Hani Hanjour when someone pointed out that "Mosear Caned" was a dangerous name to have on the list. The FBI simply backtracked from the names to determine the identities. Since most, if not all, of the September 11 hijacker identities were stolen, we remain in the dark as to who really was behind September 11.[89]

Simply plucking out a replacement name required the FBI post-9/11 to have the requisite range of internees to make this kind of selection. During their extraordinarily rapid 9/11 dragnet that rounded up hundreds of men with Arabic names, they probably did. They could easily have made him disappear in the torture gulag.[90]

Since the FBI, in the light of the Mosear Caned substitution mystery, seems to have been ready to substitute the name of an Arab with pilot qualifications for some other unsuitable name, it seems quite possible that Jarrah's name, possibly being already on the passenger manifest (particularly if he regularly flew first class), was selected for the same reason. Perhaps he was initially accused of being the pilot on Flight 93 because it did not take long to search his name and find that he had received a pilot certificate and had an old address in Germany. A little further work and – wow! – he'd studied in Hamburg, the hotbed of Islamic radicalism. As time went on, and German and other security services went to work, there was a terror trial in Germany and someone produced a video purporting to show a bearded Jarrah in October 1999, attending the wedding of Said Bahaji at the al-Quds Mosque in Hamburg with 9/11 suspects Atta, al-Shehhi, Zammar, and Binalshibh.[91] Later Binalshibh, from his anonymity within the gulag – or possibly a recliner beside a swimming pool – provided a narrative about Jarrah going to Afghanistan for three weeks and getting recruited by Osama Bin Laden. The torture gulag was where the story of Ziad Jarrah's al-Qaeda connection came from. None of the passenger calls mentioned a rogue pilot, or even a fourth hijacker. The scorched passport and its couple of inserted oddments were the only hard evidence that he'd been on the plane – and even they had survived by some kind of miracle.[92]

JARRAH AT THE CONTROLS

That Jarrah flew Flight 93 was unsupported by any evidence. It was a conspiracy theory, like Lisa Beamer's fantastic account of the hijacking.

For what the telephone calls were worth, considering the mental and emotional state of those who received them, none mentioned seeing a rogue pilot. The passengers didn't even report a fourth hijacker, let alone one at the controls of their plane.[93] Jarrah's family apparently heard FAA recordings of the rogue-pilot announcements over the airliner PA system supposedly made by Jarrah and picked up by the emergency channel: they denied it was him. No surveillance pictures before or on 9/11 showed Ziad Jarrah or any of the other Flight 93 suspects.

That should have been hugely inconvenient for the official story. It matched badly with a high-drama "meticulous re-enactment" of the events aboard Flight 93.[94] But sceptics wondered whether the truth meant anything in the context of whipping up the US public against Islam. They bore in mind that in the Pentagon's Iraq war "documents explicitly list[ed] the 'US Home Audience' as one of the targets of a *broader propaganda campaign*", according to the *Washington Post*[95] [emphasis added], and wondered whether such propaganda had extended to the events of 9/11.

As we have seen, the long-planned war was intricately connected to the 9/11 events, and in particular the "Let's Roll" recruitment slogan arising from an unrecorded, single-sourced, hearsay phone call to the Verizon Corporation.

The police and the security state supposedly knew nothing about Ziad Jarrah on 9/11, although the CIA was reported to have had someone with his identity questioned in Dubai.

Sceptical young persons in Europe did not believe the Jarrah story, and they were beyond the immediate reach of the controlled US mass media. To consolidate the case against Jarrah, intelligence operations would have got involved, and they would have set out to manufacture the consent of the youthful intelligensia through the medium that youth in particular patronized: a movie. Luckily for everyone involved, a "meticulously researched" re-enactment of the supposed life of Ziad Jarrah in Hamburg was produced. The movie was *The Hamburg Cell* and it received rave reviews from house-critics all over Europe. Later re-enactments on the silver screen followed suit and showed Jarrah at the controls of Flight 93 and listed his name among their cast credits.

THE TWO JARRAHS

We have already seen that the Atta portrayed as knowing Jarrah in *The Hamburg Cell* could not have been the Atta that "Able Danger" had under surveillance, and we've noted how often Atta appeared in two places at once.

The same applied to Jarrah. Nobody aboard Flight 93 reported a fourth hijacker, there were no CCTV photographs from Newark airport or anywhere else, and there was evidence he had a double. Even

Ziad was rarely portrayed in the English-speaking media as he appeared in a photograph taken at his home with his mother in February, 2001, when he (again) flew to Beirut to attend a family affair. This shot (left) was published in India. US-influenced media always preferred the driver's licence picture, which showed his skin as much darker (like the majority of the human race), and resembled a criminal mugshot. It better established his status as a bogeyman for the USA's fair-skinned elite.

CREDITS: Internet images, reproduced in the public interest

UK film director Antonia Bird managed to find an actor who looked like him, so the mistake was understandable (and possibly deliberate).

The official story explained Jarrah's multilingual secular westernization during his spell in the USA as a façade, adopted on the instructions of Osama Bin Laden to trick Americans.[96] Osama did not seem, however, to have instructed Jarrah to conceal his identity or go underground, the way top US officials described al-Qaeda agents as behaving.

There were at least two reported cases of mistaken identity regarding Ziad Jarrah:

Jarrah 1, at 20, was boarding at a Catholic school in Beirut, and was often in touch with the rest of his family. His parents fetched him to the family home almost every weekend by car. Not until April 1996 did he leave Lebanon for the first time, to study in Germany.[97] **Jarrah 2** leased a flat in a three-family house on East Third Street in Brooklyn, New York. A Brooklyn apartment lease from March 1995 until February 1996 carried Ziad Jarrah's name. *Landlords there identified his photograph as being identical to that of the 9/11 hijacker.*[98]

Jarrah 1 studied at the Florida Flight Training Center until 15 January 2001. Had studied there for the previous six months. His family reported he arrived in the Lebanon to visit on 26 January, five days before he supposedly passed through the UAE. His father had just undergone open-heart surgery, and Jarrah visited him daily at the hospital for over a week. Referring to this, his uncle, Jamal Jarrah, asked: "How could he be in two places at one time?" Moreover, the family said the longest Jarrah had ever gone without phoning them was ten days, back in 1997. Afghanistan's telephone system was rudimentary. In the mountains, with the Taliban rebels, it was non-existent.[99] On 30 January 2001, officials interrogated **Jarrah 2** for hours at the Dubai International Airport, in the UAE. They did this at the request of the CIA, for "suspected involvement in terrorist activities". The CIA told them that he would be arriving from Pakistan on his way back to Europe, and they needed to know where he had been in Afghanistan and how long he had been there. During the interview, the man "divulged that he had spent the previous 'two months and five days' in Pakistan and Afghanistan – the only known acknowledgment of an Afghan visit by any of the hijackers – and that he was returning to Florida. . ." It was later reported that "investigators have confirmed that Jarrah had spent at least three weeks in January 2001 at an al-Qaeda training camp in Afghanistan". US officials got the results of the interrogation before Jarrah left. "UAE and European intelligence sources told CNN that the questioning of Jarrah fits a pattern of a CIA operation begun in 1999 to track suspected al-Qaeda operatives who were traveling through the UAE." He was then permitted to leave, eventually going to the US. This story was confirmed by numerous UAE, US and European officials. No one has denied that he passed through Dubai on this date, but the CIA has not admitted to ever having ordered his questioning.[100]

The two clashing episodes were strong indications that Jarrah had a double who had stolen his identity. Identity theft was a major emerging problem in the late 1990s. The US justice department estimated annual identity thefts in 2001 at up to 700,000.[101] The US Federal Trade Commission said that identity theft was its number one source of consumer complaints, 42 percent of all complaints, in 2001.[102]

More identity problems cropped up around Jarrah's passports. He had two: one Lebanese, one German. It was Jarrah's Lebanese passport that was found after Flight 93 disappeared, as the Arabic stamp on the picture showed. Whatever happened to the German passport that he was supposed to have shown to his landlord in Florida? A German

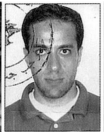

Searchers allegedly found the US entry visa of Ziad Jarrah (left) at the
Shanksville site. Luckily, the Lebanese passport picture (middle) that was with
the visa survived completely unscorched. A picture from the 1990s (right)
showed his normal appearance. Both the recovered documents apparently
had survived unstained by blood although their bearer had presumably been
reduced to gory pulp. It was briefly claimed that yet another passport had
achieved the miraculous."Two [passports] were recovered from the crash site
of United Airlines flight 93 in Pennsylvania. These are the passports of Ziad
Jarrah and Saeed al Ghamdi," Susan Ginzburg, chief counsel to the 9/11
Commission, testified on 26 January 2004 at the Hart Senate Office Building.
But the Ghamdi passport never appeared.

CREDIT: US government

nationality might have been far preferable for a man with an Arab name
who was boarding a US transcontinental flight. The Lebanese passport
was the one reportedly found at the crash site with the German work
permit of his remote relative, Assem Omar Jarrah, a picture of which
was produced in evidence at the Moussaoui trial.

The presence of any of the documents could easily have been
explained by the real Jarrah innocently being seated in first class
aboard the flight. But their retrieval from the Shanksville crater was
suspicious because:

■ The plane disappeared and witnesses said of the site: "There was
nothing there."

■ The FBI claimed the fuselage of the plane had been buried many
metres below the ground.

■ Jarrah's body, supposedly positioned at the nose of the plane, was
in a plane that according to the US government hit the ground as
fast as a bullet from a gun barrel, and was presumably immolated,

along with his ID that he either had on his person or in his carry-on bag, which would have been crushed but not burned, being underground.

▪ The photo on the entry visa, and the surname printed below, presumably contained within the passport, were both miraculously preserved from flames, while the passport picture survived the devastating impact totally unblemished.

It is very hard to resist the suspicion that the documents were somehow planted in the evidence chain to prove the presence aboard the aircraft of a qualified pilot, since none of the three hijackers reported by the passengers must have had the required qualification. This was effectively a *second* case of identity theft from Ziad Jarrah.

BUT WAS HE INNOCENT?

Ziad Jarrah was the most improbable suicide pilot of the four, as was widely realized at the time. For example, the *Boston Globe* wrote fourteen days after the events: "For [the official story] to be true, the young engineer would have had to live a double life worthy of a first-rate spy – concealing from his family, girlfriend, and friends that he was a Muslim extremist, not the religiously moderate, pro-American, fun-loving person they knew him to be."

"'It makes no sense,' his uncle, Jamal Jarrah, said in a telephone interview from the village of al-Marj, Lebanon, recalling that two days before the hijacking, his nephew called and told the family he'd be coming home for a cousin's wedding in mid-September. 'He said he had even bought a new suit for the occasion.'"[103]

Jarrah, raised a boarder at select Christian private schools, was the only alleged hijacker with a well-off family he was closely attached to and which was eloquent in his defence. Also, he had an attractive common-law wife with whom he planned to set up house soon and start a family. The parents denied he could have had anything to do with the suicide attacks. They said he might have been aboard the plane innocently, or been murdered by plotters.

"The family, which is cooperating with Lebanese authorities, said

Jarrah was a fun-loving young man and said it would have been impossible for Jarrah to have turned into an Islamic fundamentalist. They released home video of Jarrah to CNN, showing him celebrating at another couple's wedding."[104]   There was the hint of a drug connection. A *Los Angeles Times* article later referred to "bleary-eyed photographs" from his early days in Greifswald, "including one of Ziad lighting a water pipe – indicat[ing] that they did their share of partying".[105] Jarrah came from the Lebanon's Bekaa valley, a well-known hashish-production area, and his time in Florida may have been to do with drug-running in small planes. This would fit with descriptions of Atta-number two in the Sunshine State, and with Jarrah's supposed "suicide" letter, if he believed he was heading off to San Francisco on a big dope deal. An unholy combination of secret-state personnel from various countries is notoriously in control of the international drug trade.

Even Jarrah's education was disputed: the indignant family showed educational forms that proved he attended a different technical school in Germany from two "Hamburg Cell" members, disputing German authorities who said they went to the same college.

A report on 16 September 2001 said Jarrah's girlfriend reported him missing after she had not spoken to him "for some time", except that the 9/11 Commission had him calling her on the morning of 9/11, just five days earlier.[106] Formally reporting someone missing in the USA, when they had not called for only five days, would be odd.

"Jarrah is claimed to have become an associate of the Hamburg cell,

A videograb from court evidence presented in Germany purported to show a bearded Jarrah attending a wedding with high-profile Islamic militants.

CREDIT: Unknown

Part of a 757 control-panel layout mock-up presented in prosecution evidence at the Moussaoui trial in 2006. The FBI said agents found it "in a trash compactor at Days Inn, Newark Airport, Newark, New Jersey". Oddly, the Pittsburgh *Post-Gazette* said on 28 October 2001 that "back in the Florida apartment he'd left four days earlier [Jarrah had] set up a full-size, cardboard replica – three panels in all – of the cockpit of the airplane". Either he took the cumbersome layout with him to the airport hotel, or someone was planting evidence.

CREDIT: US government trial evidence release

although he never seems to have lived with the others, and cannot be confirmed to have ever known them,"[107] according to the Wikipedia entry, representing the mainstream view.

A videograb from a wedding attended by Islamic radicals in Hamburg purported to show a bearded Jarrah. He seems to have got involved with a set keen on radical Islam in Hamburg, a city well known for it. But he never lived with the so-called Hamburg Cell, as the 9/11 Commission report admitted: "In Hamburg, Jarrah had a succession of living accommodations, but he apparently never resided with his future co-conspirators [*sic*]. It is not clear how and when he became part of Atta's circle... Even with the benefit of hindsight, Jarrah hardly seems a likely candidate for becoming an Islamic extremist."[108] Also, the Commission failed to mention that he was an impressionable twenty-one years old at the time.

Jarrah's connection with the Hamburg Cell could easily be interpreted as a youthful flirtation, and his alleged journey to Afghanistan with Atta was based entirely on the tortured evidence of Ramzi Binalshibh who, by "extraordinary rendition" was in the hands of the US secret state and had not been seen for years.

The 9/11 Commission's claim that Atta drove Jarrah to the airport when he travelled to see his fiancée Aysal in Germany in July 2001 was couched in the usual "apparently" language used by all authors when they are groundlessly speculating.

THE FLORIDA PASSPORT LIE

The word "apparently" cropped up again when Jarrah was supposed to have moved into an apartment at 4641 Bougainvilla in Lauderdale-by-the-Sea with Ahmed al-Haznawi, another of the suspected hijackers. It's easy to see why the connection was only apparent, because Haznawi was reported to have shown the landlord a German passport as proof of his identity.

"One of the newly identified figures in the plot, Ziad Jarrahi [Jarrah], rented an apartment in Lauderdale-by-the-Sea for two months this summer, the owner said. Landlord Charles Lisa said Jarrahi and another hijacking suspect who shared the apartment, Ahmed Alhaznawi, both provided German passports as proof of identity."[109]

Sadly, there was no published evidence that Haznawi had ever resided in Germany or possessed a German passport. According to the 9/11 Commission, he had received instructions to obtain a Saudi Arabian passport.

"KSM told potential hijackers to acquire new 'clean' passports in their home countries before applying for a US visa. This was to avoid raising suspicion about previous travel to countries where al-Qaeda operated. Fourteen of the 19 hijackers, including nine Saudi muscle hijackers, obtained new passports. Some of these passports were then likely doctored by the al-Qaeda passport division in Kandahar, which would add or erase entry and exit stamps to create 'false trails' in the passports."[110]

Haznawi was one of these Saudi musclemen, and could not have presented the German passport that his landlord said he did, so there's something fishy about Jarrah's connection to Haznawi at that apartment. Added to which, Jarrah's passport, allegedly found at the plane crash site was Lebanese (see picture on page 115).

DEVOUT MOSLEMS IN LAS VEGAS

The Las Vegas flight allegedly made by Jarrah, and other flights to the gambling capital of the world by alleged hijackers, may have overlapped with a visit by one other suspect, or it may not. "Tracking the movements of the hijackers has been difficult, authorities said, because of their frequent use of false identification, aliases and variations of their own names."[111] But Jarrah apparently went under his own name.

A local "terrorism expert" said Las Vegas would have been an ideal place for the suspects to meet because so many visitors came from all over the world. He mentioned that Las Vegas was also an ideal place to launder money. However, he failed to add that money-laundering made it an ideal spot for drug dealers, in spite of Nevada's tough drug laws.[112]

This so-called expert did not observe that any flight by scheduled airliner would be a high risk for foreign plotters, any airport being an ID choke-point nightmare.

Drug-running would be an ideal front for the entrapment of patsy hijackers by the drug-controlling secret state, and it might explain why so many of the gang reportedly carried luggage when they did not need to, and when by so doing they increased their chances of getting interviewed and held off their plane.

THE SPEEDING TICKET

The speeding ticket would provide a hard link between Ziad Jarrah and the airport in Newark if it had not been handed out at 4:45 a.m. in a county where there are on average just seventy-eight residents per square kilometre, and thin traffic could have been expected at that

State police in Maryland ticketed Jarrah for speeding just two days before the hijackings.

CNN's website reproduced an image of a police security video that purported to show the ticketing of Ziad Jarrah for speeding on an empty street at 4:42 a.m. The ticket was later allegedly found in the rented car parked at Newark airport.

CREDIT: US police image

early hour, as demonstrated by the empty street in the tantalizing police videograb reproduced on CNN's website.

"On September 9, two days before the hijackings, a Maryland state trooper cited Jarrah for speeding on Interstate 95 in Cecil County, near the Delaware state line. Registration showed that the red 2001 Mitsubishi Galant that Jarrah drove that night was owned by Garden State Car Rental at Newark International Airport in New Jersey. After the September 11 hijackings, the car was found at the airport with the speeding citation was [*sic*] still in the glove box."[113]

The secret state evidently knew about his movements. The CIA had allegedly required someone called Jarrah to be questioned at the airport in the United Arab Emirates. Why did the Maryland police computer not show Jarrah up as a terror suspect? That could be attributable to routine police inefficiency. But why, at this late point, did Jarrah risk getting a ticket, getting questioned, getting locked up? Obviously, contact with a police officer would be extremely undesirable if he was intending to conduct an attack on America the day after next with eighteen other foreign guerrilla-warfare operatives. Just being out on the road in a remote area at a quarter-to-five in the morning would be risky, let alone speeding.

The cultist line was that, knowing he was going on a suicide mission, he was unconsciously trying to be stopped. But it was disputed whether any of the gang, apart from Atta, had yet been told they were to go on a suicide mission and not a regular hijacking. Strict secrecy, including dividing personnel into cells sealed off from each other, was intended to prevent leaks. More than half of them had risked CAPPS by checking baggage into the holds of their target planes, as if they'd thought they were going to arrive somewhere.

If the hijackers assigned to piloting were the only ones who knew that the mission involved suicide, Jarrah would be a key insider, stringently dedicated to staying out of trouble, avoiding the authorities at all times, and lying low so that he could fulfil his holy task.[114]

Sadly, Jarrah had no such profile. "Jarrah had obtained his license to fly small planes, and began training to fly large jets late in 2000. He flew to Beirut to visit his family, and then to Germany to visit his girlfriend Sengün. He brought her back to the United States for a ten-day visit, and she even attended a flight school session with him. In mid-January of 2001, he again flew to Beirut to visit his father, who was to have open-heart surgery. He then visited his girlfriend Sengün in Germany, not for the last time, and came back to the United States again. His behavior was markedly different from the other hijackers, who broke off all familial and romantic relations."[115]

He entered the USA by air approximately seven times during his residence. He took a number of scheduled flights within the country (ostensibly to research his mission and test CAPPS, according to the official story). Police found evidence that he flew to Las Vegas, capital of US organized crime, but it's not certain he ever spoke to other 9/11 suspects there.[116]

What's all wrong about this is the travel itself. With the conspirators safely inside the USA, why imperil the whole mission by passing through choke-point airports where the traveller's ID would be checked and matched against any new information, CAPPS-triggering baggage would be given secondary inspection and possibly opened, and photographs would be taken covertly?

Furthermore, from friends and family Jarrah is known to have made hundreds of transatlantic phone calls. Such calls would betray his location at any time to the secret-state investigators who were monitoring his movements, as the requested interview in the UAE proved (although the CIA denied it made the request and the 9/11 Commission did not mention the incident).

The official story of his behaviour was not consistent with the US President's description of al-Qaeda methods: "They are sent back to their homes or *sent to hide in countries around the world* to plot evil and destruction."[117] Nor did it fit with FBI director Robert Mueller's assertion that the alleged hijackers used "meticulous planning and *extraordinary secrecy*".[118] [Emphasis added.]

What it did fit, however, was the image of literally *any* person of Moslem faith, no matter how decent, prosperous, fun-loving and ambitious, as a potentially deranged suicidal killer worthy only of being murdered (as Jarrah was in Paul Greengrass's propaganda movie). That was the hidden message behind the framing of Jarrah.

4
The Shootdown

THE SITE

The case for a straightforward nosedive crash of the whole airliner, as per the official story, had never been very strong. Debris fell as far as eight miles away, leading the FBI reluctantly to consider the possibility of a shootdown or other aerial break-up. However, the corporate media cameras promoted an apparent impact site at the edge of a reclaimed open-pit mine near Shanksville, Pennsylvania, a site that soon became a shrine.

But the crash site baffled everyone who first visited it. It confused the valiant widow, Lisa Beamer. It bewildered the local coroner. The only eyewitness, if he was to be believed, was astonished to find that the plane he thought he had seen passing over his head at about forty-five feet of altitude had utterly vanished. Meanwhile, according to the official story, the plane had hit the ground nearly vertically from about 30,000 feet, travelling at maximum speed, about 580 m.p.h., or the velocity of a bullet leaving a gun barrel. The tremendous force of the impact had caused the entire plane to disappear 30 feet into the loose earth, telescoping down to a mere 30 feet in length and presumably crushing everyone and everything within beyond recognition. At

ATTACK ON AMERICA

AP: BLACK BOX FOUND IN
PENNSYLVANIA CRASH SITE

S MAY STILL BE AT LARGE ❧ 18 HIJACKERS SEIZED FOUR PLANE

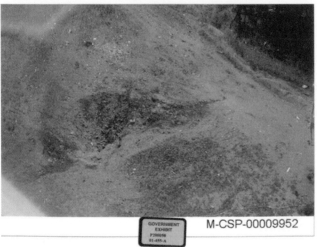

M-CSP-00009952

The television image of the Shanksville impact site (top) showed a sharply defined airliner shape, with a cone where the fuselage presumably entered the ground and clear signs of wings on either side. Viewers might not have recognized a different aerial view shown in a photograph (bottom) presented as evidence in court in 2006. The government aerial photograph showed a person standing left-of-centre in an unscorched crater examining a site that had a much more vaguely defined shape, with little trace of wing entry.

CREDITS: TV screengrab/US government

the same time, tiny fragments of human bodies were supposed to have been strewn in the branches of the trees and elsewhere around the site.

A government aerial photograph (see previous page), apparently taken very soon after the event,[1] showed a shallow crater in loose earth, with an area of scorched woods beyond it. Release of this hitherto unpublished photo revealed how the absence of crash debris must have bewildered eyewitnesses. It's hard to believe that an airliner up to 155 feet long, with two engines each weighing more than six tonnes, wings 125 feet wide, and a maximum total overall weight of 115 tonnes, could have penetrated the ground so completely as to utterly disappear. And yet this was what the FBI and the Pentagon claimed happened. They asserted that they retrieved the "black boxes" from underground excavations in this location.

A 2006 movie version of the crater also enhanced the impression of an aircraft crash by showing a cone-shaped crater with flames and smoke in it, and two charred wing craters on either side. All were absent in the aerial shot presented in court. Crudely rigged in Canada for a low-budget propaganda movie, it resembled the TV image that was supposed to be a genuine photograph.

CREDIT: A&E promotional image

M-CSP-00009868

A close-up of the actual crater (right) revealed an amorphous shape, charred soil and shards of metal debris. Some sceptics thought the site could have been faked with a bomb and planted debris.

CREDIT: US evidence photo

M-CSP-00004994   M-CSP-00009600

Left: A piece of aircraft debris was apparently revealed by a digger at the impact site at a depth of about three feet, although officials said the plane had accordioned into a crushed mass thirty feet underground. It was not clear how a large piece of one of the six-tonne engines "bounced" out of the crater to land over a mile away, as claimed by the FBI, or what became of the other engine. Jarrah's recovered passport and a clean bandana inexplicably appeared from the tangle of metal and crushed flesh that was supposed to lie far beneath the scorched morass. No available picture showed a crushed plane being removed from the crater. Right: Indian Lake marina operator John Fleegle reported that a piece of fuselage landed in the lake, about three miles from the crater. It seemed to be shown in this newly released 2006 evidence picture. If so, it was clear evidence of an aerial break-up, and possibly the shootdown that locals widely believed occurred.

CREDITS: US evidence photo/US evidence photo

A view of the burned-out woods showed shards of metal and other materials strewn over the area, but no sign of the tailplane that other crash sites showed could have survived the claimed 580 m.p.h. impact.

M-CSP-00004949

CREDIT: US evidence photo

M-CSP-00004942   M-CSP-00009733

The battered remains of the flight recorders, or "black boxes", were shown as they reportedly had been found in the rubble at the scene. They had been mounted in the tailplane that in similar crashes had survived intact.

CREDIT: US evidence photo

They also claimed to have retrieved an intact red bandana and an intact passport from hijacker bodies buried at the same location and, being in the nose of the plane, presumably utterly crushed beyond recognition. Several boxes of personal possessions reportedly were returned to relatives in the ensuing weeks, after supposedly being found at the site.

However, the government photo released in early 2006 at the staged Moussaoui trial contrasted with TV images of the supposed crash site broadcast at the time (see page 124). An image seen on MSNBC, for example, showed much clearer signs of an airliner impact, with a steep-sided cone-shape around the crater, flanked by clearly delineated wing-entry gulleys.

In spite of the media focus on the impact site, the extent of the debris field remained unexplained. The FBI propagated a vague theory that the debris field could be explained by the power of the crash spewing filmy fragments high into the air, where the wind carried them to the ground as far as eight miles away. But sceptics pointed out that the wind direction was wrong, and anyway, a photograph of the smoke from the apparent crash (see page 64) showed a plume that rose vertically into still air. Furthermore, a close-up picture of debris lying about three miles away (see page 135) showed metal parts that could hardly float on a breeze. A photograph at ground level (see page 125) showed debris mingled in with the churned earth.

One of the biggest problems with the supposed impact site was the missing engines. They should have plunged deep into the earth along with the rest of the airliner, particularly since each engine weighed about six tonnes. However, part of one engine, the FBI said, "bounced" about a mile away, while somehow the other disintegrated into small pieces. The idea that one of the engines bounced a mile, while the tailplane vanished into the earth, conflicted with photographs of the sites of similar high-speed crashes, where the tailplane normally survived intact (along with the recorders that were stored in it).

Lisa Beamer, obliged like everyone else at the time to stay about quarter of a mile away from the site, said "I didn't see a single piece of airplane anywhere." Lee Purbaugh, who was the first man at the scene, was able to walk up to the crater. "It was unbelievable," Purbaugh was reported saying, that "something that big had scattered that quick. There was nothing there."

However, close examination of the crater as shown in evidence photographs exhibited at the 2006 trial of Zacarias Moussaoui revealed that shards of debris were scattered all over the earth and mingled in it, backing the FBI's explanation that the airliner – or some of it – smashed deep into the loose earth.

On the other hand, if the aircraft really was intact when it crashed, as claimed by the official story and by the only eyewitness, then at least one of the engines should have been found in the crater and not more than a mile away. "A sector of one engine weighing one ton was found 2,000 yards away. This was the single heaviest piece recovered from the crash, and the biggest, apart from a piece of fuselage the size of a dining-room table."[2]

As for which way up the plane was, the 9/11 Commission's account went: "The airplane headed down; the control wheel was turned hard to the right. The airplane rolled onto its back... With the sounds of the passenger counter-attack continuing, the aircraft plowed into an empty field..."[3] Eyewitness Lee Purbaugh described the plane passing over his head like this: "I heard this real loud noise coming over my head," he told the *Daily Mirror*.[4] "I looked up and it was Flight 93, barely 50 feet above me. It was coming down in a 45 degree and rocking from side to side. Then the nose suddenly dipped and it just crashed into the ground. There was this big fireball and then a huge cloud of smoke."

So the 9/11 Commission, with ostensible access to the flight recorder's information, said the airliner's final nosedive had taken place in an upside-down position. And yet the only eyewitness, Lee Purbaugh, did not once mention it being upside down, something which cast suspicion on the credibility of his reported evidence.

According to the Pentagon, "the fuselage accordioned on itself more than thirty feet into the porous, backfilled ground".[5] However, the ground shown close up in a government shot of one of the flight recorders was rocky, and not porous. Also, the piece of fuselage shown in government evidence did not look accordioned enough to validate this account. A Boeing 757 is up to 178 feet and 7 inches long. To "accordion" down to 30 feet, its length would have had to be reduced by a factor of six, reducing every 10 feet of its length to just a little more than 18 inches. It was not quite clear, then, how a fragment about 5, possibly 6 or 7, feet long could have survived unless it fell from the sky on to John Fleegle's marina at Indian Lake, which would be definite evidence of a shootdown or aerial break-up.

As we have seen, there was no comprehensive investigation of the Flight 93 disaster by the US National Transportation Safety Board (NTSB), and certainly nothing like its involvement in the mid-air break-up of TWA 800.

In the TWA 800 case, the FBI was ready baldly to dismiss the reports of no fewer than *244 eyewitnesses*. Sceptics in that case took it as evidence of political tampering with the federal investigative bureau, an allegation that underpinned the sceptical case with regard to Flight 93. The motive for political tampering in the latter case involved generating, or helping to generate, popular compliance with long-term wars in the Middle East and around the world. But what were the possible scenarios the tampering might have been covering up?

MID-AIR CATASTROPHE

The mid-air catastrophe hypothesis points to a mid-air break-up of some kind.

The scenario goes like this: the principal part of the fuselage, along with a wheel and other debris, plunges through the air at a speed not far short of the speed of sound and hits the porous soil with tremendous force. There's a V-shape to the crater formed by the stub ends of the wings.

A black-ops team, although in touch with an observation flight, needs to know immediately where the largest intact part has fallen, and breaks cover to check with an available plane in the area, whereupon pilot Bill Wright innocently supplies map coordinates. Observation aircraft immediately attend the area. One of them is a military C-130, the other a white unmarked fighter-jet. Eyewitness reports of the presence of these planes will later be downplayed. The C-130 is passed off as a coincidence, reports of the white jet are ignored.

The FBI innocently keeps the public well clear for the next thirteen days. The bureau has orders to deploy agents and other searchers to find out what fell and seize it as evidence. They thus unwittingly ensure it is not tested for residues of explosives.

The rest of the debris field is quietly collected up and ignored. For example, only one close-up shot of it ever appeared in the 2006 Moussaoui trial evidence (see page 135). No aerial or satellite picture was released. Obeying a top-secret order from the security services that is handed down as instructions from the ownership, corporate media managers airbrush the debris field out of the story, believing they are acting in the public interest.

The scenario described could be the result of an airborne break-up of three kinds, listed as follows, in reverse order of likelihood.

BOMB

The only hard evidence for the existence of a bomb on board Flight 93 was the rogue pilot's reference to it in two separate announcements that were somehow relayed into air-traffic controllers' headsets. The messages were marred by unexplained radio interference of a type that had not occurred with the voices of the presumed legal pilots, recorded only moments earlier; however, they would also have to have been heard by the passengers in the cabins on board the rogue airliner, if the phone calls were credible.

The docudramas that reconstructed the events aboard Flight 93 went far beyond the bomb reported by Tom Burnett to his wife and heard about, at two removes, by Tom's sister.

Supporting Evidence for a Bomb – 1

The anonymous voice of an alleged rogue pilot announced to air-traffic controllers "Please sit down, keep remaining seating. We have a bomb on board. So sit."[6]

As shown in the transcript and played on recordings, this sounded like an explanation to passengers for a change of course. It's certainly what Thomas Burnett thought it was, and he was aboard the plane. Obviously, making the announcement did not require the existence of a bomb. Nor did mentioning a bomb seem to have been part of any agreed plan across all the rogue planes. But if the announcement reached passengers (something that was not known) it could well have triggered the few panicky rumours of the kind relayed through relatives.

On the other hand, how plausible was such an announcement? It was ostensibly addressing the passengers. But what good could such an announcement have done for the terrorists vis-à-vis the passengers? It could only be counterproductive, possibly causing an outbreak of panic in the cabin, thereby draining the three alleged hijackers' scarce resources from flying and navigating the huge aircraft as they rushed to quell the disturbance.

There was another implausible aspect of the announcement: although ostensibly intended for the passengers, it was heard by air-traffic controllers at Cleveland, and overheard by the captains of other airborne planes. Why would such a carefully planned mission involve making the elementary mistake of giving away to the authorities their rogue status and modus operandi at a time that would have put them at risk of having to face the unleashed US Air Force for up to half an hour before reaching their target?

The announcement was a clear giveaway that the pilot at the controls was a hijacker with a foreign accent. To sceptics, the bungled message sounded more like an audio-clip tailor-made for recording and exposing to the masses on TV and radio (and in court), thereby prompting widespread outrage. Why make such incriminating statements and not just stay silent, as Flight 175 was reputed to have?

On the other hand, if the passenger calls were real, they must have heard the announcement and passed on the information to the ground.

Supporting Evidence for a Bomb – 2

Flight attendant calls United mechanics and tells them: "One hijacker had a bomb strapped on and another was holding a knife on the crew."[7]

There were three hijackers that the passengers mentioned. So we had one hijacker busy holding a knife on the crew (presumably consisting of other flight attendants, because the caller was one of the crew and would hardly be calling if held at knifepoint). Another hijacker was brandishing his bomb to terrorize them. That left one hijacker to break into the cockpit, seize two experienced airline pilots, prevent them giving the alarm, drag them out of their harnesses and away from the controls and guard them in the cabin. It was not a plausible scenario.

Supporting Evidence for a Bomb – 3

A small minority of passengers reported a bomb in their phone calls.

According to the *Los Angeles Times* reporting the Moussaoui trial evidence: "The calls ... showed that most of the passengers were confused about how many hijackers had commandeered the plane, where they came from or whether their weapons were knives or a bomb or both."[8]

Tom Burnett first mentioned a bomb. The trouble was he mentioned guns also, a warning that was later discredited, although his wife was certain he would not have made a mistake. From what he is reported to have said and the time at which he said it, he seemed to have called during or just after the mysterious hijacking that nobody saw or described, and that neither pilot reported. His wife, Deena, said he had a headset for his cellphone and therefore they might not have seen him speaking. According to Deena's account of the first call, Tom Burnett was hysterical or panicky. As we saw earlier, it could therefore be reasoned that he was either envisioning weapons (guns) that didn't exist, and using a cellphone that should not have been working, or, more likely, Deena Burnett's mind was deranged by the call and its circumstances.

It's also inexplicable that the FBI, who, according to Deena, monitored calls from her husband as he made them, were not reported either discussing the bomb issue with him (through her) or giving instructions for dealing with a bomb-carrying fanatic as per the FBI handbook.

In short, Deena Burnett's report of her husband mentioning a bomb was unreliable, as was her husband's report, if he mentioned one.[9] He dismissed the bomb in a later call, anyway, as a ploy.

Jeremy Glick reportedly "called his wife [and] told her the plane had been hijacked by 'three males appearing to be Iranian . . . dark-skinned and with red bandanas on their heads' . . . Glick also told her that 'two hijackers were in the cockpit and a third had a red belt with a box that constituted some kind of a bomb'."[10] Would that "red belt" be flashing on and off, by any chance? And did it have an LCD readout on it, with big red numbers counting down towards zero? No, Glick cannot have seen any red belt and probably no bomb either. This information was filtered through the grief-stricken panic of his wife, repeating the warning given by the mysterious pilot whom nobody saw (but presumably heard).

Todd Beamer also reported a bomb. He "tried to make four calls. The first three never went through. The fourth was to a phone operator. He reported three males with knives, and 'one wearing a bomb'."[11] But Beamer was seated at the rear of the plane in tourist class, and the curtained-off first-class group of passengers were located between him and the cockpit, which was where any third hijacker not inside the cockpit (with the other two, according to Glick) would be standing to guard his comrades. Beamer was dealing in hearsay. If indeed, that is, he ever called, because the report of the call was pure hearsay, too.

Mark Bingham was supposed to have addressed his mother: "This is Mark Bingham. There are three men that say they have a bomb."[12] This, again, could be a relay of the overheard pilot's statement.

Whatever these reports said, no evidence of a bomb was produced by the FBI. It's possible that if they had found evidence of a bomb, they might have suppressed it because functioning-bankrupt United Airlines could have got hit with a class-action suit for billions. But the other thirty-odd phone calls made by the remaining nine of the thirteen passengers who called did not mention a bomb, and a bomb was not mentioned in the flight-deck recording.

If Flight 93 had been blown up by a bomb at cruising altitude, the height shown by the Flight Explorer route map, its debris area could have been expected to cover some twenty miles, all far from the flight path, as in the case of the Lockerbie crash.[13]

MECHANICAL BREAK-UP

The 9/11 Commission speculated that the rogue pilots moved the plane around violently to disrupt a passenger revolt. This led to further speculation that the rogue pilots might have succeeded in tearing a wing off, or otherwise wrecking the aircraft in mid-air. Boeing refused to discuss this possibility. Of course, such movements could just as easily have been caused by pilots attempting to avoid an approaching heat-seeking missile, fired either from the ground or from a tailing jet fighter obeying orders from within the secret state.

SHOOTDOWN

This is the point in the whole 9/11 official narrative where the government came closest to open, if paradoxical, complicity in the events, and it's the only conspiracy theory confirmed by a cabinet officer. It was defence secretary Donald Rumsfeld (last elected to public office in 1967) who said Flight 93 had been shot down, although of course his staff said it was a slip of the tongue, and not the well-recognized unconscious impulse of the guilty to confess.[14]

Suspicion of a shootdown was so widespread at the time that public eagerness to adopt the passenger-revolt story could have been caused by an unconscious denial of the possibility of an air force missile strike.[15]

The possibility of a shootdown involved radical emotional conflict in the collective psyche:

- a patriotic belief that the USAF just could not be as incompetent as it had been that morning had to exist alongside;

- an equally passionate conviction that the US government could never be complicit in killing 45 (or possibly 44 or 43 or even 40) people in an American domestic airliner.

The heroes legend was a solution to the dilemma.

The hawkish federal administration might have been inclined to admit a shootdown if it had happened. The souls lost in the airliner were a sacrifice that could be validated by a higher purpose (protecting Washington, DC). Air force scrambles had been frequent enough in the past. One report said there had been 129 scrambles within the USA in the year 2000.[16] Andrews Air Force base near Washington, DC, could scramble fighters round the clock. But secrecy is the first instinct of any war department, and reports of the passenger calls started coming in so rapidly that admission of a shootdown must have been ruled out politically because those brave passengers just might have retrieved the controls from fanatical hijackers. For the US military to have snatched victory from their grasp moments later was unthinkable.

Another reason for denial would be if the shootdown had been

Metallic debris found a mile from the impact crater, shown in a US government evidence photograph presented in the 2006 Moussaoui trial. This did not resemble the "very light material, such as paper and thin nylon, the wind would easily blow" that the FBI at the site referred to in a CNN report of 13 September 2001. "According to the NTSB, it is not only possible that the debris is from the crash, it is probable," FBI Agent Crowley was reported saying.

CREDIT: US government evidence photo

planned from the start. The Twin Towers were hit after Flight 93 had taken off, but over the next thirty-nine minutes the aircraft flew on uninformed by United Airlines or the FAA. Flight 93 only received a hijack warning forty minutes after take-off from an alert United Airlines dispatcher, United's management apparently being in a state of paralysis at the time. The pilot gave a puzzled response and the next thing he was overheard shouting was: "Get out of here." The cockpit voice recorder "started" just after the hijacking (it framed the last thirty minutes automatically). The FAA's grounding order did not come until more than fifteen minutes had passed. Why did Flight 93 fly on for so long with no warning from anyone?

Agencies attending the Shanksville site on 11 September were thinking shootdown. At the Flight 93 "crash" site, FBI agents initially did not rule out the possibility of what was neutrally termed an explosion. "Jim Marker, a Somerset, Pennsylvania County Commissioner, visited the crash site and said the FBI was investigating the possibility that the plane suffered an explosion before it crashed. The passenger who phoned Westmoreland County dispatchers also said there was an explosion, the Associated Press reported. "They are checking about a mile from the site for some debris that might show there was an explosion," said Marker. *"They do believe there was that possibility."* [17] [Emphasis added.]

The evidence certainly confirmed a shootdown. In a 13 September report logged at 6:00 p.m., CNN said: "A second debris field was around Indian Lake about 3 miles from the crash scene. Some debris was in the lake and some was adjacent to the lake. More debris from the plane was found in New Baltimore, some 8 miles away from the crash. State police and the FBI initially said they didn't want to speculate whether the debris was from the crash, or if the plane could have broken up in midair." [18]

By the next day, 14 September, the FBI had made a U-turn, and with the Air Force was coolly dismissing any talk of a shootdown. "FBI agent William Crowley discounted rumors that the military shot down the jetliner in a sparsely populated area to keep it away from the White House and other possible targets in Washington, DC. 'There was no military involvement,' Crowley said." [19] NORAD issued its own denial on the same day. "NORAD-allocated forces have not engaged with weapons any aircraft, including Flight 93," the Air Force statement said.[20]

NORAD denials might have been the truth. There were plenty of resources within the secret state that could have intervened: the US Secret Service, the CIA, and the military corporations all had access to jet fighters, missiles and pilots.

However, the original reports implicitly acknowledged that the debris field proved beyond doubt that the plane had exploded in the sky. Debris had rained down on Indian Lake, which began about 1.5 miles away from the crater, and fell 8 miles away at New Baltimore, Pennsylvania. Such a pattern did not accord with a near-vertical nose-dive into the ground of an intact jetliner, according to the experience of air-crash experts, who would have expected a plane in a vertical dive to create heaps of debris around the crash site.[21]

The only reference to an explosion in the thirty-five passenger phone calls was one that somehow went directly to Somerset County 9-1-1 emergency operator John Shaw, 29, of Youngwood, at 9:58 a.m. as the plane passed over Mount Pleasant Township.[22] "Shaw spoke to Edward Felt [*sic*] for 1 minute and 10 seconds, learning that he'd locked himself in the bathroom to make the call," a Pittsburgh paper reported. The only statement Shaw apparently made before being silenced by the FBI was: "I absolutely knew right away it was for real." If the caller had locked himself in the bathroom, he must have been calling on a cellphone, indicating that the aircraft was flying lower than about 5,000 to 8,000 feet.

The story quoted here was typical in that it identified Edward Felt as the caller, something that his brother had accepted and that he promoted at gatherings such as Universal's launch of the Paul Greengrass Flight 93 reconstruction movie in April 2006. Sadly, there was no evidence whatsoever that it was Felt who made the call, because although his brother "recognized his brother's methodical way of handling things", the caller never gave that elementary item of information always gathered first by any official on the telephone: his name.[23]

What the anonymous caller did give was, according to Shaw the operator, a clear report of an explosion: "He heard some sort of explosion and saw white smoke coming from the plane and we lost contact with him."[24] An aerial toilet in a Boeing 757 does not have a porthole, so the caller must have observed the smoke by opening the door. But the mention of smoke and an explosion on the unreleased recording of his call was later denied,[25] and the operator was not allowed to speak about it to the media.

Strangely, the 9-1-1 operator's name changed when the *Daily Mirror*'s US correspondent visited the area on the first anniversary. "Glenn Cramer, the emergency supervisor who answered it, said on the day: 'He was very distraught. He said he believed the plane was going down. He did hear some sort of an explosion and saw white smoke coming from the plane, but he didn't know where. And then we lost contact with him.' Glenn Cramer was later gagged by the FBI."[26]

Whichever operator took this anonymous call, which was always referred to as coming from Ed Felt, although such identification was pure supposition, its claim of an explosion was directly contradicted by the only eyewitness of the crash, Lee Purbaugh. He was the scrap-metal worker, reputedly hired only the day before,[27] who'd said he had a clear view of the crash.

A report quoted Mr Purbaugh: "'There was an incredibly loud rumbling sound and there it was, right there, right above my head –

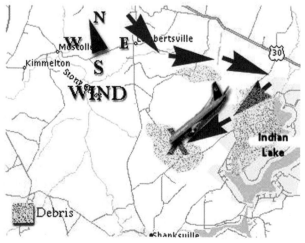

A map of the debris field showed how the wind could not have blown the debris from the impact site to where it was found.

CREDIT: www.thinkandask.com

maybe 50 feet up,' says Purbaugh, who works at a scrapyard over-looking the crash site. 'It was only a split second but it looked like it was moving in slow motion, like it took forever. I saw it rock from side to side then, suddenly, it dipped and dived, nose first, with a huge explosion, into the ground. I knew immediately that no one could possibly have survived.' "28

Mr Purbaugh then ran to the crash site and found no aeroplane. Even walking at 3 m.p.h., Mr Purbaugh would have reached the site half a mile away within ten minutes. But Mr Purbaugh's report was tainted, because although several eyewitnesses much further away than him mentioned seeing the plane possibly upside down, he only referred to the aircraft as "rocking", which fitted the official story, but he never mentioned that the plane he referred to as Flight 93 was upside down.

It's not too hard to tell whether a Boeing 757 is flying upside down or the right way up, particularly 50 feet overhead, and none of the reports of Mr Purbaugh's eyewitness evidence had him describing the airliner as upside down. And yet, according to the "black box" data supplied to the 9/11 Commission by the FBI and the Pentagon, it definitely was.

So we had unsafe evidence at the crux of the matter:

■ The only eyewitness to the "crash", who had reportedly been hired at his workplace the day before, repeated many times a wrong description of the crashing plane.

■ The only eyewitness to an explosion that might have happened in flight was anonymous, came via the hearsay report of two different operators who we were told took the same call, and the explosive content of the recorded call was suppressed.

This head-scratchingly polluted information was not clarified by the firm reports of yet more planes overhead in this out-of-the-way area of the Allegheny mountains, long after the skies had been cleared.

More than fifteen minutes before the impact, the FAA command centre had ordered all 4,546 airplanes in the air at the time to leave the skies over the whole of the USA. They were to rush to the nearest airport and land, and incoming planes were to land in Canada instead. Only military and medical flights could fly.29 There's no way such an unprecedented order, a first in the history of US aviation, at a cost of hundreds of millions of dollars to the aviation industry, could have been missed by any pilot airborne at the time. It was one of those milestone moments of an aviation lifetime that pilots recount for the rest of their days.

But there was a plane that was definitely identified as being in the area when Flight 93 disappeared – a small plane, still in the air although it was only fifteen to eighteen miles from Johnstown Cambria County Airport. WTAE-TV, the Pittsburgh channel, reported it as follows:

> [Bill] Wright was flying over Youngwood, Westmoreland County, and was getting ready to land in Latrobe under order [sic] from air traffic control.
>
> Then, an air-traffic controller asked him and his passenger to look out the window.
>
> Wright was flying a Piper Arrow when he spotted a jet crossing behind him – about three miles away. It was close enough for him and his photographer to see the United Airlines colors.
>
> Wright was flying over Youngwood for about 20 minutes before Flight 93 crashed in Stonycreek Township.
>
> Wright said that he knew that there was a problem when air-traffic controllers asked him to give them Flight 93's altitude.
>
> Wright thinks there's only one reason air-traffic controllers in Cleveland would have been asking him about the altitude. He said that it was probably because the terrorists had cut off all radio transmissions to air traffic controllers.[30]

Wright did not wonder how the air-traffic controllers had identified him as being in the right location. He went on to validate the official story's subsequent account of the rocking plane.

> "It would bank hard left, bank hard right and then back to hard left. We saw it bank three or four times before we got away from it."
>
> Wright said that may have been when several passengers were fighting back against the terrorists.
>
> "The story of the plane being taken over, that fits," Wright said.
>
> Within moments controllers ordered Wright to land immediately.
>
> "That's one of the first things that went through my mind when they told us to get as far away from it as fast as we could – that either

they were expecting it to blow up or they were going to shoot it down, but that's pure speculation," Wright said.

This report raised several questions that were not cleared up by Bush's 9/11 Commission, which in its report mentioned neither Bill Wright nor his Piper aircraft. It's hard to explain how the air-traffic controllers in the area knew that Bill Wright might be able to see Flight 93, unless its transponder had been turned back on, and that would be inexplicable, too. For example, there was no mention of turning it back on in the flight-deck tape transcript, although turning it off seemed to be mentioned.

The obvious way to explain this intervention was if the air-traffic controllers were military or secret-state personnel, who knew that the plane had been hit by a missile, by cannon fire, by chemical laser, or even some electronics-busting sound-ray, one of which had disabled the aircraft, causing it to wobble and veer, losing debris through an impact hole, and, finally, crash. These controllers would have needed to confirm that the plane was losing altitude and about to go down. Cases of airliners being hit by missiles showed that they could limp on for a couple of minutes before crashing. The wings might well rock as they struggled to keep the disabled plane airborne.[31]

This interpretation was supported by the evidence for *another* plane being in the area.

"According to the Nashua (NH) *Telegraph*, FAA employees at an air-traffic control center near Boston learned from controllers at other facilities that an F-16 'stayed in hot pursuit' of the 757... The F-16 made 360-degree turns to stay close to the 757, the *Telegraph* reported... 'He must've seen the whole thing,' the FAA employee said of the F-16's pilot. [FBI agent] Crowley confirmed that there were *two other aircraft* within 25 miles of the United flight that were heading east when it crashed, scattering debris over eight miles. He did not know the types of planes, nor could he discuss the altitudes at which they were flying."[Emphasis added.]

The US government admitted that two F-15s were positioned above New York City before 9:00 a.m. And three F-16s were patrolling over Washington, DC, by 9:40 a.m. Either F-15 jet could have flown to the Shanksville area (a military corridor) in six to eight minutes. It seemed that, from air-traffic control's first hijack warning for Flight 93 at 9:16 a.m., an F-15 could have been tailing Flight 93 by 9:22 a.m.[32]

According to sceptic author David Ray Griffin, numerous eye-witnesses saw two F-16s tailing Flight 93 minutes before it went down at 10:06, the scientifically established impact time. The official time of 10:03 would have meant deleting what was said as the missile neared and hit the airliner by cutting the crucial last three minutes off the cockpit voice recording. Subsequent to 9/11, Griffin also reported, the government released flight controller transcripts, but did not publish those for Flight 93.[33]

Again, according to eyewitnesses cited by Griffin, one of the F-16s moved closer and twice fired what were probably two sidewinder missiles, one of them catching at least one of the huge engines, and the "plane dropped", someone said, "like a stone".

Someone else heard "a loud bang" and then saw the plane's right wing dip, and then 93 plunged to earth. A Vietnam vet said he "heard a missile", a sound he knew well. In fact, the multiple accounts confirmed a missile strike.

Witnesses also saw burning debris fall from the plane "as far as eight miles away, with workers at Indian Lake Marina saying that they saw 'a cloud of confetti-like debris descend on the lake and nearby farms minutes after hearing the explosion'." Also this debris, along with human remains, was found again as far as eight miles from the site. The debris fell from the sky, and was not blasted upwards from the crater.

Witness Evidence

Eyewitness reports differed from the official story. Along the plane's route, they confirmed that the plane came from the northwest, but they said it was not nosediving. Instead it was flying low.

Rodney Peterson and Brandon Leventry noticed the plane at 2000 feet.[34] Terry Butler saw the plane at about 500 feet. Bob Blair and Linda Shepley saw the plane at 2,500 feet. Rob Kimmel saw the plane at 100 or 200 feet flying southeast. Anita McBride heard and Eric Peterson saw the plane at "maybe 300 feet". Paula Pluta (one mile away) saw the plane through her window. Tom Fritz (quarter of a mile) and Nevin Lambert (less than half a mile) saw the plane. Lee Purbaugh (300 yards) saw the plane at an altitude of forty or fifty feet till it crashed.

They said it moved strangely. Terry Butler in Stoystown: "It was moving like you wouldn't believe. Next thing I knew it makes a heck of a sharp, right-hand turn." He said the plane banked to the right and appeared to be trying to climb to clear one of the ridges, but it continued to turn to the right and then veered behind a ridge. Linda Shepley of Stoystown recalled seeing the plane wobbling right and left, at a low altitude of roughly 2,500 feet, when suddenly the right wing abruptly dipped straight down, and the Boeing 757 plunged into the earth. Peterson and Leventry in Boswell said the aircraft "dipped sharply to the left, then to the right". Tim Thornsberg, near the reclaimed strip mine, said: "It came in low over the trees and started wobbling. Then it just rolled over and was flying upside down for a few seconds . . . and then it kind of stalled and did a nose dive over the trees." Tom Fritz on nearby Lambertsville Road said: "When it decided to drop, it dropped all of a sudden, like a stone."

The officially-given speed of 580 m.p.h. did not comply with reports at the time, either. The National Transportation Safety Board and other experts estimated over 200 m.p.h. Another estimation of "law enforcement authorities" was that the speed might have approached 300 m.p.h.

Several eyewitnesses agreed that the airplane made strange sounds. Laura Temyer (several miles away in Hooversville): "I heard like a boom and the engine sounded funny. I heard two more booms – and then I did not hear anything." Michael Merringer (about two miles): "I heard the engine gun two different times and then I heard a loud bang." An unnamed witness: "He hears two loud bangs before watching the plane take a downward turn of nearly 90 degrees." Another unnamed witness: "She saw the plane overhead. It made a high-pitched, screeching sound. The plane then made a sharp, 90-degree downward turn and crashed." Lee Purbaugh (300 yards): "There was an incredibly loud rumbling sound." Charles Sturtz (half a mile): "It was really roaring, you know. Like it was trying to go somewhere, I guess." Tom Fritz (Lambertsville Road, quarter of mile) heard a sound that "wasn't quite right" and looked up in the sky. "It was sort of whistling."

Other eyewitnesses east of the impact site saw something fly in from the east: "Jim Brant, owner of Indian Lake Marina, said he rushed outside Tuesday morning when he heard the roar of jet engines overhead, then saw a fireball rise into the air . . . Mr. Brant and two of his employees arrived at the site in minutes, hoping to help survivors. He said he noticed a white plane, perhaps a jet, circling the wreckage. 'It reminded me of a fighter jet,' he said." Tom Spinelli (Indian Lake, a mile and a half) said: "I saw the white plane. . . It was flying around all over the place like it was looking for something. I saw it before and after the crash. . . He said that it had high back wings . . . the plane had no markings on it, either civilian or military." John Feegle (Indian Lake, a mile and a half): "It didn't look like a commercial plane. It had a real goofy tail on it, like a high tail. It circled around, and it was gone. . . The aircraft appeared to have an unusually tall vertical stabilizer."

Two witnesses were north to northeast of the impact site: "'As soon as we looked up, we saw a midsized jet flying low and fast,' Decker said. 'It appeared to make a loop or part of a circle, and then it turned fast and headed out.' Decker and Chaney described the plane as a Lear jet type, with engines mounted near the tail and painted white with no identifying markings. 'It was a jet plane, and it had to be flying real close when that 757 went down. If I was the FBI, I'd find out who was driving that plane.'" Susan McElwain said: "It had two rear engines, a big fin on the back like a spoiler on the back of a car and with two upright fins at the side." A total of twelve eyewitnesses observed the white jet.

Many eyewitnesses at Indian Lake observed raining debris. Some accounts state that this happened minutes after the crash, some right away: "Workers at Indian Lake Marina said that they saw a cloud of confetti-like debris descend on the lake and nearby farms minutes after hearing the explosion that signalled the crash at 10:06 a.m. Tuesday."

"Jim Brant, owner of Indian Lake Marina, said he rushed outside Tuesday morning when he heard the roar of jet engines overhead, then saw a fireball rise into the air. The wind was strong that morning, Brant said, and within minutes debris from the crash was 'falling like confetti'."

"Several minutes later, bits of white paper began to rain down , said

Carol Delasko, a secretary at the marina." Another said: "It just looked like confetti raining down all over the air above the lake."

Another witness three and a half miles away from the impact site "heard a big crash and went outside to see what it was, and stuff started falling from the sky."

Others saw debris before the crash: "Residents of nearby Indian Lake reported seeing debris falling from the jetliner as it overflew the area shortly before crashing." The official explanation that the 10 m.p.h. wind carried debris was denied by the weight of the debris reported. "Residents and workers at businesses outside Shanksville said they found clothing, books, papers and what appeared to be human remains." "By Wednesday morning, crash debris began washing ashore at the marina. Fleegle said there was something that looked like a rib bone amid pieces of seats, small chunks of melted plastic and checks."

Then it was revealed that there was *yet another* aircraft in this remote area. At 9:32 a.m., air traffic controllers in Washington, DC, "vectored an unarmed National Guard C-130H cargo aircraft, which had just taken off en route to Minnesota, to identify and follow [Flight 77]. The C-130H pilot spotted it . . . [and] attempted to follow its path."[35]

"Remarkably," noted Paul Thompson, "this C-130 is the same C-130 that is 17 miles from Flight 93 when it later crashes into the Pennsylvania countryside." By 10:08 a.m., "Cleveland flight controller Stacey Taylor has asked a nearby C-130 pilot to look at Flight 93's last position and see if they can find anything."[36]

From this, it could be gathered that Cleveland *did* have Flight 93's position, although on the flight-deck recording the alleged hijackers made no mention of restoring the transponder that they earlier discussed how to switch off.

And then, incredibly, yet *another* aircraft appeared in this out-of-the-way zone, about fifteen minutes after an unprecedented national order had grounded all flights.

"A . . . plane, described 'as a small, white jet with rear engines and no discernible markings', is seen by at least five witnesses flying low and in erratic patterns, not much above treetop level, over the crash site within minutes of the United flight crashing." One witness said the FBI told her there was no plane and did not note down her account.[37]

The reports of the white jet circling the impact site were explained unconvincingly by the FBI.

"The FBI's later explanation for the white jet was that a passing civilian Fairchild Falcon 20 jet was asked to descend from 34,000 ft to 5,000 ft some minutes after the crash to give co-ordinates for the site. The plane and pilot have never been produced or identified," the *Daily Mirror* reported.

The *Independent* commented on 13 August 2002: "The reason, as numerous people have observed, why this seems so implausible is that, first, by 10:06 a.m. on 11 September, all non-military aircraft in US airspace had received loud and clear orders more than half an hour earlier [*sic*] to land at the nearest airport; second, such was the density of 9-1-1 phone calls from people on the ground in the Shanksville area, as to the location of the crash site that aerial co-ordinates would have been completely unnecessary; and third, with F-16s supposedly in the vicinity, it seems extraordinarily unlikely that, at a time of tremendous national uncertainty when no one knew for sure whether there might be any more hijacked aircraft still in the sky, the military would ask a civilian aircraft that just happened to be in the area for help."

Another problem with the FBI's story was that eyewitnesses saw the white jet before the apparent crash or immediately after it, not descending several minutes later.

So we had:

- a Flight 93 that had been given official permission by someone unknown unprecedentedly to change course;
- a Flight 93 that had recently crossed and recrossed after turning off its transponder what might be radar "holes" where there could be poor or no detection of aircraft movements;
- air-traffic controllers who were apparently perfectly aware of the whereabouts of Flight 93, although the alleged hijackers had not mentioned turning their transponder back on;
- four armed supersonic fighters in the air, at least two of them close enough to shoot Flight 93 down, possibly all four;
- three other aircraft in the area, fifteen minutes after all US aircraft had been grounded;

- the FBI denying and ignoring eyewitness evidence of a white jet circling low;
- an ostensible impact crater uniquely devoid of sizeable aircraft debris;
- a debris trail that flowed southeast, against the northerly wind.

All these circumstances were extremely irregular and indicated that nothing straightforward was occurring, such as rogue pilots panicking and nosediving their aircraft, as the 9/11 Commission narrative had it.

A shootdown by the USAF would have been hard to keep secret. Here's an off-the-cuff list of people who would know a jet-fighter had the capability of firing and/or had fired:

- the ground crew who armed the aircraft with live weapons;
- the pilot(s);
- their ground controllers;
- the officer who issued the fire order;
- the officer who actually authorized the fire order;
- the officer in charge of the control centre from which the fire order was issued;
- everybody in the control centre from which the fire order was issued;
- the ground crew who serviced the jet after it fired the live missile.

On the other hand, the "empire" of the Pentagon contained vast resources of secret planes and covert pilots.

There was a lively debate about whether US Vice-President Richard E. Cheney issued a shootdown order after conferring with Bush, who was flying west in an unguarded US-One.[38] Another reported order from headquarters had called on pilots to defend Washington, DC, at all costs. Defense secretary Rumsfeld, who had rewritten the regulations to make himself responsible for giving any shootdown order, was in the White House videoconference. And according to the 9/11 Commission, the first time the USAF command heard about Flight 93 was at 10:07, after the airliner had disappeared.

However, the order could have come from a quite different source within the secret state.

The Impact Time

The seismic records, consolidated from four stations in the region, originally set the impact time at 10:06 a.m., which immediately became the acknowledged time of the crash and was widely published.[39] It was only later that NORAD and the 9/11 Commission got their story straight and decreed the correct impact time to have been three minutes earlier, at 10:03 a.m. There were, by then, two gold-standard crash times. Many sceptics noted that a lot could happen in three minutes, minutes that could also be removed from the end of the flight-deck recording in some remote secret-state facility. This might have been required, had the US Air Force – or some corporate fighters from the political chain of command that outranked the armed forces – actually succeeded in firing a heat-seeking missile at Flight 93. They had been ordered, after all, to defend Washington, DC, and Flight 93 was some fifteen minutes from its target.

"'The seismic signals are consistent with impact at 10:06:05,' plus or minus two seconds, said Terry Wallace, who heads the Southern Arizona Seismic Observatory and is considered the leading expert on the seismology of man-made events."[40]

However the 9/11 Commission overturned this scientific finding. "The seismic data ... are far too weak in signal-to-noise ratio and far too speculative in terms of signal source to be used as a means of contradicting the impact time established by the very accurate combination of FDR [flight data recorder], CVR [cockpit voice recorder], ATC [air traffic control] and impact site data sets. These data sets ... are based on time codes automatically recorded in the ATC audiotapes."[41]

On the other hand, from the sceptic's point of view, the seismic data were objective, whereas the FAA data might be tainted, considering the peculiar circumstances surrounding the last minutes of Flight 93.

In fact, the earlier impact time dated back to April 2002. "Family members allowed to hear the cockpit voice recorder in Princeton, New Jersey, last spring were told it stopped just after 10:03," said an anniversary report,[42] adding: "The FBI and other agencies refused repeated requests to explain the discrepancy."

"Relatives later reported they heard sounds of an on-board struggle beginning at 9:58 a.m., but there was a final 'rushing sound' at 10:03, and the tape fell silent.

'There is no sound of the impact,' said Kenneth Nacke, whose brother, Lou Nacke, Jr., is one of the passengers believed to have fought with the hijackers. Nacke confirmed that the government said the tape ended at 10:03 a.m."

"I don't know where the 10:03 time comes from," said seismic expert Terry Wallace. "Investigators typically nail down the correct times very early in a probe, experts said. Todd Curtis, who runs the Web site AirSafe.com, said the three-minute gap 'does not make sense'."

Of course, it would make perfect sense if the US Air Force, or other more mysterious jets from within the secret state, had managed to down the rogue airliner with a missile. The tape would have been doctored deep within the Pentagon, the FAA records would have been tampered with by political officials, and the 9/11 Commission would have closed ranks to cover up a mistake that could have alienated public opinion at a crucial point in the preparations for an invasion of Iraq that had begun when Bush had been appointed to the presidency.

The Timing of the Shootdown

We have seen that the military's claim that it knew nothing about Flight 93 until after it had "crashed" was false, and was made with the intention of evading an investigation. We have also seen that a shootdown could have been admissible, considering the extraordinary circumstances prevailing.

What might have made a shootdown inadmissible would be the motive and its timing, if it occurred in the middle of an unexpected and unscripted passenger rebellion. If the hijackers were in touch with hidden controllers on the ground, they might have called for help when the rebellion broke out. The resulting "help" by agencies unknown could have been a shootdown carried out in order to prevent anyone finding out what had been taking place aboard the plane, or even torturing the hijackers into revealing who controlled them. Persons on the ground could have felled the aircraft with a shoulder-launched missile while it was still at cruising altitude and before any witnesses noticed.

Alternatively, black-ops forces tipped off about what was happening on the plane might have needed to demolish secrets hidden in the aircraft's sensitive guidance equipment, or wipe out all witnesses aboard, or destroy the alleged hijackers, or a combination of all three.

Sceptics were certain that the 9/11 mission was fatally corrupted. Nothing was pure in the twenty-first century as humanity struggled over dwindling oil resources while consciously speeding towards ecological disaster. Above all, a mission was corrupt that was ostensibly conceived by men who knew a laughably pathetic patsy like Zacarias Moussaoui or a dimwit like "shoe-bomber" Richard Reid and intended to work with either of them.

How could the US administration have it both ways? It accepted that the mentally disturbed Moussaoui[43] was meant to be a pilot in the 9/11 events,[44] and, at the same time, asserted that the 9/11 events had been carried off with supreme *brio* by skilled and ruthless agents of a foreign power. So skilled, that they could hijack four airliners in a row without a single one of the eight professional aviators managing to trigger a formal hijack alert, and without being intercepted or even followed by a single US jet-fighter in the air or missile battery on the ground. Who needed a liability like Moussaoui along?

On the inscrutable evidence it's hard to reach a firm conclusion that Flight 93 was shot down, but souls gaze into the abyss of the Flight 93 disappearance and read hieroglyphics inscribed on the bones of men, women and children about primal greed, elemental murder and eternal enmity.

OTHER SCENARIOS

THE ROUTE PUZZLE

A fundamental problem that might have confused anyone who looked at a map of the 9/11 events was the duration of the flights before they reached their targets. The time spans are tabulated as follows:[45]

FLIGHT	Time in air	Time rogue	Distance from take-off to target
AA11	46 minutes	20 minutes	187 miles
UAL175	49 minutes	32 minutes	187 miles
AA77	77 minutes	46 minutes	To Pentagon: 30 miles
UAL93	81 minutes	35 minutes	30 miles

Flight 11, which apparently reached its target in twenty minutes, had the shortest rogue period. It still unnecessarily overshot its target by about half the length of the state of New Jersey, looping back to head in from the south and passing near several US Air Force bases as it went. Even the twenty minutes it took to perform this lazy curve was a long time to be in airborne control of a hijacked aircraft and heading towards New York, exposed to the possibility of interception or ground-to-air missile shootdown or even a shoot-out in the cabin.

No-nonsense mass murderers might have preferred to hijack planes from New York airports, grab control immediately after take-off and change route towards Wall Street, exposing the rogue pilots to interception or on-board resistance for only a few minutes. It seems there must have been a vital reason to fly for so long, but the 9/11 Commission, so busy excusing NORAD, gave the issue no attention.

The other rogue flights were even more perplexing.

Flight 77 spent an extraordinary forty-six minutes in the air as a rogue aircraft. And yet, it had taken off from Washington's Dulles International airport, which is about *four minutes'* flying time from its target, the Pentagon.

Flight 93 was an hour and twenty-one minutes in the air, thirty-five minutes of them with a rogue pilot at the controls. And yet, it too had left an airport that was less than *two minutes'* flying time from the "symbolic" targets, the Twin Towers.

■ Three of the four civil airliners were in the hands of rogue pilots for more than half an hour.

■ The time lapse between Flight 11 going rogue and Flight 93 doing so is an hour and fourteen minutes.

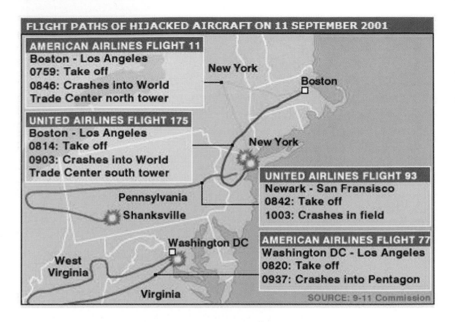

FLIGHT PATHS OF HIJACKED AIRCRAFT ON 11 SEPTEMBER 2001

AMERICAN AIRLINES FLIGHT 11
Boston - Los Angeles
0759: Take off
0846: Crashes into World
Trade Center north tower

UNITED AIRLINES FLIGHT 175
Boston - Los Angeles
0814: Take off
0903: Crashes into World
Trade Center south tower

UNITED AIRLINES FLIGHT 93
Newark - San Fransisco
0842: Take off
1003: Crashes in field

AMERICAN AIRLINES FLIGHT 77
Washington DC - Los Angeles
0820: Take off
0937: Crashes into Pentagon

New York — • Boston
New York
Pennsylvania
Shanksville
Washington DC
West Virginia
Virginia

SOURCE: 9-11 Commission

The 9/11 Commission's map of the rogue flights illustrated the long diversions that took the airliners over numerous air-force bases and at least four vulnerable nuclear power plants, an aspect the 9/11 Commission ignored. Sceptics explored various explanations, from the need to cross radar "holes", to remote-control plane-substitution scenarios. Flight 93 had the most extraordinary route of all, since it took off within sight of the WTC target. An apparent radar hole south of Cleveland was suggested as the reason for the long trip west. The text box described the flight as crashing in a field at 10:03, when neither the crash nor the time were properly established.

CREDIT: 9/11 Commission Report

These were extraordinary periods of time for out-of-control airliners to cruise the skies over Bosnywash, the world's wealthiest urbanized strip, the possessor of an unmatched imperial air force and presumably bristling with ground-to-air missiles at its numerous military air bases.

Both the air-traffic control system and the US Air Force were apparently in disarray owing to a number of confusing multi-agency exercises being conducted on that relevantly dated day, although the military said any confusion lasted only a moment. "According to General Eberhard,[46] 'it took about 30 seconds' to make the adjustment to the real-world situation. We found that *the response was, if anything, expedited* by the increased number of staff at the sectors and at NORAD because of the scheduled exercise,"[47] reported the 9/11 Commission, although how this alleged alacrity matched the non-performance of the authorities on the day was not explained. [Emphasis added.]

Confident of freedom from interference, subversive forces with black-ops security clearance could have done a lot in seventy-four minutes, but the 9/11 Commission never considered this and adhered to the amateurish-chancers-from-Afghan-caves conspiracy theory.

So there were four fuel-laden airliners being piloted by bloodthirsty Islamic fanatics. There was no limit to their hatred of the enemy. Al-Qaeda recruit Zacarias Moussaoui told a court in early 2006: "You are the head of the snake for me. If we want to destroy the Jewish state of Palestine, we have to destroy you first," adding that he had no regrets about the nearly 3,000 deaths on 9/11.[48]

These pilots were evidently out to do as much damage as possible to the Great Satan. Here they were, roaming at will in the skies over the main population and political power zone of the United Snakes of America. According to the official account, the rogue pilots had been researching this mission for more than two years, poring over the manuals they left in their rental cars and their baggage (the FBI said none of them had a laptop computer, although Moussaoui did), conducting secret meetings in Las Vegas, taking numerous unimpeded first-class flights across the country to study the cabin management of US airlines, and flying pilot-school Cessnas over possible targets. A few had even taken lessons in piloting "heavies" on professional flight-simulators, as the mentally ill Moussaoui did.[49]

Viewing the events from this airborne angle, we saw the US heartland lying spread out at the disposal of these sky pirates. They were able to strike any targets they choose. At least four prime targets lay at their mercy: nuclear power plants that were known to be vulnerable to a collision by a crippled airplane. These potentially lethal installations were all Chernobyls waiting to melt down. The undefended power stations represented the equivalent of dirty atomic bombs to an airborne attacker. Hitting them with fuel-laden airliners would have caused four nuclear catastrophes.[50] Combined, they could have resulted in a minimum of 160,000 casualties, possibly millions of long-term agonizing deaths, and the secure sealing off of trillions of dollars worth of real estate for an indefinite period. It would have been a mortifying stab at the jugular of the American giant that had dealt out equally bad radioactive punishment to civilians in Hiroshima and Nagasaki in 1945.[51]

Instead, these ruthless killers chose to throw away their lives on knocking two holes in the Twin Towers, the first of which could initially be dismissed by onlookers as incompetent piloting – as Bush reportedly quipped – and go to considerable effort to hit the Pentagon in its only unoccupied and newly fortified wedge. The fourth plane ditched over the Shanksville area, reportedly subject to the very problem inherent in flying such long distances, namely uproar in the cabin.

As noted above, there was a stark contrast between the selected targets, which were "symbolic", as the tortured detainees apparently declared, and the chance of creating widespread mayhem by hitting proper strategic targets (remember the collapse of the towers was unforeseeable). It amounted to a disconnection between the destructive ambitions of the foreign attackers and the targets that they took such elaborate risks to hit.

Examining the figures, we find that each aircraft flew hundreds of miles away before executing a U-turn to fly back to its target. In addition, Flights 77 and 93 departed from airports that lay a few minutes' flying time from the mission's target points.

ROGUE AIRLINER	Take-off distance to target	Distance actually flown to target	Extra distance involved
AA11	193 miles	328 miles	135 miles
UAL175	193 miles	368 miles	175 miles
AA77	22 miles	627 miles	605 miles
UAL93	White House 200 miles To WTC 9 miles	750 miles	550 miles

We see that the four aircraft flew (or intended to fly) more than 1,400 miles further than strictly necessary. It's unlikely that planners inside the secret apparatus of a foreign power would have spent up to five years designing a mission that so exposed itself to air force interception or military shootdown. With pilots safely in control of planes, they would select targets that inflicted a massive blow, instead of ones with symbolic value only. Above all, what possible motive would they have to fly so far before striking?

Many TV-fed people agreed with the official story: that the mission was so unthinkable, so fiendishly cunning and evil, that the USAF was knocked sideways[52] and the air-traffic controllers just couldn't cope. They would ask: what did it matter how long the planes were in the air?

It did matter for the following reasons:

- The hijackers would have had to possess inside knowledge of the inter-agency military exercises (or even a deliberate fighter-jet stand-down) planned for that day in order to be confident enough of escaping interception or shootdown for a combined total of 1,460 rogue flying miles.

- The hijackers had to control the cabin crew and the passengers who remained aboard their aircraft, who hugely outnumbered them. Added to which, hijacking and other terror rumours had been proliferating among the world's secret services that summer,[53] raising the possibility that air-marshal-type irregulars might have been placed on board these prestigious trans-continental commuter flights.[54] There was a chance, for example, that Flight 11 passenger Daniel Lewin, an Israeli multimillionaire with a history of involvement in secret-state operations, might have had some kind of security approval and drew a gun.[55]

- Toxic gas, issuing from some unknown source, might have caused survival problems. On Flight 11, attendant Betty Ong reported by in-flight phone: "We can't breathe in business class. Somebody's got mace or something."[56] The 9/11 Commission believed mace or pepper spray was used on all the planes to seal off the cockpit area, although it's hard to believe that hijackers had smuggled gas masks aboard.[57] Only men with security clearance could have done that.

■ In addition, the rogue pilot had to control his own gang. The "muscle hijackers" had all volunteered for suicide operations, according to the 9/11 Commission's hidden informants.[58] Perhaps the true nature of their mission had been kept secret. The simultaneous suicidal dedication of five people in each plane (three, possibly four, in Flight 93) might understandably have been hard to orchestrate. After the temptations of first-class flights across capitalist America and visits to hedonistic Las Vegas, there was always the chance of a spontaneous revolt in the ranks of a so-called "muscle" team, or even by one of the lone pilots supposedly aboard each aircraft.

None of these vital considerations, however, seemed to have played a part in the planning. Because the airliners were controlled by their rogue pilots for so long before crashing, there must have been a pressing reason for flying so far.

THE RADAR HOLES

It is not desirable to wander into the "tinfoil hat" area of 9/11 speculations, but the 9/11 Commission report itself was far-fetched, speculating that poor pilots not exhaustively trained, if at all, on airliners navigated them a total of 1,460 miles over a number of US Air Force bases and hit three out of four "symbolic" targets accurately at top speed.

If there was some kind of behind-the-scenes manipulation of the events, it could be concealed from both the military and the air-traffic controllers – even from the Secret Service ostensibly monitoring their screens – by exploiting gaps in radar coverage. In this regard, evidence from the radar coverage map was at least provocative. Researchers called Group8plus had the sensible idea of comparing the published routes of the rogue flights with existing maps of US radar coverage.

The map, extracted from a readily available university security study, showed the NORAD radar network, which surrounded the borders of the USA defensively, superimposed on the FAA network, which was within the country. However, it did not include the coverage of Canada, which is a full partner of NORAD. The maps were pre-9/11.

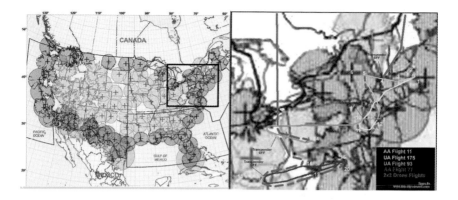

Left: Map of pre-9/11 US mechanical radar coverage, combining the known FAA system (inland) and NORAD's (coastal), published by a department at the Massachussets Institute of Technology and reproduced here in the public interest. A square shows the area magnified in the other two pictures. It does not include Raytheon's Pave Paws Early Warning Radar System, operated by the US Air Force's space command. The map would also omit any secret coverage. One key point: the map omits Canadian radar coverage. Canada is part of NORAD, and NORAD regional command at NEADS in Rome, New York, a major radar research centre, would have had access to it. Right: Northeastern part of the MIT radar map magnified, with published routes of the 9/11 rogue planes superimposed.

CREDITS: MIT/Team 8+

Close examination of the map revealed what looked like gaps in the radar coverage. White areas showed where the radar beams presumably did not reach, and several occurred in the northeastern region, where the airliners went rogue on 9/11.

The reported routes of the rogue planes were shown in different colours, superimposed on the blurry magnification of the northeast region. Some possible routes of remote-controlled aircraft (drones) were shown in mauve. Possible radar "holes" were in white in the background.

The existence of passenger remains at the crash sites would be an obvious problem for this theory if the drones were empty. However, the way the planes flew close to or across the possible radar holes remained a fascinating hint of an explanation for their long diversions in the wrong direction from their targets.

- Flight 175 flew near the tip of a radar hole, and its transponder changed identity at that point, before it recrossed the presumed radar hole.

- Flight 77's take-off point at Dulles airport in Washington, DC, was just twenty-two miles from the Pentagon. Instead, the airliner flew for half an hour across the continent, turned just after a radar hole, cut its transponder message, and again crossed the supposed radar hole to make for its target.

- Flight 93 spent fifty minutes flying the furthest across North America, and it just happened that it too reached one of the presumed radar holes, turned just after passing over it, cut its transponder message, and recrossed the hole.

Radar "holes", if indeed they existed as the map suggests, would have been usefully located for the published routes of all the rogue flights, and they would hint at an explanation of this long-standing problem of why the airliners flew so long before hitting their targets.

THE NORTHWOODS SCENARIO

This theory has to be examined, because the US military chiefs of staff themselves apparently proposed a similar scenario many years ago, in 1962. Operation Northwoods was an ingenious plane-swap deception put forward to President John F. Kennedy as a way of provoking war with Cuba. The plan came complete with unpiloted drone aircraft and planted crash debris. The document was retrieved under Freedom of Information laws and widely publicized in the months before 9/11 by an author friendly with key figures in the secret state. 9/11 Commission director Philip D. Zelikow was a Cuba–US relations expert. It would be useful to know if he knew about Operation Northwoods. Whether the document was a forgery or not, it still contained an interesting description of the plan.[59]

> An aircraft at Elgin AFB would be painted and numbered as an exact duplicate for a civil registered aircraft belonging to a CIA proprietary organization in the Miami area. At a designated time, the duplicate

would be substituted for the actual civil aircraft and would be loaded with the selected passengers, all boarded under carefully prepared aliases. The actual registered aircraft would be converted into a drone [a remotely controlled unmanned aircraft]. Take-off times of the drone aircraft and the actual aircraft will be scheduled to allow a rendezvous south of Florida.[60]

The Northwoods plan demonstrated the illusion that could be created in the air by using a remote-controlled aircraft liveried up as belonging to an airline and switching transponders. The Joint Chiefs of Staff also recorded in their Top Secret document a key element: the planting of evidence at the crash site.

c. At precisely the same time that the aircraft was presumably shot down a submarine or small surface craft would disburse F-101 parts, parachute, etc.[61]

For Cuba, the plan included the planting of evidence for the rescue teams to find. In the Shanksville context, it would take the form of plane debris, passenger evidence, and so on.

This particular version of the Northwoods Plan would *not* apply to Flight 93, however, because the passengers' remains and effects were scattered over an eight-mile-wide area at Shanksville, indicating that the plane was the same Flight 93 that took off at Newark. But why it flew for so long in the wrong direction remained a mystery that directed suspicion towards the radar "hole" it passed over twice.

And there was one media report – just one – that suggested something was wrong with the passenger story on Flight 93.

THE TWO-PLANES HYPOTHESIS

The plane-swap scenario was based on the Northwoods plan, an apparently genuine Pentagon proposal from another era of panicky fear of an exterior threat, and thus had reasonably solid credentials, however far-fetched it might have seemed. It also evoked the drone decoy planes idea that the US President had reportedly put forward, sixteen months after 9/11, in talks with UK Prime Minister Blair. Shot down by Iraq, the false-flag drone planes would have served as a pretext for the Iraq invasion.[62]

More recently, the US secret state had been covertly moving prisoners around its torture gulag, illegally using the European skies and employing illegal call signs to do so. The *Times* of London reported:

> The American military have been operating flights across Europe using a call sign assigned to a civilian airline that they have no legal right to use. Not only is the call sign bogus – according to the International Civil Aviation Organisation – so, it appears, are some of the aircraft details the Americans have filed with the air-traffic control authorities. In at least one case, a plane identified with the CIA practice of 'extraordinary rendition' – transporting terrorist suspects – left a US airbase just after the arrival of an aircraft using the bogus call sign.[63]

That the technology existed to fake the call signs and the hijack communications, and that the planes on the day could have connected with available radar "holes", was interesting evidence for the plane-swap hypothesis.

The Northwoods plan involved drone aircraft. Since 1962, when it was (supposedly) written, drone aircraft had been developed into routine weapons of imperial control from the air. One was shot down spying over Iraq on 9/11.[64]

The remains of bodies at the Flight 93 impact site were an obvious problem for the drone theory, but the radar holes remained a worrying opening for "black ops" to execute some kind of Northwoods-style plane-swap scenario that remained poorly understood.

The reason sceptics reached for the difficult plane-swap theory was that it offered one way of explaining the baffling hijackings that pilots never reported and passengers never saw. According to the plane-swap theory, the hijackings simply never took place and planes changed identity when they were swapped in the air. There were some problems with this speculation in practice, but in principle it was possible.

It required thinking "out of the box", just like the chiefs of staff had with regard to crushing the Cuban revolution. In a plane-swap all the communications from the rogue planes were staged. It would not mean the relatives, friends, air-traffic controllers and airline personnel were part of the plot: everyone on the receiving end actually got phone calls or heard radio transmissions, but they were duped by communications that were faked using the kind of voice simulation that had been common knowledge for years and was reported, for example, in the *Washington Post* in 1999.[65] In certain circles voice simulation was so well recognized that security protection against it was readily available.[66] And builders of flight simulators had been perfecting it for years.[67]

If advanced flight-simulation technology was an everyday reality in 2001, call signs could be faked, and real peoples' voices could easily be faked,[68] it was also quite easy to conceal an airborne plane from radar detection. Simply fly planes on top of one another so that they only gave one blip on the screen. Then it would be possible to swap planes in flight and conceal or change their identity using transponders.

According to the plane-swap scenario, the Flight 93 drama was propaganda from beginning to end, like the movies that depicted it, and the honest people who got sucked into the affair were the dupes of Svengalis behind the scenes.

Detailed disentangling of the complex reports of Flight 93's last ten minutes supported the plane-swap explanation.

A researcher using the pseudonym Woody Box compared all the US media reports of Flight 93's movements in the last few minutes and found them to be a mass of contradictions. However, "the numerous contradictions could be elegantly solved by postulating the existence of two different airplanes. Now, by a process comparable to the untangling of two twisted phone cords, it was possible to establish a consistent timeline for each of both planes."[69]

The researcher then set out to prove that in the narratives of the last minutes of Flight 93, the hitherto baffling on–off–on transponder sequence, along with apparently impossible changes in altitude, could be explained by the existence of two airliners, one north of Pittsburgh, one to the south. He postulated that signals from the southern one ceased and were replaced by signals from the one to the north, thereby changing the plane's identity in mid-air. The replacement drone then went on to crash, while the plane traced as Flight 93, hidden from controllers by having no transponder message, landed (possibly with its false ID'd passengers) at Cleveland airport, which luckily had been thoroughly and hastily evacuated moments earlier. This is precisely the Operation Northwoods scenario.

Basing his analysis on the 9News report above, local newspaper and radio reports from 11 and 12 September (mainly from the Akron *Beacon Journal* and the Cleveland *Plain Dealer*), statements of eyewitnesses and internet postings on the morning of 9/11 (people were listening to the radio and immediately submitted the breaking news to the net), Box made a closely argued case that the emergency landing of Delta 1989[70] at Cleveland Hopkins airport was followed by another, possibly the plane identified as United Flight 93.

If Northwoods was a faked document aimed at implicating the Pentagon and distracting attention from traitors or foreign subversives, the Woody Box hypothesis backed it up impeccably. And indeed, two prominent 9/11 researchers immediately denounced the Woody Box analysis as a hoax, arguing that the contradictions in the reports arose from sheer confusion.[71] Box rejected the charge by calling on opponents to match his double sourcing of information with their own explanation for the contradictions in the official and media narrative.

There's no doubt that the various accounts of the last few minutes of Flight 93 were very confused. Even the crash time – 10:03 a.m. or 10:06 a.m. – was disputed. Box showed that trying to attach all the reports to one plane required phenomenal aerobatics that seemed impossible. However, there were a couple of serious problems with this particular two-planes hypothesis:

> ▪ It required the complete rigging of the Shanksville crash site, which at least 400 people searched while it was an FBI crime scene. Seven boxes of "surprisingly intact mementos of lives lost" were returned to relatives from the site in subsequent months.[72] There's the Pentagon's assertion that all but one of the passengers and crew from Flight 93 were identified from their recovered remains by DNA analysis.[73]

■ It had the passengers being switched *after* the supposed crash near Shanksville, when the plane swap logically would have them being consolidated on to one plane somewhere *before* the crash. The only way Box's scenario could work would be if the passengers were all false IDs, and they disappeared back into their regular cover, but then there would be the existing deaths to explain.

■ It would contradict evidence, apparently gleaned from Flight 93's "black box", that the airliner flew upside down during its last few moments.[74]

So, while the plane-swap hypothesis interestingly explained the risk-filled duration of the rogue flights by requiring them to access possible radar "holes", finally it was unconvincing.

NO RELATIVES AT SAN FRANCISCO AIRPORT

As news of the disaster that had hit Flight 93 reached its San Francisco destination, preparations were made for receiving the relatives.

"At San Francisco International Airport, where the plane was headed, an evacuation was ordered. Bomb-sniffing dogs patrolled the hallways and a counseling center was set up for relatives of the people aboard Flight 93.

"'This is a time for compassion. It's not a time for long sermons,' said the Rev. John Delariva, a Catholic priest who is part of the airport's counseling team."[75]

However, a problem emerged.

"No family members showed up at San Francisco International Airport to greet the passengers at its normal 11:15 a.m. arrival time, said Ron Wilson, spokesman for San Francisco International Airport."

The story continued, not quoting Wilson: "That is possibly because United employees in Chicago reached many of them before they left home." It went on: "Dozens of clergy members gathered at United's VIP lounge to await survivors. San Francisco Mayor Willie Brown cancelled his trip to meet the victims' families when it appeared nobody would show up."[76]

It seemed odd that none of the friends or relatives of the approximately nine Californians aboard the flight turned up. For example, the following were known to have been resident there:

Passenger	Residence
Beaven, Alan	Oakland
Bingham, Mark	San Francisco
Bodley, Deora	Santa Clara
Burnett, Thomas	San Ramon
Corrigan, Georgine Rose	West Coast area
Garcia, Andrew	Portola Valley
Grandcolas Lauren	San Rafael
Guadagno, Richard	Eureka
Miller, Nicole	San Jose

Source: Internet searches

The news story attempted to explain their complete absence by the fact that "United employees in Chicago reach[ed] *many of them* before they left home". (But not all.) Note that this editorialization was inserted after Ron Wilson's statement, as if he had given the explanation.

Square this with Lisa Beamer's account of waiting many agonizing hours in a semi-comatose condition for confirmation from United Airlines of her husband's death. There is a three-hour time-lag across the North American continent.[77] It worked out that United Airlines had little more than three hours to do all the contact research and to reach "many of them" before they left home. Combined with the knowledge that United was also coping with the United 175 disaster at the same time, it stretched credulity.

Anyway, the friends and relatives did not need to go to the airport rendezvous to confirm their loved ones' deaths. The airport gathering was not for that purpose at all. It was a mark of respect and shared grief. "Dozens of clergy members gathered", and the Mayor was expected.

Obviously, travelling at such an alarming time was of concern, but California was not directly threatened, and the church ministers had no difficulty attending at the airport. It remains an odd thing that nobody turned up, especially considering that some of the friends and relatives, particularly Bingham's mother, Bush-supporter Alice Hoglan, and the

Burnett family, also Bush-backers, became media fixtures in the ensuing days, months and years. In 2005/6 all these no-show friends and relatives participated in a mass endorsement of the three Flight 93 cult films that were shown to a potential audience in the billions.

DID FLIGHT 93 LAND SAFELY?

The peculiar absence in San Francisco of relatives and friends of the western based passengers of Flight 93 fitted with a report, later cancelled as a mistake, that the airliner actually landed safely after the FAA grounding order at 9:45 a.m.

"A Boeing 767 out of Boston made an emergency landing Tuesday at Cleveland Hopkins International Airport due to concerns that it may have a bomb aboard, said Mayor Michael R. White. White said the plane had been moved to a secure area of the airport, and was evacuated. United identified the plane as Flight 93. The airline did not say how many people were aboard the flight."[78]

The report had been filed at 11:43:57 a.m., one and three-quarter hours after Flight 93's disappearance. Cincinnatti 9News, originators of the report, said it had come from the AP news agency. "This story has been removed from WCPO.com. It was a preliminary AP story, and was factually incorrect," the entry stated on the station's website.

WHY DESTROY FLIGHT 93?

Another problem with the plane-swap scenario was the destruction of Flight 93. If it happened on purpose, as the theory would suggest, why was it ever designed that way?

Genuine Suicide Pilot Nosedived

The complicated evidence around the disappearance of Flight 93 suggested that nothing so simple as an aborted suicide mission was involved. The shootdown evidence, and the number of aircraft in the area alone indicated other forces at work.

Destruction of Witnesses

All the witnesses from the rogue planes might have been consolidated on to one flight and destroyed in the sky by an air-to-air missile, possibly supported by land-based chemical laser,[79] over secluded Shanksville. All the human remains and scattered possessions could then be collected by unsuspecting searchers and, when passed into black-ops hands, attributed to the various crash sites from behind the scenes. Alternatively, only Flight 11 was directed north (up a radar hole) and destroyed as Flight 93. Strict government secrecy would permit this, although such a grisly scenario was too ghastly for most people even to contemplate, involving as it did the cold-blooded killing of innocent travellers. However, seventeen children and sixty-two adults had been torched to death at Waco, and heaps of body parts undeniably are part of the war industry.[80]

Destruction of Rogue Pilots

There were a couple of hints that the hijackers had special status, such as the gun (or guns) that Tom Burnett reported them carrying on Flight 93, the gun at first reported aboard Flight 11, or the gas that the 9/11 Commission said was used on all the flights, presumably requiring the raiders to don gas masks. If a genuine passenger rebellion occurred, perhaps because administered drugs in vapour form had not taken full effect, these operatives might have alerted their controllers on the ground and triggered an unplanned response: a shootdown that destroyed them and any chance that they might be questioned.

Recruitment Drive for War

The doom of Flight 93 provided an Alamo-style opportunity for Davy Crockett hero figures to emerge from military disaster. The rapid emergence on to TV screens at home of the exemplary war-widows of men portrayed as the first Crusaders, plus the heroes legend and the "Let's Roll" slogan fitted this scenario.

When it had so many devastating targets available, the aircraft's "symbolic" target in Washington, DC – either the White House or the Capitol – had never been convincing. In view of its later inexplicable collapse, Building Seven at the WTC seemed a stronger candidate, but it too would not have had the genuine strategic impact that a nuclear strike would have achieved.

Perhaps the official scenario was what had been planned all along: a staged suicide crash ostensibly caused by a passenger rebellion that served to recruit Americans into wars on Islamic regimes, except that something went wrong and the dummy plane involved had to be shot down instead. The rebellion scenario then prevented the shootdown being admitted, even by warmongers who could have scored Brownie points for it with their adherents.

The moral lesson of Flight 93's staged crash would be very simple: "They sat down as 40 and rose as one." Which happened to be the kicker line from one of the Hollywood recruitment movies.

Two stills from the Paul Greengrass film's trailer also put the recruitment message simply: "On the day we faced fear" – pregnant pause while mayhem breaks out "we also found courage." It's sad "we" didn't also find the radar holes.

REMOTE CONTROL

By this explanation, the on-board computers of an airliner took over control of the plane, leaving the pilot powerless before the instrument array. It was a method of saving hijacked airliners that had been widely discussed in the hijacking era of the 1970s and early 1980s, and became a practical reality with "fly-by-wire" technology that arrived with powerful portable computing and was installed in a new generation of aircraft. Whether the override element for bringing home hijacked aircraft was installed in the airliner fleet is unknown. Hijackings had effectively ended when the new planes were introduced. Economic efficiency would have dictated leaving them out.

However, the fact that a USAF drone was shot down while spying over Iraq on 9/11 shows that controlling aircraft remotely had become routine by that date. A combination of GPS and the US military's advanced avionics made it an easy matter to fit out individual liveried airliners with an override system. "The military has employed this capability since the 1950s," an aviation expert wrote three weeks after the 9/11 events. "Modifying and implementing the technology for use on passenger carrying aircraft in the United States would involve significant capital outlay, research and testing. But from an engineering standpoint, landing an aircraft automatically is a relatively simple matter." He was discussing Bush's disingenuous call for the defensive development of such systems.[81]

Bush's call for technology to land hijacked planes, was passed off by the media as if the capability did not already exist, although the Pentagon had been able to fly aircraft remotely since 1951. "In addition, the president said he would give grants to airlines to allow them to develop stronger cockpit doors and transponders that cannot be switched off from the cockpit. Government grants would also be available to pay for video monitors that would be placed in the cockpit to alert pilots to trouble in the cabin; *and new technology, probably far in the future, allowing air traffic controllers to land distressed planes by remote control.*"[82] [Emphasis added.]

There could have been economic motives for pretending that remote control of aircraft lay "far in the future". Fat contracts could be signed with friendly corporations for yet more spurious research mingled with pork-barrel politics – in other words, business as usual.

On the other hand, the motive could have been more sinister: to divert public attention away from the known existence of military remote-control systems. It's ominously plausible, since a senior Pentagon official at the time had been vice-president of just such a company, specializing in military remote control systems for aircraft.

So emergency landing override was available in 2001, but Bush pretended it wasn't, and called for "new technology, probably far in the future" to achieve it. It's either a tell-tale sign of deception, or it was just more of the incompetence that the 9/11 Commission blamed for 9/11.

Whichever it was, there was no shortage of evidence that remote control of four airliners on that day was feasible. On Flight 93, the probable removal of the last three minutes from the cockpit voice recorder, or even the origination of the whole recording in a sound studio, would have removed any spoken evidence of panic over the loss of control of the aircraft.

If, on the other hand, the recording was genuine, the repetition of "sit", "sit down", or "down" a total of forty-seven times over a period of five minutes might have reflected a freak-out before useless controls by bad speakers of English trying to force somebody to deal with it. The Arabic words translated as: "Inform them, and tell him to talk to the pilot. Bring the pilot back" timed at 9:45 a.m. might suggest that the rogue pilot needed the help of a qualified pilot. Perhaps it was he who at 9:48 said "Set course" and somehow got the flight plan changed, perhaps with the intention of landing the plane safely or giving away its position. Sadly, a rather important conversation conducted over the ensuing eight minutes was mostly listed as "unintelligible", proving that Jere Longman was right when he wrote that the cockpit voice recorder solved nothing.

Flight 93 appeared to have been the first scheduled trip of its kind on a Tuesday, having started as a new EWR-SFO connection a few days earlier on 5 September.[83] This innovative element might have given an opportunity for some kind of plane subsitution. An airliner modified for remote control did not need to differ from an unmodified one. The logistics of making the plane substitution would have been a challenge. However, Occam's razor loves the remote-control hypothesis, because according to it, everyone was telling the truth. Only the hands on the controls of the airliner changed.

HAVING IT BOTH WAYS

If radar holes did indeed exist that day, they would offer the only available explanation for the extended diversion of Flight 93. Something important required the long diversion to Cleveland that is not yet understood. The airliner took off so late, and travelled so far, that it flew right out of the window of plausible deniability for NORAD. Once it had U-turned southeast and flown on for half an hour, the aircraft behaved bizarrely, turning in all directions, finally wobbling, turning over on its back and crashing.

The remote-control system might have malfunctioned. The suicide pilot might have changed his mind about killing himself. The patsies possibly fell out among themselves. Perhaps air marshals planted on board took the plane over and threatened to land it safely. Possibly

Edward Green, the only known pilot among the passengers, got to the controls and radioed for help, which came in the form of a missile. Any one of a dozen things might have happened, in fact, almost anything but what the propaganda movies portrayed – as the debris field proved beyond a doubt.

The mystery of the 550-mile diversion was compounded by the complete lack of knowledge of how the hijacking was carried out, and why none of the eight airline pilots managed to give a formal hijack alert. A pilots' spokesman told the 9/11 Commission that, even if the cockpit door were fortified, he would open it if someone had a noose round the neck of one of his flight attendants. But this scenario would still leave time for one of the two pilots to issue an alert.[84]

If the multi-agency exercises being carried out on that day somehow duped the pilots of Flight 93 and eased the hijacking process, then there existed, not just a mystery around the routes, but a scandal around the exercises.[85] The 9/11 Commission ignored both the mystery and the scandal – as did the propaganda movies.

Just like all conspiracy theorists, the purveyors of the official narrative left out evidence that did not suit their version. For example, they had it both ways with their villains, who were displayed in court as absurd bunglers of dubious mental competence, like Richard Reid and Zacarias Moussaoui,[86] while their ostensible colleague Ziad Jarrah was a cool super-spy who managed to take over an airliner and seize the controls while remaining totally unobserved by any of his fellow passengers.

5
Looking Ahead

The Flight 93 controversy is almost over. Not because it was resolved, but because the forces of money, political power and prejudice are getting their way. The well-founded belief that the airliner was brought down by a third party is on the brink of relegation to the children's playground, where it might live on for a few centuries as an innocuous nursery rhyme. A $57 million memorial will be installed near Shanksville and the heroes will enter the history books, or more importantly, the history movies. Ironically, but evidently unintentionally, the memorial will be drawn up in the shape of the Islamic crescent moon.

Bush's assertion that Flight 93 heroism was "a defining moment" in US history will go down as the received line, and all talk of a shoot-down will be consigned to marginal works by unblinkered individuals. Their books and internet videos will be tolerated within limited niche markets for relatively few cognoscenti, who will be useful stooges for the worldly to mock. Nevertheless, the works will be legacies that record the suspicions and concerns of citizens at this time.

The symbol-addicted structure of the human mind will continue to throb with religious and ethnic hatred and countless individuals will be sacrificed on its pyres. The warped nature of human consciousness and

The Flight 93 memorial, as conceived in 2006, was be built in the shape of an Islamic crescent moon.

Paul Murdoch Design/Internet image

the apparently doomed urban environment that it has constructed will continue to trap us in its labyrinth.

The identity crisis that lay at the heart of the Flight 93 affair, once the shootdown issue was buried, will become central. Identity and the proof of it will become the focus of the emerging worldwide police state, its sprawling secret database handily delivered to each individual bureaucrat's computer screen by the integration priesthood. The identity of a Ziad Jarrah should never be in question again, but doubts remain on that issue.

Regarding aviation: will humanity remain prosthetically a flying animal? Some of the men who flew that day thought so: they were spending much of their lives aloft. Blithely, they gave no thought to the fact that the glorified guided missiles carrying them spewed hydrocarbon wastes into the upper atmosphere, rapidly destroying the planet's ability to reflect the sun's heat. Like millions of others, they believed the hidden persuaders who told them that air-miles were steps to a higher level of existence, and ignored the voices of reason that wished to warn them of the dangers.

What did jet travel really mean to a human being? A trip to the stars, or an embolism in unused legs? The rush of excitement as a plane defeated gravity and left the surface of the earth could easily be reproduced in the mind with pharmaceuticals, causing no impact on the environment at all. The effects of the more than 200 million tons of aviation fuel known to be used each year for civil aviation were, on the other hand, largely unknown, as responsible international bodies admitted in 2001.[1] If a street carnival looked enticing on the other side of the earth, why not get together and organize one in your own neighbourhood? If peace and quiet seemed to be available only on that desert island, why not get a few streets closed around where you lived?

The 9/11 events were only a momentary crisis for world air travel, which soon continued its apparently inexorable rise after a brief check, and in 2003 was back up to three trillion passenger-kilometres, the record set just before 9/11.

How crucial was jet travel for those in business? The suitcase on rollers, the VIP-class seat, the airborne laptop, all had become part of the business world (and all of airlines' profits). But for those who needed to contact others far away, practically everything short of a handshake was available digitally: videoconferencing, group telephone calls, video emails, photo emails, faxed signatures. In a large proportion of cases, business travel was a waste of corporate money and individuals' time, except for the prestige that it conferred to soar above the clouds on money-making errands.

How much security could the airlines really offer their customers? Confidence seemed to be unbounded: Tony Blair authorized huge new airport developments in Britain only a few months after 9/11, as if the two issues were totally unconnected. Jet airliners, which in the wrong hands were guided missiles, took off in ever larger numbers from Newark airport, in full view of Wall Street. Flight paths into London Heathrow airport continued to pass directly over the City of London. Because of 9/11, everyone had to give up their human rights except those who flew, a hugely paradoxical outcome.

The war-making state took 9/11 as permission to launch a full-scale surveillance state in the name of assuring a trustworthy identity. People had to give up their old-fashioned ideas about privacy as the USA announced in 2005 its globe-spanning US-VISIT scheme. Bermuda-based Accenture would manage the $10 billion project with, among others, techno-spook corporation SRA International, cruise-missile builders Raytheon and Abu Ghraib supplier, Titan Corporation.

The stated intention of the US scheme sounded innocuous: to "confirm the identity of people visiting the United States, note when they have overstayed their visas and alert the government if people have been identified as security risks." Actually, "the massive undertaking [would] integrate 19 legacy computer systems, provide border-crossing agents with biometric and biographical data on people entering and leaving the United States and offer links between DHS (homeland security) and other agencies such as the State Department."[2]

Travellers would notice almost nothing: "the US Customs and Border Protection Officer now uses the inkless, digital fingerscanner to capture two of your fingerscans. You first place your left index finger and then your right index finger on the scanner. The officer also takes your digital photograph. These procedures add only seconds to the overall processing time," the Department of Homeland Security cooed, while in the background waited corporations like Verichip, a fabricator of digital human-implants, the ultimate technological fix for regulating humanity.[3]

Non-US citizens noticed that the US-VISIT programme was far more ambitious than it appeared. "In many cases, US-VISIT begins overseas, at the US consular offices issuing visas, where visitors' biometrics (digital fingerscans and photographs) are collected and checked against a database of known criminals and suspected terrorists." In other words, the USA's surveillance state had to integrate with a similar police state in your own country, if you were to continue enjoying scheduled airline flights towards US cities. American regulation of the world's population lay just around the corner. Tony Blair announced in 2006 a Fortress Britain policy that also required a surveillance state in linked countries.

And it all went back to Mohamed Atta, whose identity, so elaborately researched in Bush's 9/11 Commission report, was destroyed by whistle-blowers in military intelligence. Yet, as we've seen, Atta's only role in 9/11 was probably to plant incriminating suitcases in the baggage stream.

Ziad Jarrah may well have been the unluckiest passenger who ever flew on an American airliner. His remains probably lie somewhere in American soil, unmourned, his name cursed and spat upon. All because no one could prove conclusively that he was not who the US police apparatus said he was.

The consolidation of US corporate media ownership promised to sail on untroubled by anti-trust laws, with fewer than half a dozen men controlling the news content of millions of US TV screens, and influencing billions more overseas. And within the USA's booming secret state, the hidden men would continue to pull the wires. As Edward L. Bernays, one of the founders of corporate public relations put it: "Those who manipulate the unseen mechanism of society constitute an invisible government which is the true ruling power of our country. We are governed, our minds molded, our tastes formed, our ideas suggested largely by men we have never heard of... It is they who pull the wires that control the public mind."[4]

Notes

In these notes, dates in the form xx/xx/xx are in American month/day/year format and dates in the form xx.xx.xx are in British day.month.year format.

CHAPTER 1

1. WASHINGTON – President Bush has quietly claimed the authority to disobey more than 750 laws enacted since he took office, asserting that he has the power to set aside any statute passed by Congress when it conflicts with his interpretation of the Constitution. "Bush challenges hundreds of laws, President cites powers of his office," by Charlie Savage, *Boston Globe*, 30 April 30 2006.
2. Further pictures of Bush welcoming Beamer to the capital were shown on 21 September on CBS Evening News. Congress appearance: 20 September, 10:24 p.m. ET, by the Associated Press.
3. There was always an undertow of resistance to this line. The veteran Middle East expert Robert Fisk, for example, wrote on 9/12: "So it has come to this. The entire modern history of the Middle East – the collapse of the Ottoman empire, the Balfour declaration, Lawrence of Arabia's lies, the Arab revolt, the foundation of the state of Israel, four Arab–Israeli wars and the 34 years of Israel's brutal occupation of Arab land – all erased within hours as those who claim to represent a crushed, humiliated population struck back with the wickedness and awesome cruelty of a doomed people. Is it fair – is it moral – to write this so soon, without proof, without a shred of evidence, when the last act of barbarism in Oklahoma turned out to be the work of home-grown Americans?" www.zmag.org/fiskawecalam.htm
4. NBC Evening News for Wednesday, 23 January 2002.
5. **heresy**, n. 1: any opinions or doctrines at variance with the official or orthodox position [syn: unorthodoxy, heterodoxy] [ant: orthodoxy] 2: a belief that rejects the orthodox tenets of a religion [syn: unorthodoxy]. Source: WordNet 2.0, © 2003 Princeton University.

6. "Passengers on Flight 93 may have struggled with hijackers," Reuters, 12 September, 9:45 a.m. ET.

7. The following 18 May, she proved herself a creature of the White House when she told CNN in a five-minute personal interview that she could not fault President Bush II, he had "operated on the information he had" and was doing a "fine job". The faults all lay with the intelligence services, she said.

8. The equally famous Todd Beamer call would not be reported until the following Friday night, four working days later, when the FBI had finally "had the opportunity to review the material," as United Airlines put it. Source: Beamer, Lisa, *Let's Roll*, New York, 2002.

9. Although a survey later found that 42 per cent of New York evangelicals were sceptics.

10. From an essay "The last cargo cult" by Mike Jay on www.nthposition.com.

11. Victim's mother Alice HOGLAN, victim's wife Deena BURNETT – recount the cellphone calls from relatives about what happened on the plane. ABC Evening News for Thursday, 13 September, 2001, from Vanderbilt TV news archive.

12. A&E website notes on "Flight 93" movie.

13. **cult**, n. A religion or religious sect generally considered to be extremist or false, with its followers often living in an unconventional manner under the guidance of an authoritarian, charismatic leader. The followers of such a religion or sect.

14. **revelation**, n. An uncovering, a bringing to light of that which had been previously wholly hidden or only obscurely seen. God has been pleased in various ways and at different times (Heb. 1:1) to make a supernatural revelation of himself and his purposes and plans, which, under the guidance of his Spirit, has been committed to writing. (See WORD OF GOD.) The Scriptures are not merely the "record" of revelation; they are the revelation itself in a written form, in order to the accurate presevation [*sic*] and propagation of the truth. Revelation and inspiration differ. Revelation is the supernatural communication of truth to the mind; inspiration (q.v.) secures to the teacher or writer infallibility in communicating that truth to others. It renders its subject the spokesman or prophet of God in such a sense that everything he asserts to be true, whether fact or doctrine or moral principle, is true, infallibly true. Source: Easton's 1897 Bible Dictionary.

15. **scripture**, n. Invariably in the New Testament denotes that definite collection of sacred books, regarded as given by inspiration of God, which we usually call the Old Testament (2 Tim. 3:15, 16; John 20:9; Gal. 3:22; 2; Pet. 1:20). It was God's purpose thus to perpetuate his revealed will. From time to time he raised up men to commit to writing in an infallible record the revelation he gave. The "Scripture," or collection of sacred writings, was thus enlarged from time to time as God saw necessary. We have now a completed "Scripture", consisting of the Old and New Testaments. The Old Testament canon in the time of our Lord was precisely the same as that which we now possess under that name. He placed the seal of his own authority on this collection of writings, as all equally given by inspiration (Matt. 5:17; 7:12; 22:40; Luke 16:29, 31). (See BIBLE T0000580; CANON.) Source: Easton's 1897 Bible Dictionary.

16. "Oscar-winning actress left fearing for safety after death threats over her Iraq stance," by Paul Dalgarno, Glasgow *Sunday Herald*, 30 April 2006.

17. A study published by the *Lancet* says the risk of death by violence for civilians in Iraq is now 58 times higher than before the US-led invasion. Iraq death-toll "soared post-war," BBC News, 29 October 2004.

18. Shockingly, 85 percent of the troops questioned believe they are fighting in Iraq "to retaliate for Saddam's role in the 9-11 attacks" – one of the key Iraq war myths built by Bush's frequent juxtaposition of references to Osama Bin Laden and Saddam Hussein. "America anesthetized," by Alex Sabbeth, 5 March 2006.

19. "The FBI and other agencies refused repeated requests to explain the [three-minute crash-time] discrepancy." *Philadelphia Daily News* (9/16/02) [Reprinted at: www.newsmine.org]

20. Longman, Jere: *Among the Heroes*, HarperCollins, 2002

21. Cited in Fahrenheit 911 by Michael Moore, Fellowship in Adventure films.

22. Cited in Savan, Leslie: *Slam Dunks & No Brainers*, New York, 2005.

23. Jennie Ganz, staff writer, *NSPE Engineering Times*, August/September 2002.

24. In 2006, a survey found that 82 per cent of serving military in Iraq thought they were there to avenge 9/11.

25. www.newamericancentury.org/

26. *Among the Heroes: United Flight 93 and the Passengers and Crew Who Fought Back* by Jere Longman, Hardcover, July 2002.

27. Verizon Corp. website & Beamer, Lisa: *Let's Roll*, Tyndale House Publishers, 2002.

28. On CBS Evening News for Friday, September 2001, Jefferson says she received a call from a United Airlines passenger named Todd Beamer; says he described three men hijacking the plane; says she did not tell Beamer about the World Trade Center attack; says the passengers who fought back were heroes; says she spoke to Beamer's wife from Vanderbilt TV news archive.

29. Crossway Books, November 2001.

30. *People* was owned by AOL Time Warner, a G. W. Bush donor in 2000. The corporation also owned CNN, HBO, and the largest US cable-TV grouping.

31. "Let's Roll!® Let us now praise famous widows," by Steve Perry, *Counterpunch*, 1 April 2002.

32. Another confusing concept. Although God made the world, God was not responsible for sin. See search engines.

33. "Golfer Payne Stewart dies," by Geraldine Sealey, www.ABCNEWS.com, 25 October.

34. Beamer, Lisa: *Let's Roll: Ordinary People, Extraordinary Courage*, Tyndale, August 2002, p. 5.

35. "We need a national ID card with our photograph and thumbprint digitized and embedded in the ID card," Ellison said in an interview Friday night on the evening news of KPIX-TV in San Francisco. "Bush contemplates national ID card for all citizens," Drudge Report, 23 September 2001, 20:02:37.

36. Barbara Olson's call to the Department of Justice has raised many questions.

37. Most people know that when they make a mobile call – during a 911 emergency, for example – authorities can access phone company technology to pin down their location, sometimes to within a few feet. A lesser-known fact: cellphone companies can locate you any time you are in range of a tower and your phone is on. Cellphones are designed to work either with global positioning satellites or through "pings" that allow towers to triangulate and pinpoint signals. Any time your phone "sees" a tower, it pings it. That is what happened last month when a New York City murder highlighted the existence of the built-in capability of phones to locate people even when they aren't making calls. "Reach out and track someone," by Terry J. Allen. In These Times, posted 11 May 2006.

38. Beamer, Lisa: op. cit., p. 211
39. Beamer, Lisa: op. cit., p. 187.
40. Savan, Leslie: op. cit.
41. Savan, Leslie: op. cit.
42. Beamer, Lisa: op. cit., p. 231.
43. Longman, Jere: op. cit.
44. *Pittsburgh Post-Gazette*, 22 September 2001. www.post-gazette.com/headlines/20010922gtenat4p4.asp.
45. Longman, Jere: op. cit., p. 214.
46. Longman, Jere: op. cit., pp. 216 17.
47. **faith**, n. Belief that does not rest on logical proof or material evidence. See Synonyms at **belief**. See Synonyms at **trust**. Source: The American Heritage Dictionary of the English Language, Fourth Edition, Houghton Mifflin Company, 2000.
48. "On the opening night of the RNC, Fox aired live coverage of speeches by September 11 victims' family members Deena Burnett, Debra Burlingame, and Tara Stackpole. Yet on the first night of the DNC, the network did not air any of a speech by Haleema Salie, whose pregnant daughter and son-in-law were on one of the planes that crashed into the World Trade Center on September 11, 2001. CNN and MSNBC did show Salie's speech." www.mediamatters.org, Tuesday, 31 August, 2004.
49. Its working title was *Anointed for the Call*.
50. Called: *Hello, This Is Mrs. Jefferson. I Understand Your Plane Is Being Hijacked. 9:45 a.m., Flight 93, September 11, 2001*, by Lisa Jefferson, Felicia Middlebrooks (CBS News anchor), Northfields Publishers.
51. "The ordinary terrorists," Arts.Telegraph, 31 August 2004.
52. "9/11: Behind the scenes," by Zahed Amanullah, altmuslim.com. Posted 10 January 2005.
53. "Ziad went home for the winter holiday after his first semester [in Greifswald] and upon his return seemed changed from the happy-go-lucky playboy. His cousin, Salim, noticed that he began reading radical Islamist publications." Aysel Senguen saw her fiance fall into radical Islam. She knew something was wrong but had no idea what lay ahead, by Dirk Laabs and Terry McDermott, The *Los Angeles Times*, 27 January 2003.
54. 9/11 Commission Report, Chapter 7, Note 190.
55. *Los Angeles Times*, 23 October 2001. The newspaper changed its tune later, supposedly as evidence emerged from a trial in Germany.
56. "The stolen election of 2004: Welcome back to hell," by Larry Chin, Online Journal Associate Editor. Source: www.fromthewilderness.com.
57. On Discovery's website.
58. "Find ways to blend in with your opponent and control him," the instructor, Bert Rodriguez, had told Jarrah back in May, when he walked into US-1 Fitness, a gymnasium in Dania Beach, Florida, and paid $500 cash for the course. *Pittsburgh Post-Gazette*, 28 October 2001.
59. NYT, 9 September 2005.
60. www.imdb.com.
61. Henshall, Ian, co-author *9/11 Revealed*, London & New York, 2005.

62. Griffin, David Ray: "Flights 11, 175, 77, and 93: The 9/11 Commission's Incredible Tales," 4 December 2005. www.911truth.org/article.php?story=20051205150219651

63. Brook-Lapping website.

64. In a review of *United 93* by Brian Lowry. www.variety.com/VE1117930271.html.

65. Oneillus, www.imdb.com/title/tt0481522.

66. Maureen Clare Murphy, *Electronic Iraq*, 10 November 2003.

67. BBC News online, 15 May 2003. http://news.bbc.co.uk/1/hi/programmes/correspondent/3028585.stm.

68. Contribution claim here: http://la.indymedia.org/news/2003/04/47530.php. MSNBC was an NBC joint venture with Microsoft, a corporation that had kicked in $2.4 million to get Bush elected.

69. www.universalstudios.com.

70. By Kirk Honeycutt, HollywoodReporter.com, 20 April.

71. "*United 93* to open the Tribeca Film Festival." Source: Universal Pictures, 29 March 2006.

72. *United 93* website for Greengrass's comments. Criticism by Keith Uhlich, *Slant Magazine*, 2006.

73. Composite CVR and ATC transcript released by US government prosecutors at the 2006 Moussaoui show trial, and Beamer, Lisa, op. cit.

74. Unsourced by Gere Longman, *Among the Heroes*, HarperCollins, 2002. 9/11 Comission Report gives: UAL record, Flight 93 EWR ACI passenger history, Sept. 11, 2001.

75. BBC News online, 23 September 2001. http://news.bbc.co.uk/1/hi/world/middle.east/1559151.stm.

76. http://911research.wtc7.net/cache/planes/evidence/ tomflocco.Lawyers.blackboxs.htm.

77. *Daily Telegraph*, 23/09/2001. http://tinyurl.com/fi5f.

78. http://archives.cnn.com/2001/WORLD/meast/09/18/inv.terror.jarrah.

79. 9/11 Comission Report, p. 456, Note 74.

80. Supposedly along with Jarrah's relative's work permit. http://en.wikipedia.org/wiki/Assem.Omar.Jarrah.

81. BBC News online, 13 Feburary 2006. http://news.bbc.co.uk/1/hi/uk.politics/4708444.stm.

82. President Bush's approval rating has fallen to its lowest mark of his presidency, according to a new Harris Interactive poll. Of 1,003 US adults surveyed in a telephone poll, 29 percent think Mr Bush is doing an "excellent or pretty good" job as president, down from 35 percent in April and significantly lower than 43 percent in January. It compares with 71 percent of Americans who said Mr Bush is doing an "only fair or poor" job, up from 63 percent in April. "Bush's ratings hit new low, poll shows," *Wall Street Journal* online, 12 May 2006.

83. All phonecall details from Complete 911 Timeline, Open Content project managed by Paul Thompson.

84. Longman, op. cit.

85. Note that this presumes the hijackers would not want calls made, although more than thirty calls have been reported.

86. Quotation from the contemporary Verizon/GTE Airfone website.
87. "In the back of the plane, 13 of the terrified passengers and crew members made 35 air phone calls and two cell phone calls to family members and airline dispatchers, a member of an FBI Joint Terrorism Task Force testified Tuesday." From: "Prosecutors play Flight 93 cockpit recording," by Greg Gordon, McClatchy Newspapers, 12 April 2006.
88. This 9-1-1 call, which should have been automatically recorded, has never been released.
89. 911research.wtc7.net
90. It was Mrs Olson's employer, CNN, that broke the story at 2:00 a.m. next day.
91. Olson must have originally said his wife called on a cellphone because he knew that such impossible calls could never show on a bill. When he switched his story to an Airfone, he must have believed that American had such phones on its 757s. Anyway, it kicked the billing question into touch for the time being. The 9/11 Commission feebly tried to close the issue by stating that all Flight 77 calls (of what type is not stated) went to an unknown number. Keane Commission Report, Chapter 1, Note 57: 'The records available for the phone calls from American 77 do not allow for a determination of which of four "connected calls to unknown numbers" represent the two between Barbara and Ted Olson, although the FBI and DOJ believe that all four represent communications between Barbara Olson and her husband's office (all family members of the Flight 77 passengers and crew were canvassed to see if they had received any phone calls from the hijacked flight, and only Renee May's parents and Ted Olson indicated that they had received such calls). The four calls were at 9.15 for one minute, forty-two seconds; 9.20 for four minutes, thirty-four seconds; 9.25 for two minutes, thirty-four seconds, and 9.30 for four minutes, twenty seconds.' (Refs: FBI report, "American Airlines Telephone Usage," 20 September 2001; FBI report of investigation, interview of Theodore Olson, 11 September 2001; FBI report of investigation, interview of Helen Voss, 14 September 2001; AAL response to the Commission's supplemental document request, 20 January 2004.)
92. ALEXANDRIA, Virginia (CNN) – Prosecutors asked a judge to rethink granting 9/11 families suing airlines access to evidence gathered for the criminal case against al-Qaeda terrorist Zacarias Moussaoui.

US District Judge Leonie Brinkema's 7 April order requires prosecutors to provide copies of all unclassified aviation security documents to attorneys representing September 11 families in a civil lawsuit pending in New York.

Prosecutors called the order "unprecedented" and urged Brinkema to withdraw it. The motion was filed by Chuck Rosenberg, the US attorney for the Eastern District of Virginia.

Brinkema's order would allow the families' attorneys access to "highly sensitive" law enforcement documents and could compromise the continuing investigation into the September 11, 2001, terrorist attacks. The inquiry is "the largest criminal investigation in our nation's history, which is still ongoing," the motion says.

"This order will likely provoke negative consequences for numerous criminal cases in the future," prosecutors said. Rosenberg requested a May 19 hearing.

American and United airlines each lost two passenger jets to al-Qaeda hijackers on September 11, 2001.

Among the 65 plaintiffs in the civil case is Mike Low, whose daughter, Sara, was a flight attendant on the first plane to strike the World Trade Center. He testified as a government witness in the criminal case.

The plaintiffs sued the airlines for wrongful death in 2002, rather than accept compensation from a federal fund that gave $7 billion to families. Brinkema agreed with their attorneys that legislation creating the victims compensation fund protected the rights of nonparticipating families to bring a negligence claim.

In their motion, prosecutors argued that the aviation security documents are specially selected materials provided to a small group of attorneys cleared to handle sensitive evidence in the Moussaoui case.

"The government never contemplated this material would be disclosed more widely for use in private civil litigation," the motion says.

Ron Motley, an attorney who successfully argued for access to the documents last month, said he would reply to the government's motion next week.

"We have not asked the government to give the 9/11 victims one single thing they didn't provide to Moussaoui's lawyers," Motley said.

The order would require the government to begin turning over copies of documents two weeks after a verdict is returned in Moussaoui's trial.

The plaintiffs have struggled with the Transportation Security Administration to obtain pre–September 11 aviation security documents.

"It is amazing what some agencies think is secret," Brinkema said before issuing her order last month. "As a culture, we need to be careful not to be so wrapped up in secrecy that we lose track of our core values and laws."

The families' pursuit was triggered by the revelation early in the Moussaoui trial that TSA lawyer Carla Martin improperly coached witnesses. Martin, who had prepared aviation security documents and witnesses in the case, sent witnesses transcripts and commentary by e-mail, even though a court order required scheduled witnesses to ignore the proceedings.

Martin's e-mail chain revealed she had been communicating with airline attorneys, and the families' attorneys suspected collusion.

From: "Judge Leonie Brinkema granted 9/11 families access to documents used in the Zacarias Moussaoui case," "US seeks to keep evidence from 9/11 families," "Prosecutors ask Moussaoui judge to reconsider order," by Phil Hirschkorn, CNN, 26 April 2006.

93. Barbara Olson was reported by her husband as asking the same baffling question.

94. Taken from the 9/11 Commission's evidence and referenced in writer/director Dylan Avery's persuasive documentary "9/11 Loose Change".

95. http://filmcritic1963.typepad.com/reviews/

96. http://www.timesonline.co.uk/article/0,,13509-1735385,00.html. Cf. the ostensible crash site: http://img.photobucket.com/albums/v124/eelpie/flight93crashsite.jpg.

97. Pilots have four methods of instantly giving the hijack alarm on a Boeing 757, including a button on the joy-stick.

98. *Pittsburgh Post-Gazette*, 28 October 2001.

99. By Brian Lowry, *Variety*, 19 April 2006.

100. *United 93* production budget:
http://www.the-numbers.com/movies/2006/FLT93.php;
9/11 Commission budget: http://www.9-11commission.gov/about/faq.htm#q5.

101. Flight 93 took off at 8:42 that morning, a few minutes before the Flight 11 struck the WTC. It was not hijacked until 9:28. It is simple fact that the FAA, American Airlines and

the military knew about the 911 hijacking before Flight 93 took off. Before its cockpit was seized two planes had hit the World Trade Center. The 9/11 Commission report states it clearly: "As news of the hijackings filtered through the FAA and the airlines, it does not seem to have occurred to their leadership that they needed to alert other aircraft in the air that they too might be at risk." From: "American Airlines could have saved that flight; instead they tried to keep the hijackings secret. What you won't see in *Flight 93*, the film," by James Ridgeway, counterpunch.com, 28 April 2006.

CHAPTER 2

1. USA Today, 5 November 2001.
2. Reuters, 9/13/01.
3. "FBI does not rule out shootdown of Penn. airplane," Reuters, 9/13/01
4. CNN transcript, NTSB Chairman Jim Hall Opens TWA Flight 800 Final Report Review, aired 22 August 2000.
5. 9/11 Commission Report, p. 15ff.
6. Longman, Jere: op. cit.
7. 9/11 Comission Report, p. 30. This and the following paragraphs draw on David Ray Griffin's essay
'Flights 11, 175, 77, and 93: The 9/11 Commission's incredible tales," 4 December 2005.
8. 9/11 Commission Report, p. 29.
9. Some short passages here are excerpted verbatim from David Ray Griffin's essay
'Flights 11, 175, 77, and 93: The 9/11 Commission's incredible tales," 4 December 2005.
10. Griffin, D. R., op. cit.
11. America Remembers, MSNBC Dateline, 11 October 2002. Cited in Thompson, Paul: Complete 9/11 Timeline. www.cooperativeresearch.org.
12. (9:36 a.m.): Flight 93 Turns Around, Files a New Flight Plan. Flight 93 files a new flight plan with a final destination of Washington, reverses course and heads toward Washington. [*Pittsburgh Post-Gazette*, 11/28/2001; Longman, 2002; MSNBC, 10/3/2002; *Guardian*, 11/17/2001] Radar shows the plane turning 180 degrees. [CNN, 10/13/2001] The new flight plan schedules the plane to arrive in Washington at 10:28 a.m. [Longman, 2002]. From: Thompson, Paul, op. cit.
13. These and subsequent paragraphs by Gregg Zoroya, USA Today, 11 September 2002.
14. http://www.tomburnettfoundation.org/tomburnett.transcript.html.
15. "Widow of hijack hero breaks ranks to sue United Airlines," by Sarah Baxter, London *Times*, 11 September 2002.
16. 9/11 Comission Report, p. 13.
17. Cited in Thompson, Paul: Complete 9/11 Timeline. www.cooperativeresearch.org. Sources: *Toronto Sun*, 10/16/2001; *Pittsburgh Post-Gazette*, 11/28/2001; ABC News, 10/12/2001; Longman, 2002; MSNBC, 8/30/2002
18. Longman, Jere: op. cit.
19. As long as other interference and safety problems with PEDs can be overcome. See IEEE Spectrum Online, March 2006: http://www.spectrum.ieee.org/mar06/3069/5. Sadly, the article's research does not differentiate between attempted calls and calls that made a connection.

20. 9/11 Commission Staff Statement No. 17.
21. "The Burnetts," by Gregg Zoroya, USA Today, 9/11/2002.
22. Written and delivered by Rev. Dr. Paul S. Nancarrow, 4 May 2003, St George's Episcopal Church, St Louis Park, Minnesota, "Where Everyone Has a Place at Christ's Table".
23. Sources: EgyptAir voice recorder doesn't change theory of deliberate crash, The EgyptAir Flight 990 cockpit voice recorder, 8 December 1999.
24. Specialist's Factual Report of Investigation, DCA00MA006.
25. "Three-minute discrepancy in tape: Cockpit voice recording ends before Flight 93's official time of impact," by William Bunch, *Philadelphia Daily News*, 16 September 2002.
26. "Flight 93 families bash FBI theory," by Peter Maer, CBS, 8 August 2003.
27. *Philadelphia Daily News*, 16 September 2002.
28. CNN, 7/23/2004.
29. SFGate.com, 4/13/2006.

CHAPTER 3

1. Items 1–5 are according to the FBI's affidavit submitted to Judge David Cohen in Maine, available at http://tinyurl.com/bfsuw. Note that the affidavit refers to the contents of Atta's "bags that *did not make it* onto the flight out of Boston". [Emphasis added.]
2. "Fitting together the puzzle of Osama Bin Laden's network as arrests reach 150," Washington, Associated Press, 5 October 2001, 12:00 p.m. ET.
3. http://www.freerepublic.com/focus/f-news/535850/posts. The "very odd" instruction manual later featured prominently in the demonization of Atta. For example, *Time* led its front-page feature with the following: ". . . Let's poke inside Mohamed Atta's brain the night before he helped slaughter 7,000 people [*sic*]. 'You have to remind yourself to listen and obey that night, for you will face situations that will require your obedience 100 percent,' reads a letter found in Atta's luggage and in the belongings of two other hijackers." *Time* magazine, 8 October 2001.
4. "At least one of the young religious zealots carried a copy of specific handwritten instructions from Mohamed Atta." Beamer, Lisa, op. cit., p. 193.
5. "Unraveling 9-11 Was in the Bags," Newsday (Melville, New York, KRT, via News-Edge Corporation, 18 April 2006, 09:20 a.m. PDT.
6. Robert S. Mueller III, head of the FBI, in a speech to the Commonwealth Club of San Francisco, USA, 19 April 2002.
7. August/September 2001 – According to a detailed 13-page memo written by Minneapolis FBI legal officer Colleen Rowley, FBI headquarters ignores urgent, direct warnings from French intelligence services about pending attacks. In addition, a single Supervisory Special Agent (SSA) in Washington expends extra effort to thwart the field office's investigation of Zacarias Moussaoui, in one case rewriting Rowley's affidavit for a search warrant to search Moussaoui's laptop. Rowley's memo uses terms like "deliberately sabotage", "block", "integrity", "omitted", "downplayed", "glossed over", "mis-characterize", "improper political reasons", "deliberately thwarting", "deliberately further undercut", "suppressed", and "not completely honest". These are not terms describing negligent acts but rather, deliberate acts. FBI field agents desperately attempt to get

action, but to no avail. One agent speculates that Bin Laden might be planning to crash airliners into the WTC, while Rowley ironically noted that the SSA who had committed these deliberate actions had actually been promoted after11 September. Source: Associated Press, 21 May 2002.

8. Once the official conspiracy theory had been established in the mass media, those same manipulators working behind the scenes may have felt that the superfluous uniforms strategy needed jettisoning. On the first anniversary of the events, a report duly appeared on the suspect WorldNetDaily, ridiculing the uniform reports. In a report datelined Washington (quoted above), WorldNetDaily wrote: "The clothing found in one of hijacking ringleader [*sic*] Mohamed Atta's bags wasn't a pilots' [*sic*] uniform, as first reported, but his paradise wedding suit, says an [unnamed] American Airlines employee who was with authorities when they first opened his luggage."

"Alongside the navy suit – which was eerily laid out as if Atta were in it, with a sapphire-blue necktie looped under a crisp dress-shirt collar and neatly knotted– was a bottle of cologne. At the foot of the bag, which had been locked, was a fancy leather-bound Koran painted gold. 'It was like opening a casket,' the [unnamed] American employee said in an exclusive WorldNetDaily interview." The report continued: "The clothing found in Atta's bag has previously been described as a pilots' uniform. But there were no markings or any other signs that indicated so, the [unnamed] American employee says. 'It was a suit,' he said. 'It was not a pilot's uniform.'"

Sadly, this so-called paradise wedding outfit was never mentioned in the FBI affidavit, and neither were uniforms. We are evidently reading racist propaganda.

Besides trying to cancel the phoney-uniforms reports using an unnamed source, the story tried to clear up the baggage check-in anomaly. "Atta was forced to check his two larger bags, described as soft-sided with roller boards, because the 19-seat commuter plane he flew to Boston allows passengers just one carry-on bag each, says a US Airways Express [i.e. Colgan] employee who works at the ticket counter where Atta checked in." (Are they ostensibly quoting Tuohey, whom the FBI was helping to avoid publicity at the time?)

"Atta intended to carry on all three of the bags he initially brought with him to Portland International Jetport in Maine earlier that morning, [unnamed] sources there say."

WorldNetDaily's attempt to alter the 9/11 record on the baggage is interesting because it addresses the baggage issue without explaining, or even addressing, Atta's mysterious connecting flight. If Atta, the slick, controlled, and ruthless professional, cherished an unrealistic wish to carry on two full-sized suitcases at Portland, in order to take them with him to his death, why did he fly to Boston from Portland, and not embark directly at Boston? Clearly, he had to remain situated in Portland so that the opening of the incriminating baggage remained plausible.

WorldNetDaily's ridicule of the planted reports of uniforms being discovered in the baggage is not even accurate. Compare the original disinformation. The *Boston* Globe reported on 18 September 2001 that "an FBI report first obtained by *Der Spiegel* shows that when agents went through one of Atta's bags, which did not make the transfer from a connecting flight from Portland, Maine, they found airline uniforms". Note the plural. It is not one suit that is supposedly being mistaken for an airline uniform, but at least two.

The *Globe*'s disinformation continued: ıInvestigators are trying to determine if Atta or any of his associates used the uniforms to gain access to areas of Logan Airport that would normally be secure, sources said. They are also trying to determine if the uniforms were connected to a break-in last April at the Hotel Nazionale in central Rome, in which two American Airlines pilots said they were robbed of their uniforms, badges, and airport access badges."

9. 9/11 Commission Report, p. 1, Note 1.

10. See Bakan, Joel, *The Corporation: The Pathological Pursuit of Profit and Power*, Free Press, New York, 1 March 2005.

11. See FBI affidavit at http://tinyurl.com/bfsuw.

12. "Bin Laden Prime Suspect in Attacks," by George Gedda, Associated Press, 9/11/ 2001.

13. Neil MacKay, Glasgow *Sunday Herald*, on 16 September.

14. PENTTBOM data: Kean evidence, 16 June 2004. Mystery investigation: Chap. 1, Note 1 cites Michael Tuohey interview of 27 May 2004 and Tom Kinton interview of 6 November 2003, and also the Portland International Jetport site visit on 18 August 2003, but no mention of FBI investigation files.

15. "Portland police interviewed two employees at the Portland Public Library who are sure they saw Atta on several occasions. Spruce Whited, head of security at the library, said he first saw a man he is convinced was Atta in April 2000 [before Atta's supposed arrival in the USA, according to the FBI timeline]. He said the man came to the library several times, using the computers. 'I only recognized him [presumably from the FBI photo graph] because he'd been here a few times,' he said." Kathy Barry, a reference librarian, also reported seeing Atta. But the FBI apparently was not interested. "Whited said no investigators have asked to look at the library's computers (. . .) He said the FBI had not interviewed him." In spite of Whited's concerns, AP reported on 20 September, 2001, that "Police Chief Michael Chitwood said based on what authorities know, the men 'have no long-term connection nor have they been in Maine prior to this'." *Portland Press Herald*, 10/5/01, sourced at Group8+.

16. *Newsday*, 30 September 2001.

17. "Airline ticket agent recalls Atta on 9/11," AP, 7 March 2005. http://www.foxnews.com/story/0,2933,149635,00.html.

18. 9/11 Commission's Note 91 on p. 532.; also p. 451.

19. Published on the Reuters intranet on 22 June 2004; emphasis added.

20. FBI says, "No hard evidence connecting Bin Laden to 9/11." http://www.teamliberty.net/id267.html.

21. In a 2006 story published in *Newsday* and written by an op-ed columnist who was also the author of a history of the US Secret Service, this appeared:

The report did not say how many bags were checked in Portland, nor did it differentiate them by their contents. But three commission staff members who helped prepare the report said there were two pieces. Two staff members, John Raidt and R. William Johnstone, said it was clear both bags belonged to Atta. "He plopped both of them down on the luggage rack," Raidt said. "Alomari just stood by." from: "Unraveling 9-11 was in the bags. Luggage that didn't get put on hijacked jet provided information about terrorists, say former investigators," by Michael Dorman, *Newsday*, 17 April 2006.

22. Susan Ginzburg, Commission senior counsel, testified on 26 January 2004 that a "passport was recovered from luggage that did not make it from a Portland flight to

Boston on to the connecting flight which was American Airlines flight 11. This is the passport of Abdul Aziz al Omari".

23. See affidavits at: http://www.cooperativeresearch.org/timeline/images/fbi.10.jpg.

24. "Hundreds of investigators descended on Logan International Airport on Tuesday trying to determine how terrorists commandeered two nearly identical jetliners... More than 150 state police detectives joined FBI and other federal investigators at Logan, said State Police Lt. Paul Maloney. He and other officials refused to discuss details of the investigation." From: "Massport: Logan chosen by terrorists for proximity," by Justin Pope and Denise Lavoie, Associated Press, 7:30 p.m., 09/11/01.

25. "Unraveling 9-11 was in the bags. Luggage that didn't get put on hijacked jet provided information about terrorists, say former investigators," by Michael Dorman, *Newsday*, 17 April 2006.

26. Ginzburg's evidence, cited above.

27. Calvin Woodward, Associated Press, 11 September 2002.

28. AP, 05.10.01, *Sydney Morning Herald*, 15.09.01, *Boston Globe*, 18.09.01.

29. Here are the words of James K. Lechner, FBI agent, in his affidavit seeking permission from Judge David M. Cohen to examine Atta's rental car: "Subsequent to the departure of AA11, American Airlines personnel at Logan discovered two bags that had been bound for transfer to AA11 but had not been loaded onto the flight prior to its departure. These two bags, a green TravelGear bag bearing American Airlines tag number US138530 and a black Travelpro bag bearing American Airlines number US138259, were checked to passenger Atta. These two bags were checked on 11 September 2001 at Portland, Maine, and were marked to be transferred at Logan from an inbound flight from Portland to AA11 ... On September 11, 2001, Unites States Magistrate Judge Lawrence P. Cohen of the United States District Court for the District of Massachussetts issued a warrant authorizing a search of the two bags."

30. 9/11 Commission Report, p. 1.

31. "Unraveling 9-11 was in the bags. Luggage that didn't get put on hijacked jet provided information about terrorists, say former investigators," by Michael Dorman, *Newsday*, 17 April 2006.

32. Find them here: http://www.fbi.gov/pressrel/pressrel01/100401picts.htm.

33. *New Yorker*, 10/01/01.

34. "Seven minutes later, Atta apparently took a call from Marwan Al Shehhi, a longtime colleague, who was at another terminal at Logan Airport. They spoke for three minutes Between 6:45 and 7:40, [the men] checked in and boarded Flight 11, bound for Los Angeles. The flight was scheduled to depart at 7:45" the 9/11 Commission reported. Note that he "apparently" took a call from Shehhi. This was a significant assumption made on the very first page of the Commission's thick report. No available photographic evidence put Shehhi at the airport or anywhere else in Boston. Source: 9/11 Commission Report, pp. 1–2.

35. http://www.fas.org/irp/congress/2002.hr/092602mueller.html.

36. ibid.

37. http://www.fas.org/irp/congress/2002.hr/092602mueller.html.

38. e.g. AFP, 9/22/01, Berliner Zeitung, 9/24/01

39. *Berliner Zeitung*, ibid.

40. "A secret Pentagon unit had Mohammed Atta, the 9/11 ringleader, in its crosshairs 13 times before the 2001 attacks, a US congressman has claimed citing the unit's records.

"Curt Weldon, a Republican representative, said on Tuesday data produced by the US military intelligence unit code-named Able Danger showed Atta's name 13 times.

"The unit used data mining to investigate the al-Qaida network.

Weldon said: 'Thirteen times we have hits in the data that's still available, that we were told was destroyed.'

"Weldon cited recent analyses of data gathered by Able Danger before the 2001 attacks on New York and Washington.

"Two military officers – an active-duty captain in the Navy and a lieutenant colonel in the Army Reserve – have recently said publicly that they were involved with Able Danger and that the program's analysts identified Mohamed Atta, the Egyptian-born ringleader of the Sept. 11 attacks, by name as a potential terrorist by early 2000.

"They said they tried to share the information with the Federal Bureau of Investigation in the summer of 2000, more than a year before the attacks, but were blocked by Defense Department lawyers. FBI officials, who answer to the jurisdiction of Mr. Specter's committee, have confirmed that the Defense Department abruptly canceled meetings in 2000 between the bureau's Washington field office and representatives of the Able Danger team.

"The Pentagon had said that it interviewed three other people who were involved with Able Danger and who said that they, too, recalled the identification of Mr. Atta as a terrorist suspect. Mr. Specter said his staff had talked to all five of the potential witnesses and found that 'credibility has been established' for all of them. Source: "Pentagon bars military officers and analysts from testifying," by Philip Shenon, Washington, *New York Times*, 30 September 2005.

41. June 3: Atta arrives in Newark, New Jersey aboard a Czech Airlines flight from Prague with a six-month tourist visa for the US. He has shaved off his beard, has begun to wear western-style clothing again and appears to have a large amount of money at his disposal.

http://www.abc.net.au/4corners/atta/maps/timeline.htm.

42. Two military officers – an active-duty captain in the Navy and a lieutenant colonel in the Army Reserve – have recently said publicly that they were involved with Able Danger and that the program's analysts identified Mohamed Atta, the Egyptian-born ringleader of the Sept. 11 attacks, by name as a potential terrorist by early 2000. . . The Pentagon had said that it interviewed three other people who were involved with Able Danger and who said that they, too, recalled the identification of Mr. Atta as a terrorist suspect. Mr. Specter said his staff had talked to all five of the potential witnesses and found that 'credibility has been established' for all of them. Source: "Pentagon bars military officers and analysts from testifying," by Philip Shenon, Washington, *New York Times*, 20 September 2005.

43. http://www.informationclearinghouse.info/article7545.htm.

44. *The Hamburg Cell*, 2004.

45. See www.MadCowprod.com. All these have appeared in the mainstream mass media, as well as in the much better realized material of such sunbelt stars as Daniel Hopsicker of Miami and Mark Howell, of Key West fame. The latter provide fascinating reading from a zone where knowledge of the criminal milieu is vital for everyday life.

46. Word seems to have gone around about the bombing connection. Here it appears as a bus bombing in Israel. "Atta, who has been linked by international intelligence authorities to a bus bombing in Israel, was on a US government terrorist 'watchlist'. . . and was listed as an accoicate [*sic*] of Osama bin Laden's al-Qaida organization." Source: "Atta's trail of terror passed through Las Vegas," by John L. Smith, Thursday, 20 September 2001, *Las Vegas Review-Journal* http://www.reviewjournal.com/lvrj_home/2001/Sep-20-Thu-2001/news/17037273.html.

47. Wikipedia is the online encyclopedia that publishes user-edited entries.

48. *Respekt*, 10 November 2003.

49. "As the FBI's investigation has developed, Atta's shrouded pattern of activity has emerged. He was in almost constant movement in the weeks leading up to Sept. 11. On Aug. 6 Atta rented the first of three cars and drove 3,204 miles. In a final automobile trip, which ended Sept. 9, Atta logged more than 1,000 miles. He was one of 13 suspected terrorists who received Florida driver's licenses since May 1." Source: "Atta's trail of terror passed through Las Vegas," John L. Smith, Thursday, 20 September 20 2001, *Las Vegas Review-Journal*.

50. *Newsday*, 11/18/01.

51. Noted in Michael Moore's *Fahrenheit 911*.

52. Beamer, Lisa: op. cit.

53. "There is no scientific proof that anyone was dead prior to the crash," he said. By David Jones, *Daily Mail*, 27 July 2002.

54. "Flight 93: Forty lives, one destiny," Dennis B. Roddy, Cindi Lash, Steve Levin and Jonathan D. Silver, *Pittsburgh Post-Gazette*, 28 October 2001.

55. Quoted on AviationExplorer.com.

56. FBI report: "Knives found at the UA Flight 93 crash site," undated.

57. 9/11 Commission, Staff Statement 17.

58. http://www.fromthewilderness.com/free/ww3/011805_simplify_case.shtml.

59. Ruppert, Michael C., *Crossing the Rubicon*. Gabriola Island, Canada, 2004. Ruppert's secret service monitoring FAA screens assertion is not referenced.

60. Trillion in the US is one million million.

61. "More money for the Pentagon," CBS News Correspondent Vince Gonzales reports, while its own auditors admit the military cannot account for 25 percent of what it spends.

"'According to some estimates we cannot track $2.3 trillion in transactions,' Rumsfeld admitted." Source: "The war on waste," CBS Evening News, Los Angeles, 29 January 2002.

62. Operation Northwoods, ostensibly discovered by James Bamford. Well publicized and available on any search engine. It described a scenario remarkably similar to the events of 9/11, as a means of triggering war with Cuba. The plan has been described as a hoax planted by a foreign power wishing to point the finger of blame at the Pentagon. See: "Operation Northwoods: The counterfeit," by Carol Valentine, October 2001.

63. *Washington Business Journal*, 11 September 2001, by Taylor Lincoln, *Potomac Tech Journal*.

64. http://cjonline.com/stories/091301/ter_heropassengers.shtml.

65. http://www.sentel.com/html/presidentsmessage.html.

66. "Also by this time, 'everyone' in the United Airlines crisis center 'now knew that a flight attendant on board had called the mechanics desk to report that one hijacker had a bomb strapped on and another was holding a knife on the crew'." *Wall Street Journal*, 10/15/01.

67. According to the Barbara Olson call, the pilot of Flight 77 was not killed either.

68. Interview with Jama Jarrah, CBC *Fifth Estate*, 10 October 2001.

69. For another detailed description of the alleged hijackers besides that published by the 9/11 Commission, see McDermott, Terry, *Perfect Soldiers, The 9/11 Hijackers: Who They Were, Why They Did It*, New York, 2005. For suicide bomber phenomenon, see: *Suicide Bombers: Allah's New Martyrs* by Farhad Khosrokhavar, *Making Sense of Suicide Missions* by Diego Gambetta, *Osama: The Making of a Terrorist* by Jonathan Randal, *Masterminds of Terror: The Truth Behind the Most Devastating Attack the World Has Ever Seen* by Nick Fielding, *Suicide Terrorism* by Ami Pedahzur.

70. Ibid., note 53.

71. 9/11 Commission Report, Chapter 7, Note 190.

72. "Suicide hijacker's phone call to girlfriend, Jarrah called his girlfriend on 11 September," by Rob Broomby, BBC correspondent in Berlin, Tuesday, 19 November, 2002.

73. OTTAWA – "Some of Pierre Trudeau's closest friends were not aware of the extent of the former prime minister's involvement in a fascist-type secret organization in the 1940s until the publication of a book this week, but his participation was a reflection of the dominant intellectual currents in Quebec Roman Catholic circles at the time. Closest friends surprised by Trudeau revelations." By Hugh Winsor, Special to the *Globe and Mail*, Saturday, 8 April 2006.

74. By Sheila MacVicar and Caroline Faraj, 1 August 2002, CNN.

75. 9/11 Commission Report in Note 19 Chapter 1 cites: UAL record, Flight 93 EWR bag loading status, Sept. 11, 2001; UAL record, Flight 93 EWR [Newark code] ACI [Airports Council International] passenger history, Sept. 11, 2001; UAL record, Flight 93 EWR full bag history, Sept. 11, 2001; TSA report, "Selectee Status of September 11th Hijackers," undated; FBI report, "The Final 24 Hours," 8 December 2003.

76. "Certain al Qaeda members were charged with organising passport collection scemes to keep the pipeline of fraudulent documents flowing. To this end, al Qaeda required jihadists to turn in their passports before going to the front lines in Afghanistan. If they were killed, their passports were recycled for use. The operational mission training course taught operatives how to forge documents. Certain passport alteration methods, which included susbtituting photos and erasing and adding travel cachets, were also taught. Manuals demonstrating the technique for 'cleaning' visas were reportedly circulated among operatives. Mohamed Atta and Zakariya Essabar were reported to have been trained in passport alteration." 9/11 Commission Report, p. 169.

77. "Airports screened nine of Sept. 11 hijackers, officials say," by Dan Eggen, *Washington Post*, Saturday, 2 March 2002; Page A11 Link http://www.washingtonpost.com/wp-dyn/articles/A26149-2002Mar1.html.

78. "Hijack plotters used S. Florida as a cradle for conspiracy," by Andres Viglucci & Manny Garcia, , *Miami Herald*,15 September 2001.

79. Kean report, p. 95.

80. "Armed Forces DNA Indentification Laboratory personnel were crucial in identifying victims." From the definition of the Armed Forces Medical Examiners (AMFE) at the Pentagon's medical division at Walter Reed Army Medical Center in northern Washington, DC. The AFME are responsible for determing the cause and manner of death of members of the Armed Forces on active duty. The AFME is also responsible for identify-

ing bodies of military personnel. Sourced from the WebFairy: http://history.amedd.army.mil/memoirs/soldiers/afme.pdf.

81. By Daniel Sieberg, CNN, 21 September 2001. http://edition.cnn.com/2001/US/09/21/inv.id.theft/.

82. Robert S. Mueller III, head of the FBI, in a speech to the Commonwealth Club of San Francisco USA, 19 April 2002.

83. "Binalshibh was captured in Pakistan on September 11, 2002, after a gunbattle in Karachi. He was subsequently turned over to the United States, which is holding him in an unknown location." www.wikipedia.com. Also: http://news.bbc.co.uk/2/hi/south.asia/2257456.stm.

84. This phrase is used in echo of the President's bad-taste witticism when informed that a plane had hit the WTC fourteen minutes earlier: "That's some bad pilot." http://www.commondreams.org/headlines03/0822-05.htm.

85. An inscribed plinth found by French invaders in Egypt that allowed scholars to decrypt ancient Egyptian hieroglyphics.

86. "Unraveling 9-11 was in the bags, Luggage that didn't get put on hijacked jet provided information about terrorists, say former investigators," by Michael Dorman, *Newsday* 17 April 2006.

87. Discovered by Allan Wood, a researcher associated with Paul Thompson's 9/11 Time-line project. CNN BREAKING NEWS America Under Attack: List of Names of 18 Suspected Hijackers Aired September 14, 2001 – 10:11 ET http://transcripts.cnn.com/TRANSCRIPTS/0109/14/bn.01.html.

88. "Federal Aviation Administration records show [Hanjour] obtained a commercial pilot's license in April 1999, but how and where he did so remains a lingering question that FAA officials refuse to discuss." http://www.whatreallyhappened.com/hanjour.html

89. http://xymphora.blogspot.com/2005/06/mosear-caned.html.

90. Report: "108 died in US custody" (AP). At least 108 people have died in American custody in Iraq and Afghanistan, most of them violently, according to government data provided to the Associated Press. Roughly a quarter of those deaths have been investigated as possible abuse by US. personnel. CBS News, Washington, 16 March 2005.

91. Wikipedia, Said Bahaji

92. Longman, Jere, *Among the Heroes*, New York, 2002. Longman's book is selling poorly on Amazon (#362,867), obviously another coincidence.

93. Longman, Jere, op. cit. confirmed by the 9/11 Commission Report.

94. But don't these inconsistencies prove that the phone calls were genuine? Not necessarily, because the original script might have involved three hijackers, for reasons unknown.

95. "Military plays up role of Zarqawi, Jordanian painted as foreign threat to Iraq's stability," by Thomas E. Ricks, *Washington Post*, 10 April 2006.

96. "Jarrah also appears to have projected a friendly, engaging personality while in the United States. Here he is, hair frosted, proudly displaying the pilot certificate he received during his flight training in Florida. Yet this is the same person who only a year earlier had journeyed from Hamburg to Afghanistan and pledged to become one of bin Ladin's suicide operatives." American Radio Works, public radio.

97. *Los Angeles Times*, 10/23/01; *Boston Globe*, 9/25/01.

98. Longman, Jere, op. cit., pp. 101–2

99. Longman, op. cit.

100. CNN, 8/1/02; *Chicago Tribune*, 12/13/01; CNN, 8/1/02; CNN, 8/1/02.

101. 2002 Federal Trade Commission Study press release.

102. www.myidfix.com.

103. "Hijack suspect lived a life, or a lie," by Elizabeth Neuffer, *Globe*, 9/25/2001.

104. "Hijacking suspect's family claims mistaken identity," CNN, 18 September 2001.

105. "Aysel Senguen saw her fiance fall into radical Islam. She knew something was wrong but had no idea what lay ahead," by Dirk Laabs and Terry McDermott, *Los Angeles Times*, 27 January 2003.

106. "German, Afghan links to suspect," CNN, 16 September 2001. 9/11 Commission Report, Chapter 7, Note 190.

107. Wikipedia: Ziad Jarrah

108. 9/11 Commission Report, p. 163. The Jarrah case resembles that of M. S. Kahn, the accused London 07/07 suicide bomber, who supposedly had a similar sudden Islamic transformation. For the official version, see:
http://www.officialconfusion.com/77/themen/menpre77/
110306independentKhanLEAfile.html;
for the unofficial one, see:
http://team8plus.org/e107_plugins/forum/forum.viewtopic.php?2684.last.

109. "Hijack plotters used S. Florida as a cradle for conspiracy," by Andres Viglucci and Manny Garcia, *Miami Herald*, 15 September 2001.

110. 9/11 Commission Report, p. 235.

111. "Five terrorists visited LV, Men made total of six trips between May, August," *Las Vegas Review-Journal*, 28 September 2001.

112. Atta-number-two was seen on board one of the offshore casino ships owned by convicted DC lobbyist and racketeer Jack Abramoff. See: works of Daniel Hopsicker at www.madcowprod.com.

113. September 11 hijacker questioned in January 2001. Sources: "CIA was interested in his travels in Afghanistan," by Sheila MacVicar and Caroline Faraj (CNN's Mike Boettcher, Dana Bash, and Elise Labott contributed), 1 August 2002. Posted: 8:24 p.m. EDT (00:24 GMT).

114. This makes the official claim that Atta drove thousands of miles in his last month so hard to explain.

115. www.answers.com: entry for Ziad Jarrah.

116. "Authorities would not say whether the Las Vegas visits of Jarrah and al-Shehhi overlapped. Each is thought to have departed within days of their arrival." *Las Vegas Review-Journal*, 26 September 2001.

117. Associated Press, 20 September 2001.

118. *Sydney Morning Herald*, 1 May 2002.

CHAPTER 4

1. It would be interesting to know which aircraft took this picture, showing as it does no rescue services in attendance and no local curiosity-seekers.

2. "We all know the inspiring story of Flight 93, of the heroic passengers who forced the hijacked plane to the ground, sacrificing themselves to save the lives of others. The only trouble is: it may simply not be true." John Carlin reports from Shanksville, Pennsylvania. Independent.co.uk, 13 August 2002.

3. 9/11 Commission Report, p. 14. (It's an odd idea that the attack could have continued while the plane was upside down.)

4. 9/13/02.

5. Longman, Jere, op. cit.

6. http://edition.cnn.com/2006/LAW/04/12/moussaoui.trial/index.html.

7. "Also by this time, 'everyone' in the United Airlines crisis center 'now knew that a flight attendant on board had called the mechanics desk to report that one hijacker had a bomb strapped on and another was holding a knife on the crew'." *Wall Street Journal*, 10/15/01.

8. "Flight 93 calls aired in court: At Moussaoui trial, voices of passengers, attendants show confusion, fatalism," by Richard Serrano, *Los Angeles Times*, 12 April 2006.

9. Furthermore, in the wake of the disaster, Mrs. Burnett's younger sister spoke on her behalf, thus giving third-hand hearsay. "...Burnett's younger sister, Mary Margaret Burnett, 32, said from their parents' home in Minnesota." Source: "Reports of resistance to terrorists on flight emerge," by Steve Mills and Andrew Martin, *Chicago Tribune*, 13 September 2001.

10. *Los Angeles Times*, ibid.

11. *Los Angeles Times*, ibid.

12. www.StandDown.net, "Exposing NORAD's wag: The 911 window dressing tale," by Mark R. Elsis, Lovearth.net, 8 January 2003.

13. Libyans were convicted for this bombing, but controversy still surrounds the event. Flight PA 103 took off from Heathrow at 18:25 on 21 December 1988 bound for New York. At 19:03 radio contact with the aircraft was lost.

14. In a 2004 Christmas Eve address to US troops in Baghdad, Rumsfeld referred to the "the people who attacked the United States in New York, shot down the plane over Pennsylvania." http://www.cnn.com/2004/US/12/27/rumsfeld.flt93/.

15. Laura Temyer of Hooversville: "I didn't see the plane but I heard the plane's engine. Then I heard a loud thump that echoed off the hills and then I heard the plane's engine. I heard two more loud thumps and didn't hear the plane's engine anymore after that." (*She insists that people she knows in state law enforcement have privately told her the plane was shot down*, and that decompression sucked objects from the aircraft, explaining why there was a wide debris field.) [Emphasis added.] *Philadelphia Daily News*, 12/15/2001, cited by Paul Thompson at: www.cooperativeresearch.org.

16. "Today, any aircraft with radio problems is suspect, no problem routine. Fighter jets are scrambled to babysit suspect aircraft or 'unknowns' three or four times a day. Before Sept. 11, that happened twice a week. Last year, there were 425 unknowns – pilots who didn't file or diverted from flight plans or used the wrong frequency. Jets were scrambled 129 times." by Linda Slobodian, *Calgary Herald*, 13 October 2001.

17. *San Jose Mercury News*, 12 September 2001, Wednesday, Domestic News section.

18. http://911research.wtc7.net/cache/disinfo/deceptions/cnn.blackbox93.html.

19. "Black box recovered at Shanksville site," by Richard Gazarik and Robin Acton, *Pittsburgh Tribune Review*, 14 September 2001.

20. *Tribune Review*, ibid.
21. "If the aircraft has come down vertically with relatively low energy, the wreckage will be contained in a relatively small area, dependent on the size of the aircraft, of course." David F. King, a Principal Inspector at England's Air Accidents Investigation Branch in Farnborough, Hampshire, and an air-crash expert for the past thirty years, interviewed by PBS-TV's Nova programme.
22. "Felt reaches 911 just before crash," by Richard Gazarik, *Pittsburgh Tribune Review*, Sunday, 8 September 2002. This legend-puffing story fails to mention that Felt reported signs of an explosion.
23. "Investigators *believe* this was Edward Felt, the only passenger not accounted for on phone calls." Longman, Jere, op. cit. [Emphasis added.]
24. Paul Thompson has compiled the full references for this officially suppressed detail on his website www.cooperativeresearch.org. In outline they are: Associated Press, 10/12/2001; ABC News, 10/11/2001; ABC News, 10/11/2001.
25. Longman, Jere, op. cit.
26. *Daily Mirror*, ibid.
27. "Lee Purbaugh, 32, working just his second day at Rollock Inc." also "A handful of people working near or driving through a rural area of Somerset County watched as the plane flipped over and disappeared,". The crash in Somerset: "It dropped out of the clouds," *Pittsburgh Post-Gazette*, Wednesday, 12 September 2001. This story is based on the reporting of staff writers Bob Batz, Tom Gibb, Monica L. Haynes, Ernie Hoffman, Ginny Kopas, Cindi Lash, and James O'Toole.
28. The *Independent*, 13 August 2002.
29. Various officials claim credit for the order, from the Transportation secretary right down to the man on the spot in the command center. www.StandDown.net, "Exposing NORAD's wag: The 911 window dressing tale," by Mark R. Elsis, Lovearth.net, 8 January 2003.
30. WTAE-TV: The Pittsburgh channel, "Pilot witnesses Flight 93's final moments, Pilot's widow seeks answers." POSTED: 3:49 p.m. EDT, 19 September 2001.
31. A Korean Airline 747 was hit by two Russian missiles in 1983, yet continued to fly for two more minutes. Korean Air, 10/1/1983, cited by Paul Thompson in 9/11 Timeline, www.cooperativeresearch.org.
32. Thompson, Paul, op. cit.
33. Griffin, David Ray, "The new Pearl Harbor: Disturbing questions about the Bush administration and 9/11 chapter," New York, 2004. Chapter 3, pp. 49–55.
34. Independent 9/11 researchers collated this data. All the sources are given by John Doe on Democratic Underground at: http://www.democraticunderground.com/discuss/duboard.php?az=view_all address=125x28985.
35. 9/11 Commission Report, p. 25.
36. Thompson, Paul, op. cit. The timeline gives loads of mass-media sources for this.
37. http://www.cooperativeresearch.org/context.jsp?item=a1006treetop.
38. Cheney: Bush OK'd shootdown of rogue planes WASHINGTON (CNN) – In the moments after it became apparent that the United States was under attack Tuesday, President Bush authorized the military to shoot down any unauthorized civilian aircraft that might have been heading toward the White House or the Capitol, Vice President

Dick Cheney said Sunday. "We decided to do it," Cheney declared on NBC's "Meet the Press", 16 September 2001 Posted: 11:42 a.m. EDT (15:42 GMT).

39. In spring, 2002, earth scientists Won-Young Kim and G. R. Baum published "Seismic observations during September 11, 2001, terrorist attack" in a report to the Maryland Department of Natural Resources. They established the time of the crash at 10:06:05, give or take five seconds. Their conclusion was based on the analysis of the seismic records from four seismic recording stations ranging from 92 to 217 miles away.

40. *Philadelphia Daily News* (9/16/02) [Reprinted at: newsmine.org].

41. 9/11 Commission, Note 168, p. 462.

42. *Philadelphia Daily News* (9/16/02) [Reprinted at: newsmine.org].

43. http://www.tmcnet.com/usubmit/2006/04/16/1576037.htm.

44. http://www.cbsnews.com/stories/2006/04/13/ap/national/main-D8GVB5POG.shtml.

45. All times calculated from the 9/11 Commission Report, pp. 32–33.

46. Gen. Erberhard was promoted after 9/11, and now runs Northcom, the USA's first-ever domestic military command.

47. 9/11 Commission Report, Chapter 1, Note 116.

48. Moussaoui stands by 9/11 attacks, BBC News online, 13 April 2006.

49. "Defence lawyers say Moussaoui's life should be spared because of his limited role in the attacks, evidence of mental illness, and because his execution would only fulfil his dream of martyrdom." BBC News online, 13 April 2006.

50. Bush wants to build lots more, and build them around the world. "I think we ought to start building nuclear power plants again. I think it makes sense to do so. Technology is such that we can do so and say to the American people, these are safe...We're also going to work with other nations to help them build nuclear power industries." Bush, 20 February 2006 at Johnson Controls, lithium battery makers.

51. In his 1999 book *Downfall*, historian Richard Frank analysed the many widely varying estimates of casualties caused by the bombings. He concluded "The best approximation is that the number is huge and falls between 100,000 and 200,000." Most of the casualties were civilians.

52. E.g. "The coordinated assault on New York and Washington caught the United States completely off guard. Focused largely on guarding against bombing threats to overseas targets, US authorities concede they were ill-prepared for hijacked jetliners purposely crashed on American soil." From a collection of contemporary reports at: http://www.emergency.com/2001/11sep01-terror1.htm.

53. "In his testimony, [Richard A.] Clarke [head of the Counterterrorism Security Group] commented that he thought that warning about the possibility of a suicide hijacking would have been just one more speculative theory among many, hard to spot since the volume of warning of 'al Qaeda threats and other terrorist threats, was in the tens of thousands – probably hundreds of thousands'." 9/11 Commission Report p. 345.

54. "There were only 33 armed and trained federal air marshals as of 9/11. They were not deployed on US domestic flights, except when in transit to provide security on international departures. This policy reflected the FAA's view that domestic hijacking was in check – a view held confidently as no terrorist had hijacked a US commercial aircraft anywhere in the world since 1986." 9/11 Commission Report, p. 85.

55. September 11, 2001: Israeli Special-Ops Passenger Shot or Stabbed by Hijackers? An FAA memo written on the evening of 9/11, and later leaked, suggests that a man on Flight 11 was shot and killed by a gun before the plane crashed into the WTC. The "Executive Summary," based on information relayed by a flight attendant to the American Airlines Operation Center, stated "that a passenger located in seat 10B [Satam Al Suqami] shot and killed a passenger in seat 9B [Daniel Lewin] at 9:20 a.m." (Note that since Flight 11 crashed at 8:46, the time must be a typo, probably meaning 8:20). A report in Israeli newspaper Ha'aretz on September 17 identifies Lewin as a former member of the Israel Defense Force Sayeret Matkal, Israel's most successful special-operations unit. [United Press International, 4/6/2002] Sayeret Matkal is a deep-penetration unit that has been involved in assassinations, the theft of foreign signals-intelligence materials, and the theft and destruction of foreign nuclear weaponry. Sayeret Matkal is best known for the 1976 rescue of 106 passengers at Entebbe Airport in Uganda. [*New Yorker*, 11/29/2001] Lewin founded Akamai, a successful computer company, and his connections to Sayeret Matkal remained hidden until the gun story became known. [*Guardian*, 10/15/2001] FAA and American Airline officials later deny the gun story and suggest that Lewin was probably stabbed to death instead. [*Washington Post*, 4/2/2002; United Press International, 4/6/2002]. From: www.cooperativeresearch.org

56. (8:21 a.m.): Flight 11 Attendant Ong Phones in Hijack Report, Officials Doubt Validity Betty Ong. [Source: The *Eagle-Tribune*]

Flight 11 attendant Betty Ong calls Vanessa Minter, an American Airlines reservations agent in North Carolina, using a seatback Airfone from the back of the plane. Ong speaks to Minter and an unidentified man for about two minutes. Then supervisor Nydia Gonzalez is patched in to the conference call as well. Ong says, "The cockpit's not answering. Somebody's stabbed in business class and ... I think there's mace ... that we can't breathe. I don't know, I think we're getting hijacked." A minute later, she continues, "And the cockpit is not answering their phone. And there's somebody stabbed in business class. And there's ... we can't breathe in business class. Somebody's got mace or something ... I'm sitting in the back. Somebody's coming back from business. If you can hold on for one second, they're coming back." As this quote shows, other flight attendants relay information from the front of the airplane to Ong sitting in the back, and she periodically waits for updates. She goes on, "I think the guys are up there [in the cockpit]. They might have gone there – jammed the way up there, or something. Nobody can call the cockpit. We can't even get inside." The first four and a half minutes of the call is later played in a public 9/11 Commission hearing. Ong apparently continues speaking to Gonzalez and Minter until the plane crashes. [9/11 Commission, 2/27/2004; *New York Observer*, 3/11/2004] 9/11 Commissioner Bob Kerrey, who has heard more recordings than have been made public, says that some officials on the ground greet her account sceptically: "They did not believe her. They said, 'Are you sure?' They asked her to confirm that it wasn't air-rage. Our people on the ground were not prepared for a hijacking." [*New York Times*, 5/18/2004 Sources: Bob Kerrey]
From Paul Thompson's 9/11 Timeline. www.cooperativeresearch.org.

57. Again, the 9/11 Commission cites evidence that the Commission itself found inexplicable, i.e. Atta's baggage from the unexplained Portland connecting flight. "Reports included the presence of mace and/or pepper spray in the cabin, and indications that passengers had difficulty brathing. We believe this indicates that the terrorists created a

"sterile" area around the cockpit by isolating the passengers and attempting to keep them away from the forward cabin, in part, by using mace or pepper spray. Pepper spray was found in Atta's checked luggage that was recovered at Logan Airport." 9/11 Commission, Staff Statement 4.

58. "While training at al Qaeda camps, a dozen of [the Saudis] heard Bin Ladin's speeches, volunteered to become suicide operative, and eventually were selected as muscle hijackers for the planes operation...After the selection and oath-swearing, the operative would be sent to KSM for training and the filming of a martyrdom video, a function KSM supervised as head of al Qaeda's media committee." 9/11 Commission Report.

59. Operation Northwoods, part of Operation Mongoose, which included a terror campaign on US soil.

http://www.gwu.edu/-nsarchiv/news/20010430/.

60. Cited in Bamford, James, *Body of Secrets*, New York, April 2001, pp. 85–86.

61. Operation Northwoods, p. 11.

http://www.gwu.edu/-nsarchiv/news/20010430/northwoods.pdf.

62. Mr Bush told Mr Blair that the US was so worried about the failure to find hard evidence against Saddam that it thought of "flying U2 reconnaissance aircraft planes with fighter cover over Iraq, painted in UN colours". Mr Bush added: "If Saddam fired on them, he would be in breach [of UN resolutions]." Blair–Bush deal before Iraq war revealed in secret memo, PM promised to be "solidly behind" US invasion with or without UN backing, by Richard Norton-Taylor, The *Guardian*, 3 February 2006.

63. US military planes criss-cross Europe posing as civilian flights, by Jon Swain and Brian Johnson-Thomas, *The Times*, London, 19 February 2006.

64. CNN Washington bureau, 23 September 2001.

http://archives.cnn.com/2001/WORLD/asiapcf/central/09/22/ret.afghan.plane/

65. "When seeing and hearing isn't believing," by William M. Arkin, Special to: washingtonpost.com, Monday, 1 February 1999.

http://www.public-action.com/911/voice-simulation/index.html

66. http://www.voice-security.com/Demo.html.

67. A 1999 research paper describes it:

http://www.beta-research.com/121099abstract.html.

68. For nothing, actually, using Shareware from this website.

http://www.sharewareconnection.com/virtual-personality-.htm

69. Over 100,000 viewers visited this article on one website alone. "Plane swap over Pennsylvania: Flight 93 and his doppelganger," by Woody Box, 16 January 2006.

http://journals.democraticunderground.com/woody%20b

70. Delta 1989's suspected hijacked status was confirmed by military officers in their testimony to the 9/11 Commission, who mention it in their report: "Boston Center immediately began speculating about other aircraft that might be in danger, leading them to worry about a transcontinental flight – Delta 1989 – that in fact was not hijacked. At 9:19, the FAA's New England regional office called Herndon and asked that Cleveland Center advise Delta 1989 to use extra cockpit security." 9/11 Commission Report, Chapter 1 "We have some planes".

71. Victoria Ashley/Jim Hoffman (911research.wtc7.net).

72. "Flight 93 victims' effects to go back to families," by Steve Levin, *Pittsburgh Post-Gazette*, 30 December 2001. MercutioATC, a poster on Democraticunderground.com wrote on January 24th, 2006:
"Investigators yesterday appeared to be initially searching in the immediate area of the plane's impact – a soot-singed crater and a V-shaped gash in the adjacent trees. They have recovered some human remains, pieces of plane seats and seat belts and a few personal items, including check books, clothing and a singed Bible, but said they haven't found anything larger than an ordinary briefcase or telephone book."
http://www.post-gazette.com/headlines/20010913scene0913...
"Miller said he had identified 12 of the victims through dental records and fingerprints. He is refusing to release the names of those victims, saying he does not want to upset their families . . . He said DNA testing would be used to identify the other victims, a process that could take months."
http://www.post-gazette.com/headlines/20010929somerset0...
"Evidence collection teams late Wednesday recovered the first recognizable human remains from the crash of United Airlines Flight 93 in Somerset County."
http://www.pittsburghlive.com/x/search/s.47536.html.
There is no shortage of news articles reporting the discovery of human remains. There were even identifications made using dental records and fingerprints *before* DNA testing was done that identified the remains as having come from UAL93 passengers.
73. Sourced from the WebFairy:
http://history.amedd.army.mil/memoirs/soldiers/afme.pdf.
74. "The airplane headed down, the control wheel was turned hard to the right. The airplane rolled onto its back." 9/11 Commission Report, p. 14.
75. "Hijacked passenger called 911 on cell phone, September 11, 2001." Posted: 11:35 p.m. EDT, Shanksville, Pennsylvania (AP).
76. We checked the authenticity of this report with Lisa Fernandez. Find the text at:
http://www.spring.net/yapp-bin/public/read/porch/86.
Credited as: "Passenger called wife from cell phone shortly before Pittsburgh crash," by Paul Rogers and Lisa Fernandez, Knight Ridder news service (no date). The headline is also listed as a story collected after 9/11 at:
http://www.brothersjudd.com/blog/archives/2004/09/links.from.911.aftermath.1.html.
It is also listed as: *San Jose Mercury News*, 12 September 2001, Wednesday, Domestic News section. Thanks to Nick Kollestrom and G.H. for this reference.
77. The 11:15 a.m. PST arrival time in San Francisco would have occurred at 2:15 p.m. on the East coast. With the crash having been confirmed at about 10:30 EDT in Pennsylvania, and California relatives leaving their homes at, say, 10:15 a.m. PST (1:15 p.m. EDT) to make the rendezvous at San Francisco airport.
78. "UAL Flight 93 landed safely at Cleveland Hopkins Airport, Plane lands in Cleveland – bomb feared aboard," Reported by 9News Staff, Web produced by: Liz Foreman, 9/11/01 11:43:57 a.m.
79. "World's first ray gun shoots down missile," Redondo Beach, www.spacedaily.com, 7 June 2000. The Army's Tactical High Energy Laser Advanced Concept Technology Demonstrator (THEL/ACTD) has successfully demonstrated its ability to detect, track, engage and destroy a Katyusha rocket armed with a live warhead. The rocket in flight was

successfully intercepted and destroyed in field testing at the Army's High Energy Laser Systems Test Facility, White Sands Missile Range, New Mexico.

80. Late 2004 estimate by the UK professional medical journal, The *Lancet*. The Pentagon has said that it does not count numbers of enemy civilian dead. Story link: http://www.cnn.com/2004/WORLD/meast/10/29/iraq.deaths/.

81. "Thwarting skyjackings from the ground: Automated airplane landing systems could bring a hijacked airplane 'home'," by Alan Staats, Special to FACSNET, Posted 2 October 2001.

82. "Bush to increase federal role in security at airports, *New York Times*, 28 September 2001.

83. Some researchers assert that Flights 11 and 77 were never scheduled to fly, but the claim has not been made for Flight 93, except that it appeared to be a new scheduled listing. There is also a claim that an aircraft with the same tail number as the plane that was Flight 93 was sighted two years later.

84. The "prevailing Common Strategy of cooperation and nonconfrontation meant that even a hardened cockpit door would have made little difference in a hijacking. As the chairman of the Security Committee of the Air Line Pilots Association observed when proposals were made in early 2001 to install reinforced cockpit doors in commerical aircraft, 'Even if you make a vault out of the door, if they have a noose around my flight attendant's neck, I'm going to open the door'." 9/11 Commission Report, p. 85.

85. Rep. Cynthia McKinney managed to insert a question about the war-games into the Congressional Record. http://www.copvcia.com/free/ww3/030105.mckinney.question.shtml.

86. Moussaoui demonstrated his competence by getting himself into prison before and during 9/11. "ALEXANDRIA, Virginia (Reuters) – Defense lawyers trying to save Zacarias Moussaoui's life presented evidence on Monday that the September 11 conspirator was a schizophrenic who had an abusive father and an unsettled childhood. Witnesses were brought forward." Source: "Moussaoui said mentally ill, mistreated as child," by Deborah Charles, Reuters, Monday, 17 April 2006.

CHAPTER 5

1. The IPCC Special Report recognized that the effects of some types of aircraft emissions are well understood, revealed that the effects of others are not, and identified a number of key areas of scientific uncertainty that limit the ability to project aviation impacts on climate and ozone. Statement form the International Civil Aviation Organizations (ICAO) to the 15th Sesssion of the UNFCCC. Marrakesh, 30 October, 2001.

2. "Accenture secures US visit," by Nick Wakeman, *Washington Technology*, Vol. 19 No. 5, 06/07/04.

3. "US-VISIT: How it works," from the DHS.gov website, under a terror alert warning that never went below amber, or "Elevated: significant risk of terrorist attacks," although no known terror attack had happened on US soil since 2001.

4. Bernays, Edward L., *Propaganda*, New York, 1928.

Appendix:
United Airlines Flight 93 CVR Transcript

The cockpit voice recording (CVR) transcript is reset from the evidential PDF. This is the transcript that the judge in the 2006 Moussaoui trial ordered released. The translations from Arabic (bold face) are from the US government, which also determined which voices were "unintelligible". A possibly crucial thirteen-minute conversation leading to the end of the flight is all marked "unintelligible". The initial passage in which "sit" or "sit down" is repeated many times is usually represented as culminating in the silencing of a stewardess, but since the CVR only records voices on radio or in the cockpit, and the connecting door presumably was shut (because no passenger or cabin crew member reported the events), this is implausible. Of the possible two versions deduced from the reports of the bereaved, the one they heard with a "positive" ending suggesting the passengers gained entry to the cockpit and possibly took control of the plane, the other indicating the passengers never entered (adhered to by the 9/11 Commission) this is clearly the "negative" version, with many voices shouting the religious motto instead of one voice as the plane plunges to its doom. It is not known why certain lines the passengers remembered hearing in 2002 no longer appear in the transcript.

Time (EDT)	Transcript
09:31:57	*Ladies and Gentlemen: Here the captain, please sit down keep remaining seating. We have a bomb on board. So sit.*
09:32:09	*Er, uh ... Calling Cleveland Center ... You're unreadable. Say again slowly.*
09:32:10	*Don't move. Shut up.*
09:32:13	*Come on, come.*
09:32:16	*Shut up.*
09:32:17	*Don't move.*
09:32:18	*Stop.*
09:32:34	*Sit, sit, sit down.*
09:32:39	*Sit down.*
09:32:41	Unintelligible... **the brother.**
09:32:54	*Stop.*
09:33:09	*No more. Sit down.*
09:33:10	**That's it, that's it, that's it, down, down.**
09:33:14	*Shut up.*
09:33:20	Unintelligible.
09:33:20	*We just, we didn't get it clear ... Is that United Ninety-Three calling?*
09:33:30	**Jassim.**
09:33:34	**In the name of Allah, the Most Merciful, the Most Compassionate.**
09:33:41	Unintelligible.
09:33:43	*Finish, no more. No more.*
09:33:49	*No. No, no, no, no.*
09:33:53	*No, no, no, no.*
09:34:00	**Go ahead, lie down. Lie down. Down, down, down.**
09:34:06	**There is someone ... Huh?**
09:34:12	*Down, down, down. Sit down. Come on, sit down. No, no, no, no, no. No.*
09:34:16	*Down, down, down.*
09:34:21	*Down.*
09:34:25	*No more.*
09:34:26	*No more. Down.*
09:34:27	*Please, please, please...*

09:34:28 *Down.*
09:34:29 *Please, please, don't hurt me. . .*
09:34:30 *Down. No more.*
09:34:31 *Oh God.*
09:34:32 *Down, down, down.*
09:34:33 *Sit down.*
09:34:34 *Shut up.*
09:34:42 *No more.*
09:34:46 **This?**
09:34:47 *Yes.*
09:34:47 Unintelligible.
09:34:57 **One moment, one moment**
09:34:59 Unintelligible.
09:35:03 *No more.*
09:35:06 *Down, down, down, down.*
09:35:09 *No, no, no, no, no, no. . .*
09:35:10 Unintelligible. . .
09:35:15 *Sit down, sit down, sit down.*
09:35:17 *Down.*
09:35:18 **What's this?**
09:35:19 *Sit down. Sit down. You know, sit down.*
09:35:24 *No, no, no.*
09:35:30 *Down, down, down, down.*
09:35:32 *Are you talking to me?*
09:35:33 *No, no, no.* Unintelligible.
09:35:35 *Down in the airport.*
09:35:39 *Down, down.*
09:35:40 *I don't want to die.*
09:35:41 *No, no. Down, down.*
09:35:42 *I don't want to die. I don't want to die.*
09:35:44 *No, no. Down, down, down, down, down, down.*
09:35:47 *No, no, please.*
09:35:57 *No.*
09:37:06 **That's it. Go back.**
09:37:06 **That's it.** *Sit down.*
09:37:36 **Everything is fine. I finished.**
09:38:36 **Yes.**

09:39:1 1	*Ah. Here's the captain. I would like to tell you all to remain seated. We have a bomb aboard, and we are going back to the airport, and we have our demands. So, please remain quiet.*
09:39:21	*Okay. That's ninety-three calling?*
09:39:24	**One moment.**
09:39:34	*United Ninety-Three. I understand you have a bomb on board. Go ahead.*
09:39:42	*And center exec jet nine fifty-six. That was the transmission.*
09:39:47	*Okay. Ah. Who called Cleveland?*
09:39:52	*Executive jet nine fifty-six, did you understand that transmission?*
09:39:56	*Affirmative. He said that there was a bomb on board.*
09:39:58	*That was all that you got out of it also?*
09:40:01	Affirmative.
09:40:03	*Roger.*
09:40:03	*United ninety-three. Go ahead.*
09:40:14	*United ninety-three. Go ahead.*
09:40:17	*Ahhh.*
09:40:52	**This green knob?**
09:40:54	**Yes, that's the one.**
09:41:05	*United ninety-three, do you hear the Cleveland center?*
09:41:14	**One moment. One moment.**
09:41:15	Unintelligible.
09:41:56	*Oh man.*
09:44:18	**This does notwork now.**
09:45:13	*Turn it off.*
09:45:16	**... Seven thousand ...**
09:45:19	**How about we let them in? We let the guys in now.**
09:45:23	**Okay.**
09:45:24	**Should we let the guys in?**
09:45:25	**Inform them, and tell him to talk to the pilot. Bring the pilot back.**
09:45:57	**In the name of Allah. In the name of Allah. I bear witness that there is no other God, but Allah.**
09:47:31	Unintelligible.
09:47:40	**Allah knows.**
09:48:15	Unintelligible.
09:48:38	*Set course.*
09:49:37	Unintelligible.

09:51:27	Unintelligible.
09:51:35	Unintelligible.
09:52.02	Unintelligible.
09:52:31	Unintelligible.
09:53:20	**The best thing: The guys will go in, lift up the ...** Unintelligible **... and they put the axe into it. So, everyone will be scared.**
09:53:27	**Yes.**
09:53:28	**The axe.**
09:53:28	Unintelligible.
09:53:29	**No, not the ...**
09:53:35	**Let him look through the window. Let him look through the window.**
09:53.52	Unintelligible.
09:54:09	**Open.**
09:54:11	Unintelligible.
09:55:06	*You are ... One ...*
09:56:15	Unintelligible.
09:57:55	**Is there something?**
09:57:57	**A fight?**
09:57:59	**Yeah?**
09:58:33	Unintelligible. **Let's go guys. Allah is Greatest. Allah is Greatest. Oh guys. Allah is Greatest.**
09:58:41	*Ugh.*
09:58:43	*Ugh.*
09:58:44	**Oh Allah. Oh Allah. Oh the most Gracious.**
09:58:47	*Ugh. Ugh.*
09:58:52	*Stay back.*
09:58:55	*In the cockpit.*
09:58:57	*In the cockpit.*
09:58:57	**They want to get in there. Hold, hold from the inside. Hold from the inside. Hold.**
09:59:04	*Hold the door.*
09:59:09	*Stop him.*
09:59:11	*Sit down.*
09:59:13	*Sit down.*
09:59:15	*Sit down.*
09:59:16	Unintelligible.

09:59:17	**What?**
09:59:18	**There are some guys. All those guys.**
09:59:20	*Let's get them.*
09:59:25	*Sit down.*
09:59:29	**What?**
09:59:30	**What.**
09:59:31	**What?**
09:59:36	Unintelligible.
09:59:37	**What?**
09:59:39	Unintelligible.
09:59:41	Unintelligible.
09:59:42	**Trust in Allah, and in him.**
09:59:45	*Sit down.*
09:59:47	**Unintelligible.**
09:59:53	*Ahh.*
09:59:55	Unintelligible.
09:59:58	*Ahh.*
10:00:06	**There is nothing.**
10:00:07	**Is that it? Shall we finish it off?**
10:00:08	**No. Not yet.**
10:00:09	**When they all come, we finish it off.**
10:00:11	**There is nothing.**
10:00:13	Unintelligible.
10:00:14	*Ahh.*
10:00:15	*I'm injured.*
10:00:16	Unintelligible.
10:00:21	*Ahh.*
10:00:22	**Oh Allah. Oh Allah. Oh Gracious.**
10:00:25	*In the cockpit. If we don't, we'll die.*
10:00:29	**Up, down. Up, down, in the** *cockpit.*
10:00:33	**The** *cockpit.*
10:00:37	**Up, down. Saeed, up, down.**
10:00:42	*Roll it.*
10:00:55	Unintelligible.
10:00:59	*Allah is the Greatest. Allah is the Greatest.*
10:01:01	Unintelligible.
10:01:08	**Is that it? I mean, shall we pull it down?**
10:01:09	**Yes, put it in it, and pull it down.**

10:01:10	Unintelligible.
10:01:11	**Saeed.**
10:01:12	*... engine ...*
10:01:13	Unintelligible
10:01:16	**Cut off the oxygen.**
10:01:18	**Cut off the oxygen. Cut off the oxygen. Cut off the oxygen.**
10:01:34	Unintelligible.
10:01 :37	Unintelligible.
10:01:41	**Up, down. Up, down.**
10:01:41	**What?**
10:01:42	**Up, down.**
10:01:42	*Ahh.*
10:01:53	*Ahh.*
10:01:54	Unintelligible.
10:01:55	*Ahh.*
10:01:59	*Shut them off.*
10:02:03	*Shut them off.*
10:02:14	*Go.*
10:02:14	*Go.*
10:02:15	*Move.*
10:02:16	*Move.*
10:02:17	Turn it up.
10:02:18	**Down, down.**
10:02:23	**Pull it down. Pull it down.**
10:02:25	*Down. Push, push, push, push, push.*
10:02:33	**Hey. Hey. Give it to me. Give it to me.**
10:02:35	**Give it to me. Give it to me. Give it to me.**
10:02:37	*Give it to me. Give it to me. Give it to me.*
10:02:40	Unintelligible.
10:03:02	**Allah is the Greatest.**
10:03:03	**Allah is the Greatest.**
10:03:04	**Allah is the Greatest.**
10:03:05	**Allah is the Greatest.**
10:03:06	**Allah is the Greatest.**
10:03:07	*No.*
10:03:09	**Allah is the Greatest. Allah is the Greatest.**
10:03:09	**Allah is the Greatest. Allah is the Greatest.**

9/11 Revealed
by Ian Henshall and Rowland Morgan

Challenging the facts behind the War on Terror

"The authors of *Revealed*, both radical journalists, have subjected the official version of what happened to intense scrutiny and found huge gaps." Nick Fielding, *Sunday Times*

The lead up to 9/11 and the events of that day are littered with big questions. How did it happen? Who benefited? Are we really convinced by the explanation we have been given? Henshall and Morgan find answers in a shocking and persuasive new take on the day that became a turning point in history.

To order a copy of *9/11 Revealed* please fill in the form below:

Name: ....

Address:..

.... Postcode:.......................

Daytime Tel. No. / Email (in case of query): ....

Three ways to pay:

1. **For express service telephone the TBS order line on 01206 255 800 and quote "FLI". Order lines are open Monday–Friday 8:30 am – 5:30 pm**

2. I enclose a cheque made payable to TBS Ltd for £......

3. Please charge my: [ ]Visa [ ]Mastercard [ ]Amex [ ]Switch (Switch issue no.......)

Card number: .... Expiry date:...............

Signature.......................... (your signature is essential when paying by credit card)

Please return forms (*no stamp required*) to FREEPOST RLUL-SJGC-SGKJ, Cash Sales/ Direct Mail Dept., The Book Service, Colchester Road, Frating, Colchester CO7 7DW.

Enquiries to readers@constablerobinson.com
www.constablerobinson.com

Constable and Robinson Ltd (directly or via its agents) may mail, email or phone you about promotions or products. Tick box if you do not want these from us [ ] or our subsidiaries [ ].